CULTURE, IDENTITY AND POLITICS

Research in Ethnic Relations Series

Through Different Eyes: The Cultural Identity of Young Chinese People in Britain
David Parker

Britannia's Crescent: Making a Place for Muslims in British Society
Danièle Joly

Housing, 'Race', Social Policy and Empowerment
M.L. Harrison

Religion, Class and Identity
The State, the Catholic Church and the Education of the Irish in Britain
Mary J. Hickman

Migration, Citizenship and Ethno-National Identities in the European Union
Edited by Marco Martiniello

Ethnic Conflict and Development: The Case of Guyana
Ralph R. Premdas

Ethnic Conflict and Development: The Case of Fiji
Ralph R. Premdas

Social Citizenship for Whom?
Thomas Faist

'Race', Education and Work: The Statistics of Inequality
David Drew

Ethnicity and Development in Nigeria
Okwudiba Nnoli

The South Asian Petty Bourgeoisie in Brtain
An Oxford Case Study
Shaila Srinivasan

Culture, Identity and Politics

Ethnic minorities in Britain

Edited by

TERENCE RANGER
YUNAS SAMAD
OSSIE STUART

Avebury
Aldershot • Brookfield USA • Hong Kong • Singapore • Sydney

Published by
Avebury
Ashgate Publishing Limited
Gower House
Croft Road
Aldershot
Hants GU11 3HR
England

Ashgate Publishing Company
Old Post Road
Brookfield
Vermont 05036
USA

British Library Cataloguing in Publication Data

Culture, identity and politics: ethnic minorities in Britain
1. Minorities – Great Britain 2. Minorities – Great Britain – Political aspects 3. Group identity – Great Britain 4. Great Britain – Ethnic relations
I. Ranger, T.O. (Terence Osborn), 1929– II. Samad, Yunas
III. Stuart, Ossie
305.8'0941

Library of Congress Catalog Card Number: 96-83254

ISBN 1 85628 571 5

Reprinted 1996

Printed and bound by Athenaeum Press. Ltd.,
Gateshead. Tyne & Wear.

Contents

Note on contributors

Dr Claire Alexander is a British Academy Post-doctoral Research Fellow, in the Faculty of Social Science, at The Open University. She is author of *The Art of Being Black*, Oxford University Press, Oxford, in press.

Dr Sue Benson is the Newton Trust Lecturer in Social and Political Science at University of Cambridge. She has written extensively on race and ethnicity in Britain and Nigeria and is the author of *Ambiguous Ethnicity: Interracial Families in London*, Cambridge University Press, Cambridge, 1981.

Dr Beatrice Drury is a Research and Development Officer, on the Young Homeless Project in Leamington Spa and was a Research Fellow at the Centre for Research in Ethnic Relations, Warwick University. She was editor with J. Rex of *Ethnic Mobilisation in a Multicultural Europe*, Avebury, Aldershot, 1994.

Dr John Eade is Principal Lecturer, Department of Sociology and Social Policy, Roehampton Institute. He is author of *The Politics of Community: the Bangladeshi Community in East London,* Avebury, Aldershot, 1989, editor with M. Sallnow, *Contesting the Sacred: the Anthropology of Christian Pilgrimage,* Routledge, London, 1991 and *Living the Global City,* Routledge, London, forthcoming.

Professor Stuart Hall, is Professor of Sociology, at The Open University. He has research interests in cultural theory and cultural studies, political sociology, the media, race, ethnicity and cultural identity. His publications include, *Resistance through Rituals: Youth Subcultures in Post-war Britain*, Unwin Hyman, London, 1989; *The Popular Arts,* Pantheon, New York, 1964; *Policing the Crisis: Mugging, the State, and Law and Order,* Macmillan, London, 1978; *The Hard Road to Renewal : Thatcherism and the Crisis of the Left,* Verso, London, 1988 and *Race, Ethnicity, Nation: The*

Fatal Triangle, the W.E.B. Dubois Lectures, Harvard University Press, forthcoming.

Dr Mary Hickman is Director of Irish Studies at the University of North London. She is author of *Religion, Class and Identity: State, the Catholic Church and the Education of the Irish in Britain*, Avebury, Aldershot, 1995 and is directing a research project for the Commission for Racial Equality entitled 'Discrimination and the Irish Community in Britain'.

Cathie Lloyd is a Research Fellow at the Centre for Research in Ethnic Relations, Warwick University. She has published extensively on anti-racist movements and strategies in Europe. She is currently researching on anti-racist discourse in France. Formerly she was a senior researcher at the Commission for Racial Equality.

Professor Terence Ranger is Professor of Race Relations, St Antony's College, Oxford. He has worked extensively on race and ethnicity in Africa and particularly in Zimbabwe. He was editor with Eric Hobsbawm of *The Invention of Tradition*, Cambridge University Press, Cambridge, 1983; author of *The Invention of Tribalism in Zimbabwe,* Mambo, Gweru, 1985; and author of 'The Invention of Tradition Revisited' in Terence Ranger and Ofumeli Vaughan, eds., *Legitimacy and the State in Twentieth Century Africa*, St Antony's/Macmillan, London, 1993. He is now working on the twentieth century history, including the history of ethnicity, in northern Matabeleland.

Dr Yunas Samad is a Lecturer in the Department of Social and Economic Studies, Bradford University. He is the author of *Nation in Turmoil: Nationalism and Ethnicity in Pakistan 1937-1958*, Sage, Delhi 1995 and is presently collaborating on an ESRC project on 'Globalisation, Ethnic Minority Media and the Representation of Islam'.

Dr Ossie Stuart is a part-time lecturer at the Roehampton Institute and the School of Oriental and African Studies, London University. Formerly he was a Research Fellow at the Social Policy Research Unit, York University. He has written extensively on race, ethnicity and disability and is the author of *Sport in Africa*, Macmillan, London, 1993.

Dr Steve Vertovec is Principal Research Fellow at the Centre for Research in Ethnic Relations, Warwick University. He is the author of *Hindu Trinidad: Religion, Ethnicity and Socio-Economic Change*, Macmillan, London, 1992; editor of *Aspects of the South Asian Diaspora*, Oxford University Press, Delhi, 1991; co-editor of *The Urban Context: Ethnicity, Social Networks and Situational Analysis,* Berg, Oxford, 1995 and *Islam in Europe: The Politics of Religion and Community,* UCL Press, London, in press.

Dr Pnina Werbner is a Senior Lecturer in Social Anthropology at Keele University, and Research Administrator of the International Centre for Contemporary Cultural Research based at Keele and Manchester. She has written extensively on migration, ethnicity and Islam in Britain. Her publications include *The Migration Process: Capital, Gifts and Offerings among British Pakistanis,* Berg, Oxford, 1990; *Black and Ethnic Leaderships in Britain: the Cultural Dimensions of Political Action*, co-edited with Muhammad Anwar, Routledge, London, 1991; *Economy and Culture in Pakistan: Migrants and Cities in a Muslim Society*, co-edited with Hastings Donnan, Macmillan, Basingstoke, 1991; and `Person Myth and Society in South Asian Islam', Special issue of *Social Analysis*, Adelaide, 1990 and *Islam, Diaspora and Millennium: The Political Imaginaries of British Pakistanis*, forthcoming.

1 Introduction[1]

Terence Ranger

The breakdown of the black/white dichotomy

The dominant paradigm in British race relations has until recently been the black/white dichotomy. Within this parameter research, debate and policy initiatives concerned with discrimination, disadvantage and political mobilisation have taken place. But this simple dichotomy has broken down. Blackness defined as the common experience of oppression by non-whites has given way to a myriad of externally imposed or self-asserted ethnicities. Blackness defined as the property of people of African descent - though constantly and fiercely reiterated - has also been eroded. What Paul Gilroy calls the 'pluralization of black identities' has involved a movement from 'the comfort of cultural sameness [in] homogenous and unchanging black communities' to the 'familiar but deeply resented divisions based on class, ideology and money, ... sexuality, gender and generation' (1993a, pp. 2-3). Even whiteness is being increasingly deconstructed as a growing experience of Europe reveals its legacy of racism between white and white. Everywhere - whether in Britain or in Europe itself - there has been an assertion of ethno/cultural rather than race/colour identities.

The forces, which have produced this 'pluralization', have been themselves plural and ambiguous and there have been many and sharply contrasting assessments of its significance for good or ill. Aziz Al-Azmeh, for instance, offers a completely negative account both of the causes and the consequences. In his view, 'the recent transition, most specifically in Britain, from structural considerations of immigration to a culturalist notion of ethnic diversity' has 'definite structural foundations'. For non-whites it is the product of 'spatial segregation, social involution and ghetto formation'. Meanwhile, whites have developed an ideology of 'differentialist culturalism'. This has the double effect of breaking up the solidarities of oppression and of mystifying a 'social reality of stunning diversity'. False constructs of community, defined in terms of religion/culture have emerged from this interaction of involution and ideology (1993, pp. 1-3).

One result of this has been an 'over-Islamicisation of Muslims' - and equally an 'over-Hinduisation of Hindus', an 'over-Africanisation of blacks', etc. (Al-Azmeh 1994). Another has been the way in which both Right and Left traditions of British political thought have come to express themselves within the assumptions of 'differentialist culturalism'. Thus the ideology embraces 'both a libertarian streak and a segregationism ... as mirror images'. It holds together both 'anti-racist heterophilia' and 'racist heterophobia' and even finds room for 'racist heterophilia', which desires co-existence 'in mere spatiality'. Al-Azmeh deplores these consequences in Britain, and equally deplores the consequences of global culturalism, which he sees as an abandonment of the project of development. Britain and the West now relate to the world not as modernisers but through a descent into ethnology The result is the 'over-Croatisation' of the Croats, etc., etc. (1993, pp. 5-6, 1994).

Al-Azmeh calls for unequivocal anti-culturalist and anti-essentialist politics; the re-assertion of the Grand Narrative of progressive modernisation; the revalidation of the nation states of the Third World. Somewhat similarly, the British black scholar, Harry Goulbourne, has deplored the rise of the ethnic paradigm in Britain and has called for the British nation state 'to resume its historic responsibilities'; to act as the broker between communities and identities; to sustain and develop a shared civic culture (1991, p. 238).

There is, on the other hand, another tendency in the recent literature. Whatever may be the reasons for and effects of white differentialist culturalism, some scholars insist that blacks themselves have to break away from the old simple dichotomy. So Stuart Hall argues in this volume: 'The experience of being black in the world, and the range of expressive and creative forces which are accessible to it; of the variety of cultural languages that it can now speak, cannot be funnelled through the tiny eye of the negative experience of racism. Because that is simply to accept that I am nothing but the inverse of how I am seen ... It is not possible to occupy black identity at the end of the twentieth century in the heart of Europe in that monological way. So what you are seeing now ... is blacks increasingly understanding the multiplicity of identities that they are going to need'. If ethnicity is the name of the contemporary game, then blacks must be, and are, supremely equipped to play it. If culture is to be the mark of identity, then blacks must be, and are, multifariously culturally creative.

Certainly there are, as Al-Azmeh warns, dangers of involution and of cultural over-determination. But, so Hall insists, if one is sufficiently aware of these dangers it is possible for blacks to make the dangerous journey back to the sources and to return safely to modern times without being trapped in a static primordialism. Hall is even prepared to speak, as he did in a plenary lecture to the December 1993 London University conference on Language and Empire, about tactical essentialism. In reality, of course, the sources are richly varied and allow for the imagination of 'the multiplicity of identities that they are going to need'. Indeed blacks can emerge from the journey with the inspiration for enlarged rather than enclosed identities, allowing them 'to live with hybridity [in] an interdependent world of migrated peoples'. Blacks can then be as universal as Goulbourne wants them to be but also have 'the resources to be able to be productive, creative, to explore their own histories, to tell their own stories'.

Certainly, too, there are the structural factors which Al-Azmeh emphasises. Yes, says Hall, 'we're talking about operating a very constrained system, but nevertheless, even within those constraints, it is possible to use the identity question as a way of levering spaces open'.

Whatever may be their different assessment of the balance of libertarian rather than segregationist potentialities in the politics of cultural difference, however, all these scholars agree on the invented or imagined character of ethnic identity. Al-Azmeh insists that the ethnic revival is a product of 'modern European irrationalist thought'. Paul Gilroy argues that both black essentialism and ethnic assertions, far from being anti-western and pre-modern, are in fact 'Western and modern', and 'derive from a history of ideas that has been integral to modern racial typology and white supremacy' (1993a, p. 9).[2] The recent explosion of ethnicity in Britain is the most recent product of forces and ideas which have been operative first in Europe and then in the world since at least the nineteenth century.

An Africanist and Asianist response

Over the last five years a particular style of analysis of ethnic relations has grown up at St Antony's College, Oxford. At its core has been a group of scholars who began work as social historians of Africa and Asia but who have now also turned their attention to the question of ethnicity in Britain and Europe. The two Africanists are Professor Terence Ranger and Dr Ossie Stuart; the two Asianists are Dr Yunas Samad and Dr Tazeen Murshid. All four have treated questions of identity in Africa or Asia. Ranger has written extensively about the invention or imagination of African tradition, and particularly the tradition of primordial ethnicity (1983, 1993). Stuart has explored the ingredients of African urban identities in Bulawayo after the Second World War (1989). Samad has studied nationalism and ethnicity in Pakistan (1995a, 1995b); Murshid has written about nationalism and ethnicity in Bangladesh (1993, 1995). The Africanists have been particularly influenced by *The Invention of Tradition*; the Asianists by Benedict Anderson's *Imagined Communities* (1983).

These four social historians carried out their research quite independently of each other and do not in any sense form a school. But they all bring to the analysis of ethnic relations in Britain a common set of assumptions, derived from their African and Asian work. They agree on the constructedness rather than the primordiality of ethnicity. They agree on the complex interaction of external and internal factors in constructing it. Colonial administrators and their missionary and antiquarian colleagues classified and invented and imposed ethnicities as a way of defining/confining their subjects; then many of those subjects took up the new identities and imagined them much more deeply and profoundly as a way of making space for themselves. They agree that the construction of ethnicity requires to be studied historically rather than merely stated as a post-modernist proposition. In each case, though they assert that contemporary African and Asian ethnicities are recent phenomena, they also assert the need to study historical process over at least a hundred years and sometimes for much longer than that. Like other Africanists and Asianists they have developed techniques for studying changing metropolitan ideologies; imperial inventions and categorisations; the working misunderstandings of the colonial men-on-the-spot; the findings of colonial science; the work of missionary linguists; the ethnographic discourse of African and Asian rural organic intellectuals, who participated in the invention of ethnic identities; the cultural nationalist discourse of ideological brokers, who imagined the content of ethnicities once invented; the lived-out contributions of workers and peasants.

Turning to the study of race relations in Britain and Europe, these social historians naturally found themselves at home in the new world of culturalist notions of ethnic diversity. While the work of sociologists and geographers on educational and employment differentials, on spatial segregation, and other structural considerations of immigration, obviously remained very important, it seemed that their own social historical assumptions, techniques and comparative findings might be usefully applied to the British debate about differentialist culturalism.

For one thing, the varying propositions that have been advanced in the British debate strike immediate Africanist and Asianist echoes. Al-Azmeh's account of non-white segregation and introversion; of the white ideological combination of an anti-racist heterophilia, a racist heterophobia and a racist heterophilia desiring co-existence in mere spatiality, can hardly fail to be powerfully evocative for a South Africanist. South Africanists have documented liberal segregationism and apartheid *volkekunde* ethnography as well as sheer racism and anti-racism. They have discussed ethnicity as a fruit of African introversion, documenting Bantustan pseudo-ethnicity and, above all, the over-Zuluisation of the Zulu (Dubow 1989, Maré 1993, Rich 1984, Marks 1992, Vail 1989).

Stuart Hall's vision of a potentially enlarging debate about class, generation and gender within the parameters of a constantly re-imagined identity, on the other hand, has parallels in John Lonsdale's splendidly subtle and dense concept of moral ethnicity. Lonsdale is all too aware of the manipulation of ethnicity by the colonial and post-colonial state in Kenya. This he calls political tribalism. But analysing the case of the Kikuyu, in particular, Lonsdale insists that tribe does not mean a unit of consensus and unquestioned shared values, but rather an arena for debate about what it means to be Kikuyu (or Luo, or Ganda, or whatever). One cannot a priori determine whether any particular ethnicity is progressive or reactionary in effect; there is a constant struggle between different imaginers of ethnic identity; between young and old, men and women, radicals and conservatives, exclusive and inclusive definitions of identity. In this struggle space is sometimes levered open and sometimes foreclosed. Ethnicity is not moral in itself but it constitutes the ground on which fundamental moral debate takes place (1992).[3]

The central problem for Africanist students of ethnicity is how to reconcile South African and Lonsdalian analyses. South African historians and anthropologists find it impossible to apply the notion of moral ethnicity to the beastly realities of tribal war, but it may be that they ought to do so. Is the debate among the Zulu about Zulu identity any less intense or various in its potential than the debate among the Kikuyu? Is the outcome not equally important? On the other hand, should not an enthusiastic chronicler of the Luo of Western Kenya,[4] like Professor Atieno Odhiambo, with his belief in the legitimacy of the Luo nation and the amorality of the Kenyan state, pause to consider the role of structural involution in producing Luo self-consciousness (Odhiambo 1990)?

Since the central problem for students of British ethnicity is how to reconcile Al-Azmeh's sort of interpretation with Stuart Hall's, it seemed possible that a comparison between the Africanist, and similar Asian, literature and the debate about Britain's ethnic diversity would be illuminating. For one thing, it would confirm that the processes of ethnic categorisation and ethnic self-assertion that have been so striking in Britain in the past decade are a recent manifestation of much wider and older phenomena, deeply rooted in the imperial encounter with indigenous societies. For another thing, it would suggest ways of analysing British ethnicities and insist that such analysis must be historical as well as anthropological and sociological. It would enable comparison and contrast between ethnic and confessional definitions in Asia and Africa and their reformulation in Britain. Taking up Paul Gilroy's insistence on routes as well as roots (1993b), it would be able to show that identities within Africa and Asia have been formed as much by the comings and goings of traders, hunters, and pilgrims as by the growth of communities in settled environments. It could provide a jumping off point from which to follow Asians and Africans as they moved along their complex and painful paths towards Britain.

It was in this spirit that the four social historians of the St Antony's cluster began their own studies of British and European ethnicity.[5] It was in this spirit, too, that the weekly St Antony's Ethnic Studies Seminars have been organised, increasingly with the assistance of Dr Claire Alexander, whose anthropological study of young black identities in London gave splendid proof of the potentialities of a study of levering space open by means of ethnic imagination (1992). And it was in this spirit, finally, that the May 1992 Workshop on 'Culture, Identity and Politics: Ethnic Minorities in Britain' was organised.

This book has grown out of that 1992 Workshop, although its contents do not fully reflect the presentations made there. Thus we have not been able to include Raphael Samuel's or Diana Jeater's papers, while we have added chapters by Mary Hickman and Pnina Werbner. But the book still falls into the three parts planned for the Workshop, each reflecting the preoccupations of Asianist/Africanist social historians as transferred to the study of ethnicity in Britain.

The first part of the book is concerned with history, reflecting our anxiety to set both the black/white dichotomy and the differentialist culturalism which has succeeded it in a long historical sequence. The second part of the book is concerned with methodology and in particular with the question of how the discipline of social anthropology, which had so much to say about ethnicity in Asia and Africa, can contribute to its understanding in Britain. The third part of the book is concerned with illustration - with case studies of the contrasting imagination of British Asian and British black identities.

Historical perspectives on ethnicity in Britain

Two historical presentations were made at the Workshop, one by Raphael Samuel on racism and anti-racism in British history, and one by Cathie Lloyd on anti-racist traditions in France. Two large points emerged from these presentations. Raphael Samuel used history to deconstruct both the black/white dichotomy and the assumptions of the more recent differential culturalism. Cathie Lloyd's paper suggested great contrasts between the potential of French and British national traditions for sustaining effective anti-racism in the present. Both points can be, and were, debated.

Raphael Samuel declared that in our revisionist age not only race but racism were due to be deconstructed. Racism has come to be defined as the abuse of power by whites in order to repress and discriminate against blacks. Anti-racism has come to be defined as argument and action that exposes and combats white oppression of non-whites. These definitions, argued Samuel, could only be applied to British history after the second world war, though, as we shall see he had his reservations even about that. But they certainly could not be applied earlier.

There certainly were blacks in early modern England and they were certainly the object of prejudice. But from the mid sixteenth century onwards, the essential marker of first English and then British identity was not whiteness but Protestantism. The significant Other for the construction of English and British identity was not the blacks but the Celts. Celtic speech was the prime marker of the outsider; Celtic societies, whether in Gaelic Ireland or in the Scottish Highlands, were relegated to the backwardness of tribalism. The prime victims of racism were the Catholic Irish, despised, dispossessed, disenfranchised and deported in Ireland itself, and crudely stereotyped and exploited when the need for manual labour brought hundreds of thousands of them to industrialising England. In such a context anti-racism was more centrally represented by the Catholic Emancipation movement than by the campaign for the abolition of slavery. Nor had all the victories of this traditional anti-racism yet been won. Masked by the recent focus on non-whites, the Irish still suffered much discrimination and many disabilities.

Having thus disposed of the centrality of the black/white dichotomy for the greater part of British history, Samuel also criticised the idea that recent ethnic categorisation and self-assertion was itself a new recent feature of British social and political life. There had been a constant stream of European immigrants and refugees - Huguenots, Jews, Poles. Each had struck its own balance between cultural retention and cultural assimilation; each had made its own connections with native British traditions of radicalism. London's East End, in particular, had witnessed generations of ethnicity and of radicalism. The fact that the new ethnicities were Bangladeshi and Somali did not, in his view, cut off what was happening in the East End today from this long history of struggle. To see racism and ethnicity solely in terms of white and non-white would be to abandon any hope of making connections with previous traditions of immigrant struggle and political radicalism and to surrender the white population of the East End into the hands of the National Front.

In putting forward these challenging propositions Samuel was, of course, drawing upon a good deal of recent historical work on the construction of Britishness. Linda Colley's (1992) magisterial *Britons: Forging the Nation, 1707-1837,* published at about the same time as Samuel's presentation, makes a somewhat similar case. Colley, too, stresses the centrality of Protestantism - Britons 'defined themselves as Protestants struggling for survival against the world's foremost Catholic power'. She emphasises the centrality of English as a language and the Otherness of speakers of Welsh and Gaelic. In a striking passage she describes British response to Catholic Irish immigration:

> In some areas of Great Britain, traditional prejudices had actually become even sharper because of the recent flood of Irish immigrants. Back in the 1780s, the number of Irish men and women living on the mainland was probably little more than 40,000. But by the time of the 1831 census, there were some 580,000 Irish in Britain, close to 5 per cent of the labour force ... The bulk of them were young adults, disproportionately illiterate and unskilled [and] they undercut British-born manual labour in those northern and Scottish cities where they were concentrated. All these cities petitioned strongly against Catholic emancipation in 1829

Some parallels are obvious. The 1991 census reveals that blacks and Asians now comprise some 5 per cent of Britain's population, concentrated in the cities. (People of Irish descent now come to closer to 10 per cent.). But then, as now, racism did not depend only on propinquity or on threat to jobs and houses. Colley shows that bitter opposition to Catholic emancipation was voiced in areas which saw no immigrants. Opponents acted 'not so much from what they knew, as from what they felt'. And what they felt was threat to British national identity - 'many ordinary Britons saw themselves as being part of a native tradition of resistance to Catholicism which stretched back for centuries, and which seemed, indeed, to be timeless' (1992, p. 330).

So far, then, Colley's picture corresponds to Samuel's. She does, however, add Empire as a dimension in the construction of British identity. But the relevant chapter is called Peripheries and its emphasis is entirely on the American Empire and the revolution in British sensibilities provoked by the War of Independence. India rates two references in her Index; the West Indies and Africa none. Unlike Catholic Emancipation, the abolition of slavery features in Colley's account not as the climax of a great struggle over the definition of national identity, nor as a victory for anti-racism over racism. It features instead as an occasion for the manifestation of an assured and complacent British moral superiority.

Now, all this is a salutary corrective. If we focus internally, on British society itself, it has to be accepted that before the twentieth century blacks and Asians did not constitute the significant Other and Irish Catholics did. But the question which necessarily arises, both from the perspective of the history of Africa, Asia and the Caribbean and from the perspective of the routes by which identity is constructed, is whether one can sensibly focus internally. Neither Colley nor Samuel would deny for a moment that many Britons were encountering Africans and Asians outside Britain in imperial and colonial contexts of unequal power and exploitation throughout the eighteenth and nineteenth centuries. Nor would they deny that the use of unequal power by these Britons did much to produce defined and stereotyped ethnicities in the extra-European world. But could the encounter have been so one-sided? Did not the routes which took Britons to India and West Africa and the West Indies, and then brought them back to Britain, contribute to definitions of Britishness as well?

Many scholars have recently answered this question positively. Linda Colley herself asserts in her introduction a proposition which she does not develop in her book:

> Great Britain was an invention forged above all by war. Time and time again, war with France brought Britons into confrontation with an obviously hostile Other and encouraged them to define themselves collectively against it. They defined themselves as Protestants struggling for survival against the world's foremost Catholic power. They defined themselves against the French as they imagined them to be, superstitious, militarist, decadent and unfree. And, increasingly as the wars went on, they defined themselves in contrast to the colonial peoples they conquered, peoples who were manifestly alien in terms of culture, religion and colour (1992, p. 5).

Other historians have made this point much more strongly. Catherine Hall, asking many of the same questions for Britain in the middle and late nineteenth century which Linda Colley posed for an earlier period, has come up with significantly different answers. Both make use of campaigns for parliamentary reform and the passage of reform acts in order to focus upon debates over who should be included in the political nation. Colley's book climaxes with the 1832 Reform Act which she sees as a reconstitution of the nation after the traumas of Catholic Emancipation. Hall's recent work climaxes with the 1867 Reform Act. This time, she argues, the debate about who deserved to join the British political nation was inextricably linked with events in Jamaica. The black/white dichotomy replaced the Catholic/Protestant dichotomy as the context for the definition of British identity. British sympathy for the emancipated Negro had by the 1860s been replaced by mass enthusiasm for European nationalist movements; the debate over Reform co-incided with the debate over the Morant Bay uprising in Jamaica and its repression by Governor Eyre; reactionary protestations that parliamentary reform was advocated by 'Nigger Philanthropists' had to be countered by the assertion that the new voters were 'Englishmen like ourselves'; the extension of the franchise in Britain was counter-pointed by its abolition in Jamaica. Reformers might desire the extension of the 'British genius for self-government' to colonies of white settlement and proclaim that 'Our Colonies are the Centre of our Civilisation', but they agreed that for many years to come black Jamaicans would be unfit to vote (Hall 1994).

Catherine Hall's work is explicitly a result of questioning the past from the perspective of our current post-colonial identity crisis. We are all, she says, post-colonial subjects whether ex-rulers or ex-ruled. And of course post-colonialism has collapsed those old distinctions between periphery and metropole and outer and inner. As many scholars have recently pointed out, the once neatly stereotyped and classified colonial peoples - set aside in a static tribal or caste universe that seemed to have little to do with the progressive dynamic of British society and institutions - have now arrived as post-colonial peoples in the metropolis itself. 'The arrival of post-colonial peoples challenges the notions of progress, law and order, Western liberalism and civility', writes Ossie Stuart. 'The history of colonialism is a counter to the normative history of the West' (1994).

And here we come to a challenge to Samuel's second proposition - that black and Asian immigration since the second world war is qualitatively similar to the long sequence of previous immigrations. The incoming of fugitives from European tyrannies did not challenge British notions of progress and liberalism, however much there were tensions over housing and jobs in the areas where they settled. But if Stuart is right that the idea of metropolitan progress was linked to the idea of colonial backwardness, the metropole being defined by contrast to the periphery and vice versa, then when these two separate histories come together inside Britain it produces an entirely new crisis of identity. The white majority reacts by striving to maintain the old distance between centre and periphery, but now within national boundaries. It persists with the ascription to blacks and Asians of 'fixed primordial identities' just as these were ascribed under colonialism. Yet 'these migrants imagine their identities afresh and by so doing transform this society' (Stuart 1994, Brah 1993).[6]

Colley writes that 'the manner in which Great Britain was made ... may well be the means of its unmaking in the future'. Protestantism is now merely residual; France is now a partner in the European Community; the 'massive overseas Empire' has been lost. Where now is British identity? Catherine Hall adds that since not only Britishness but whiteness came during imperialism to be defined by contrast to the colonial African, Caribbean and Asian Other, post-colonialism demands both an effort to imagine a nation state which includes British black and Asian identities and also an effort to imagine white identities not rooted in empire.

For these and other reasons it is not so easy to integrate blacks and Asians into British radical traditions as Samuel suggests. As Michael Keith has remarked, the current exhibition on the peopling of London, with its message of continuity and change, stops more or less dead in 1945, despite offering a guide in Bengali. In the contemporary politics of the East End, indeed, the exhibition runs the danger of producing a dangerous anti-Semitism because of its appearance of over-representing the Jewish immigrant experience at the expense of the Muslim (1994).[7]

Yet while it may be necessary to debate with some of Samuel's propositions, nevertheless his presentation has left an important mark on this book. After the conference was over the organisers commissioned from Mary Hickman a paper on the Irish experience in Britain which appears as its first chapter. Hickman's account first documents the extremities of racist discrimination against Irish immigrants in nineteenth century Britain and then goes on to explain why the Irish have since dropped out of discussion on race relations. This has partly been a consequence of the centrality of the black/white paradigm. But it has mainly been the result of a peculiar process of segregation and involution. Hickman argues that the children of Irish immigrants were set aside in their own church schools. She also argues that religion - Catholicism - was equated to culture and became the main marker of Irish ethnicity, rather than nationality or any tradition of political action. But Catholicism - once the defining Other for a Protestant Britain - became increasingly respectable and Anglicised. Beginning as an agent of segregation it increasingly became an instrument of assimilation.

There are both parallels and contrasts here with recent Asian immigration. As Aziz Al-Azmeh complains, Islam has come to be regarded as culture just like Irish Catholicism. There is a demand for separate Muslim schools. But these are hardly likely to end up as instruments of Anglicisation. Other ways will have to be found to mask the Muslim presence. Meanwhile, the masking of the Irish barely conceals their continued centrality to definitions of British identity. Racism remains central to British national identity, writes Hickman, 'and the foremost struggle about the boundaries of the United Kingdom is taking place in Northern Ireland ... Explanations of the present conflict in Northern Ireland are rooted in stereotypes which echo the rationality/irrationality divide of 19th century conceptions of the differences between the English and the Irish'. Coming to terms with British post-colonialism requires an unmasking of relationships with the Irish as well as a confrontation in the metropole with imperial black and Asian ethnic stereotypes.

Cathie Lloyd's presentation needs less extended discussion since in a revised form it appears as a chapter in this book. Like Raphael Samuel, she emphasised that key historic triumphs of anti-racism had little to do with the white/black dichotomy, the 1791 Emancipation of the Jews playing something of the same role in France that the 1829 Catholic Emancipation Act played in Britain. Like Linda Colley, she saw the abolition of slavery in France more as a self-regarding display of virtue than as a practical transformation of racial relationships. But Lloyd's chapter significantly heightens one of the issues raised by Samuel.

By contrast to Colley's account of the ingredients of British national consciousness, Lloyd writes that 'the theme of universalism/difference, however, was central to myth making ... and process of legitimation of French national identity, thus binding antiracism and national identity together in a complex way'. As Lloyd shows, the universalism of the Enlightenment was profoundly ambiguous in its implications. It legitimated egalitarianism and secularism; it also legitimated nationalism and the French imperial civilising mission. Yet, as she writes, 'the Enlightenment still acts as a powerful magnet to all forms of "progressive" thought in France ... [and] has a specific resonance for antiracists'. Hence, 'there has been a continuous struggle to appropriate the ideas of the Enlightenment', which has meant, among many other things, much unease among French anti-racists with the idea of ethnicity. Lloyd asserts that the 'parameters of the [French] debate are quite different to that in Britain'. And this raises sharply the question, which we have already briefly discussed - whether there is anything either in the establishment or the counter-establishment traditions of British patriotism to which contemporary anti-racism can appeal.

There has, of course, been a tradition of radical British universalism, speaking for liberty and the Rights of Man. But this has not recently had a very good press. Linda Colley depicts John Wilkes, for instance, as representing a 'swaggering and intolerantly Little English patriotism' rather than any sort of fraternal universalism. 'Wilkes became the personification of liberty, and liberty was the hallmark of Englishness' (1992). Addressing a Δ1990 conference on the National Curriculum in History convened by Raphael Samuel, Paul Gilroy made the same sort of point about the whole tradition of British left nationalism.

> I hold to the view that a great deal of New Left historiography is articulated in an explicitly nationalistic register. Certainly the great power and authority of the New Left historians should not lead us to overlook the way in which their work [contains] a rather volkish tradition of national popular radicalism seemingly transmitted with only minor interruptions from Putney Heath to Greenham Common.

This 'doggedly ethnocentric' historiography of radicalism offers 'a language of national belonging and patriotism [which] has acquired a series of racial referents that cannot spontaneously be dislodged by a pure act of will' (Gilroy, 1993a, pp. 66-7).

In this address, and in his subsequent monograph, Gilroy argued for 'rewriting British history to the point at which it ceases to be recognizably British at all', suggesting in particular 'an Atlantic perspective'. But what is striking is how little British content Gilroy's Atlantic perspective contains. When Gilroy undercuts Afrocentric essentialism by emphasising how much the great black American intellectuals drew from Europe, it is not British ideas that inspire them. Douglass, Du Bois and Richard Wright respond to German and French philosophy (1993b). Or as Gilroy told Raphael Samuel's conference: 'Edward Wilmot Blyden, Martin Delaney, Alexander Crummell, James Theodore Holly and the rest of the intelligentsia of the black Atlantic world were, to varying degrees, indebted to the nationalist thinking of Herder, Schleiermacher, Hegel and von Treitschke' (1993a, p. 65). It is as though there was nothing in the British tradition, even in its heyday and still less now, which could be made use of by black thinkers.

From an Indian Ocean, if not an Atlantic, perspective this seems strange. Indianists and Africanists are well used to appeals by black and Asian intellectuals to British doctrines of universalism. Black South African leaders - before they were submerged by the rising tide of segregationism - extolled the promise of 'Equal Rights Under the Flag' (Marks 1994). Nineteenth century Indian intellectuals responded enthusiastically to the modernising ideologies of Utilitarianism. 'Well into the 1870s', writes Tapan Raychaudhuri, the emerging Indian national consciousness 'rejoiced that India was part of a glorious world-wide empire, and nurtured hopes a steady progress under Britain's providential guidance' (1988). In Raychaudhuri's view, Indian nationalism and the subsequent Indian nation state were products of this nineteenth century encounter. There is, of course, a paradox here. According to Colley, Wilke's radicalism was a Little Englander dissent from imperial definitions of Britain. The universalism to which African and Indian modernisers were appealing was an imperial rather than a dissenting ideology. Moreover, both in Africa and in India these modernisers were betrayed; equality under the flag gave way to all the structured inequalities of classified ethnicity, caste and communalism.

Obviously there is no possibility of a revival of imperialist universalism. But some at least of the authors we have cited are reluctant to cede the day to ethnic and cultural differentialism. Aziz Al-Azmeh insists that the globalising project of modernisation which Afro-Asian nation states inherited from European empires is still the only viable Grand Narrative, compared to which Islam is 'a historical romance' (Al-Azmeh 1994). Harry Goulbourne appeals to metropolitan traditions of British universalism, which he sees as the product of struggle between liberalism, radicalism and immigrant agency:

> Entry and settlement for all groups have been fraught with difficulties and sometimes open and violent conflict. During the course of such conflict, as well as many others which were completely independent of ethnic considerations (such as class, regional or democratic interests) Britain developed a civic culture which has contributed massively to notions such as the rule of law, parliamentary sovereignty, individual freedom, and certain common assumptions about individual freedom and group tolerance in a wider social collectivity. There are, of course, many drawbacks in both the statement and practice of these commonalties; they nonetheless constitute the basic essentials from which post-imperial Britain can strive to build a more fair society (1991, p. 238).

Historical debate thus sets up the fundamental question of this book - how to balance continuity and innovation. Can contemporary Britons make use of anything from their national past or do they have totally to re-imagine themselves? Is contemporary ethnicity merely the latest version of decades of immigrant politics or does it represent something quite new - the Empire coming home to roost? Are contemporary black and Asian ethnicities in Britain continuities of identities rooted in Africa, the Caribbean and South Asia, or are they innovative and transforming self-assertions? Are British political, social and economic structures inherited from the imperial era in any case more important than self-definitions, no matter how creative? Is ethnicity, in short, the project of post-imperial European nation-states, abandoning any universalising idea of development, or is it the project of the once colonised, bringing new energy and life back to the metropole? These are European analogies to the Africanist need to balance political tribalism and moral ethnicity, or the Indianist debate on whether communalism is merely cynically manipulated false consciousness or whether it also represents positive elements of local popular protest against the exploitative state.

It is plainly critically important to find analytical modes for resolving these questions, whether in Africa, India or Britain. In Africa and Asia analysis of ethnicity has until recently been the preserve of social anthropology but there is currently intense debate about whether anthropology can any longer generate valid propositions. The second section of this book, therefore, consists of a debate about what happens when anthropologists turn to study ethnicity in Britain.

The debate over anthropology

Africanists and Indianists are very familiar with the idea that anthropology is in crisis. African and Asian nationalist movements resented a division of intellectual labour that treated Europeans historically and the rest of the world anthropologically. Social history has therefore been respectable in independent Afro-Asia, while anthropology has had to disguise itself. South African anthropologists, given the opportunity to learn from developments in the rest of Africa and the time to do something about it, have worked hard to redeem their discipline. They have repented of past Anglophone assumptions that tribal societies were ancient and homogenous, and repudiated the legitimation given to apartheid by Afrikaner *volkekunde* ethnography. But this has not saved them from a fresh apprehension of disaster. Two South African anthropologists have recently documented 'a self-perception by many that the discipline is in disarray, as though the uncertainties of moving from apartheid South Africa to black majority rule have pushed South African anthropology into a state of liminality' (Gordon and Spiegel 1993).

In some ways this crisis of self-confidence is curious, since ethnicity as a topic has recently become both politically urgent and academically respectable in South Africa.[8] And whatever the errors of the past, the work of Southern African anthropologists on ethnicity has had much to offer. (Thus the Southern African literature on urban tribalism has things to say which are still relevant to the study of ethnicity in Britain, where it is so much a phenomenon of the cities). But anthropological approaches to ethnicity remain suspect in South Africa even as the topic itself has become urgent.

This is because anthropological work is held to come down too heavily on the subjective rather than on the structural determinants of ethnicity. Cultural identity - a notion as suspect to many South African intellectuals as it is to Aziz Al-Azmeh - is seen as pre-eminently an anthropological concept. Those radical South African intellectuals who do deal in terms of cultural discourse emphasise contradiction, dissent, peripherality rather than the core-concepts of homogenous societies. The participant-observation method of anthropology seems to privilege consciousness (and false consciousness) rather than to help in understanding the mega-structures of post-industrialism; the notion that ethnicity is primordial - even if the word is not intended by anthropologists to imply changeless antiquity - cannot help but suggest essentialist rather than constructionist definitions. Social historians are seen as better able to balance African imagination of ethnicity with colonial intellectual manipulations and socio-economic constraints.[9]

These issues are also at stake in the debate between Sue Benson, John Eade and Pnina Werbner that makes up the second section of this book. The argument amongst them is about much more than the defects or merits of a discipline. The question is primarily how to study ethnicity in Britain and only secondarily whether anthropology is an appropriate way of doing it.

Much of this argument is conducted in terms familiar to Indianists and Africanists, but from their perspective there is a paradox in Sue Benson's way of opening it. Benson asserts that anthropologists have been much happier studying British Asian ethnicities than studying British black identity.

Asian ethnicities seem to represent culture and community in recognisably ethnographic ways, with boundaries sharply defined by language and religion, while blacks present no such clear demarcations.

The paradox is both academic and existential. Anthropologists have been much more central to discussion of identity in Africa than they have been in India. In Africa more or less all rural societies have in the past been defined as tribal, while in India only minority mountain and forest peoples have been so classified. Anthropological studies of these tribals have been peripheral to analysis of rural India, while for a long time anthropologies of African tribes were assumed to represent the whole truth about rural Africa.[10]

And this relates to the existential paradox. In Britain today everyone talks of Asian ethnicities. But in India itself ethnicity has until recently largely been absent, or at least repressed, from discussion of majority identities. Caste, class, communalism are perceived as the major categories of self-identification - distinctions that have to be either overcome or redefined in order to create ethnicities. In India tribals are so called because unlike more sophisticated people they have ethnicity. In Britain, however, much Asian sophistication is manifestly being invested in the imagination of ethnic identities.[11] Meanwhile, there are of course classic African ethnicities in Britain, in the shape of Yoruba Associations and Igbo Clubs. But the great majority of blacks in Britain, as children of the diaspora, have no tribal affiliations.[12]

All this means that there can be no direct transfers of anthropological expertise from India and Africa and no assumption that contemporary ethnicity in Britain is continuous with known and studied Indian and African identities. Nor is the old Africanist concept of detribalisation - deployed as a way of accounting for all those Africans who manifestly did not fit into an ethnic paradigm and also as a way of explaining social breakdown - any help in understanding the situation of British blacks. In studying ethnicity in Britain anthropologists have to start from the beginning.[13]

It is Sue Benson's contention that they have been unready to do so. She argues that the first specifically anthropological voice within the race relations field was James Watson's collection *Between Two Cultures* (1977). It was reminiscent, she says, of the Africanist classics of British structural-functionalist anthropology, both in its sequence of chapters, each dealing with a different ethnicity, and its assumption of the authenticity of the subjectivity of the migrants themselves, and hence of the anthropological account. The emphasis of this early anthropological work was on 'community and cultural life', terms drawn from extra-European studies with little consideration what they might mean in this different context. Benson stresses the silence in these texts:

> on questions of racism, power and domination [which] had some uncomfortable resemblance to that earlier silence on questions of racism, power and domination in the colonial encounter.

This was no accident since 'British social anthropology developed its distinctive character in the context of imperialism'. For Benson, in fact, these domestic field-studies reproduced the weaknesses of their Africanist antecedents, and her critique echoes current South African suspicions of anthropology. 'A particular kind of anthropology, one focused upon an organic view of culture, comes to stand for anthropology as a whole'. So the account of culture focuses distortingly upon the normative and those elders who express it. Moreover, 'the very assertion of the central authenticity of the actors' own experiences and concepts renders invisible the fine connections that run back and forth between agency and structure, representation of the self and representation by others'. In Benson's view this anthropology of British ethnicity both puts too much emphasis upon the subjective and gets the subjective wrong.

Benson's critique is developed by John Eade. Eade makes his own explicit reference to the development within Africanist anthropology from studies of rural tribes to studies of urban ethnicity. This example has been drawn on by anthropologists in Britain to cope with the absence of 'isolated, homogenous communities' yet nevertheless to fulfil their aim of listening to articulate black and Asian voices. Only to study discrimination and disadvantage, such anthropologists argue, is to define blacks and Asians merely as victims rather than as agents.[14] But how to set about listening to the voices of articulate agents within the minority communities? And here the idea of urban ethnicity is invoked, since ethnicity implies cultural definition and it is by means of creative use of imported cultural traditions that black and Asian organic intellectuals resist their enclosure by the white majority. Once the problematic has been defined in this way, then anthropologists appear supremely equipped to deal with it.

Eade accepts the need for 'internal voices to be heard properly'. He also accepts that anthropologists of British ethnicity have recently paid attention to 'racial differentiation and conflict, power imbalance and class'. He knows that their model of ethnicity is far removed from any idea of unchanging cultural consensus and that they stress instead creativity and re-deployment of cultural resources. In this sense they do not assert any primordial essential identity. Nevertheless, he thinks their work is still fatally marred by 'essentialist and primordialist assumptions'. In this anthropology, ethnic minority communities are distinguished:

> by a social and cultural essence ... The essential characteristics of ethnic groups are revealed in their social and cultural institutions, which are seen as primordial, i.e. fundamental in terms of providing a structural foundation upon which other institutions rest and requiring intense loyalty.

Hence one has to focus on ethnic group centres; on family, inter-familial networks, language, religion and place of origin.

Like Benson and the contemporary critics of South African anthropology, Eade believes that this focus on the primordial core of ethnic identity over-emphasises boundaries; over-states continuity; over-privileges men and elders; forecloses debates about identity. Like them, too, he prefers:

> an emphasis upon the social construction of individuals and groups through discursive narratives and practices, a relational, de-centred and

non-possessive approach towards power and resistance, and an insistence on discontinuity, divergence and heterogeneity.

Eade does not wish to assist in the 'construction of authentic communities', which then become the objects of public policy and legitimate representative ethnic spokesmen. He prefers to study deconstruction rather than construction; dispute rather than consensus; 'competing claims to knowledge and rival modes of resistance'.

Pnina Werbner's work is cited by both Benson and Eade. She thus occupies the invidious position of being what she calls a 'subject/victim of a fiction of representation by fellow anthropologists'. The details of her response are best left to her chapter. But its central argument is very relevant to the set of issues discussed in this Introduction. Briefly, she insists that competition, rivalry, discontinuity, and divergence must all themselves have a context. For Pakistanis in Britain, that context has been provided by an initial construction of identity by the first generation. These came into a void of strangerhood, non-relationship. They filled the void by making friends. 'Friendship isn't a given - it is a voluntary act of identification'. Pakistanis 'came as strangers to each other' but they made the most enduring bonds of friendship with each other. Through this friendship they created 'multiplex relationships out of that void, that initial emptiness'. Ethnic identity, in no sense given, was made out of myriad ties of family and friendship; it was both purposeful and implicit. Although manifestly and recently created - in fact because of its newness and vulnerability - this ethnicity came to insist upon cores and boundaries.

It is out of this context that rivalry and competition springs. 'This process of ethnicity or community formation is not a once-and-for-all, single event: it is a continuous, unfolding process of discovery and argument'. Two great changes have taken place. The former young first generation immigrants have become conservative elders, insisting on their core values. 'For the younger generation ... or for women, the sociality forged in bridging the world of strangerhood may be very oppressive'. So there is inter-generational and gendered struggle. Moreover, Pakistani numbers have grown so large that friendship clusters have grouped on the basis of class, political ideology, religious belief. 'Community was by now no longer a group of consociates who lived together. Community had become, in effect, a kind of argument through practice'. Yet community is more than a rhetorical trope. It exists in relation to other asserted identities; it exists as the arena of debate.

John Lonsdale makes use of the concept of moral ethnicity. Pnina Werbner speaks of the moral community. It is not a unity. It is full of conflict, of internal debate about moral values and the relationship to others. It involves fierce competition for leadership. It also involves competition for the right to name. Who are we? What do we stand for? What are we to be called? Here we reach once again the question of the special role of anthropology in studying ethnicity. Werbner's work is characterised by Benson and Eade as quintessentially anthropological. Yet Lonsdale's is a project of social and intellectual history. And so, essentially, is Werbner's. Lonsdale describes how a combination of Kikuyu patriarchs, rural entrepreneurs and Christian literates created an ideology of self-improvement and acquisition: this was their definition of Kikuyu core values rather than his. He also describes how younger, poorer men and women developed counter-ideologies of reciprocity. In the same sort of way, Pnina Werbner insists that it is not her methodology that creates an impression of a coherent Pakistani ideology, dominated by male elders. She is describing what they have created - and describing also the oppositions and counter-definitions which have arisen. Authentic communities may indeed become the objects of public policy, in a British equivalent to political tribalism. But for Werbner they are authentic because they involve moral debate. This debate requires to be taken seriously and to become part of the intellectual history of contemporary Britain.

Case studies of Asian and black ethnicity in Britain

The third section of this book consists of five case studies, three on Asian and two on black identities. In their richness of detail these chapters eminently deserve to be read for themselves. But they also raise general questions directly related to this Introduction.

It is striking that all three of the Asian case studies deal with religious identity, while religion is nowhere mentioned in the two case studies on blacks. Evidently there has been an ethnicisation of Asian religion in Britain, while black identity draws relatively little on religious sources. We must ask what difference this makes to the terms of debate within moral community. Does religious ethnicity place male elders in a dominant position? Are norms which are stated in religious terms particularly inflexible? Does this difference in the construction of ethnicity mean that there is an existential reflection of the disciplinary dichotomy stated by Sue Benson? Do Asians have cultures while blacks have hybridity?

As we have seen, Aziz Al-Azmeh insists that religions are not identical with cultures and that when the two are confused and conflated the result is the over-Islamicisation of Muslims, the over-Hinduisation of Hindus, etc. As we have also seen, in India itself religion has often been sharply distinguished from ethnicity. Nor is it by any means inevitable that religion will come to be an ethnic marker when believers find themselves a minority overseas. A recent study of South African Muslims, for example, notes that there has been much debate among them on how to observe Islam in a *dar al-harb* (home of the infidel). South African Muslims come overwhelmingly from the Indian and Coloured populations. Apartheid offered them ethnic identities, creating a special Malay category for Coloured Muslims. But from the 1970s there has been pressure from intellectuals to regard ethnicity as unIslamic. Rejecting the apartheid categorisation of Coloured Muslims as Malays, Islamic spokesmen insisted that Muslims 'identify themselves primarily as members of one religious group and emphasize the *umma* (community) both locally and worldwide' (Ridd 1994).

Yet in Britain ethnicity has not been rejected as unIslamic - or unHindu. British national identity is no longer defined, as it once was, in terms of Protestantism. Together with Empire, the confidence that Britain is the favoured nation of a Protestant Jehovah has long vanished. But into the fragmented, secular and uncertain consciousness of the contemporary white majority, there have been sharp intrusions of Asian religious ethnicity. Beatrice Drury's chapter on the self perceptions of young Sikh women finds that they explain the differences between them and whites or blacks 'in terms of religion and socio-culture', thereby reducing these differences 'to their ethnicity'. Steven Vertovec's conference paper asserted that 'settlement and institutional change in Britain has fostered and reified notions of "Hinduism" and "Hindu community" as ethnic phenomena'. Yunas Samad writes of a new term: British Muslim, remarking that 'the appropriation and usage of this term was an implicit recognition that religious identification was the major characteristic of British people originating from South Asia'. In fact, the conflation between Asian religion and ethnicity has already gone so far in Britain as to appear inevitable.

Yet, as both Vertovec and Samad document, the ethnicisation of Asian religion has been a recent process. Vertovec's discussion of Hinduism in Britain makes a direct connection with those processes of imperial classification which have been discussed above. He stresses the multiplicity and discontinuity of Indian sects and castes and emphasises that 'it was only after the arrival of, and colonisation by, Europeans' that the idea of a religion, an 'ism', came into being. 'The most prominent factor in such conceptualisation was the hegemonic presence of the British Raj'. Missionaries, Orientalists, and administrators combined to reify, select and define; indigenous revival movements made their own syntheses of Hinduism; these were then appropriated by early regional and pan-Indian nationalists. Gandhi made a major contribution to the re-invention of Hinduism. In twentieth century India great diversities have persisted but 'the notions of "Hinduism" and "Hindu community", which have been created in rather recent history hold considerable sway throughout Indian society and politics'.

The emergence of an ethnic Hinduism in Britain, however, is not a mere continuance of these Indian processes. Vertovec insists that 'the ideological formulation of "Hinduism" in Britain has been patterned by a host of unique contextual factors'. The process has been in some ways not unlike Pnina Werbner's discussion of the networks of friendship through which the first generation of Pakistanis filled the void of strangeness. Despite the enormous variety of their original castes, sects, and places of origin, first generation young male Indian migrants formed 'loosely-knit associations or committees ... to organize for all - regardless of area, sect or social group/caste of origin - modest celebrations of "All-India" holy days'.

Thereafter, as re-union with wives and children combined with secondary migration to build up numbers, there was a proliferation of regional and sectarian/devotional associations and temples. But the original impulse to generalisation and community has persisted and in a third phase a number of umbrella organisations have emerged in order to co-ordinate Hindu activities and to express common interests. Meanwhile, state school Religious Education has presented a generalised version of Hinduism, which is mirrored by the simplified and generalised representations promoted by many British Asian organisations. Thus 'British "Hindus" are being represented, and are increasingly representing themselves, as a single "faith": at the same time they are moving ... towards reproducing themselves as a "community"'.

Some parts of this analysis apply also to the emergence of British Muslim identity. As Edward Said and many others have shown, imperial Orientalism produced a reification of Islam as well as virtually creating Hinduism (Said 1978). British schools' Religious Education in World Faiths presents a simplified version of Islam along with its simplified version of Hinduism. Many British whites, occupying their own post-Christian world, treat real, living World Faiths with an almost awed respect, very different from that accorded to merely cultural manifestations of ethnicity. Out of all this has emerged the single, monolithic model of Islam which provoked Aziz Al-Azmeh into insisting on Islams as well as upon Modernities (Al-Azmeh 1993). However, all this does not simply deliver an Islamic ethnic identity since, after all, the notion of a single, universal Islam is supposed to override ethnicities. British ethnic Islam has been a product of the sequences of friendship and household formation described by Pnina Werbner and Steve Vertovec, as well as of the availability of funds from Saudi Arabia and Iran and the respect accorded to Islam in British official ideology.

The three Asian chapters in this book also raise the question of the consequences of this ethnicisation of religion - or confessionalisation of ethnicity - for youth and for women. Here we confront a question also now under much discussion by Africanists - whether ethnicity is yet another thing that men do to women, whether women are themselves the key bearers of ethnicity, or whether there is a complex mix of the two.[15]

In their discussion of the reproduction of British Muslim and Hindu communities, both Werbner and Vertovec emphasise the central role of women. Vertovec sees the domestic sphere as the 'foremost environment' for religious nurturing among British 'Hindus'. 'Hindu' women are the main agents of religious transmission (Vertovec cites Logan 1988). In the debate over how best to analyse British Islamic ethnicity, we have already noted John Eade's criticism of too great a focus on kinship and the household and his own preference for a study of the social construction of individuals and groups. But to this Werbner replies that she has not operated on some a priori assumption of the centrality of the domestic. Rather she has described the reality of the moral community constructed by the first male Pakistani generation. She adds that 'for the younger generation or for women, the sociality forged, in bridging the world of strangerhood may be very oppressive'. Religious definitions of moral ethnicity, in short, may make self construction of individuals through discursive narrative particularly difficult.

Thus in her conference presentation Beatrice Drury showed her young Sikh women constantly having to consider the force of religious tradition when making their decisions about conduct. Very few of her informants have been initiated into the full Sikh Code of Conduct and thus become 'a dedicated, religious Sikh'. The great majority say that their parents have put no pressure on them 'to be religious' - 'My Dad says that it's up to us when we get older'. Yet they nevertheless regard sections of the Code as binding upon them and as salient to Sikh identity. 'Nanak started a new religion. different from the Hindus and Muslims ... You feel that after all that struggle, you must be proud to be a Sikh, even a bad one!'; 'It's because of our religion. We have rules which Christians don't have'; 'I prefer to marry a Sikh because of the religion'.[16]

So far as Hinduism and Islam are concerned, religious essentialism has generated among whites not only an almost exaggerated respect but also its counterpart - a profound belief among radicals that Hinduism and Islam are by definition patriarchal and oppressive. What is missing in discussions of British Islam particularly is the sense that like other religions, and Christianity in particular, it is a mixture of the transcendent and the earthy; the comic as well as the severe; offering opportunities for liberation as well as for repression. The case of Salman Rushdie appears to have shown that Islam is no joking matter and no matter for debate either. From either perspective - of respect or condemnation - it seems especially difficult for young people, and particularly young women, to construct discursive or dissident identities within the Islamic moral ethnicity.

The contrast here with the chapters on black identity seems complete. Claire Alexander's discussion of the self-consciousness of black youth admits that they do not have 'a complete freedom of expression'. But the 'constraints of power' which she identifies are external and springing from the white majority and its institutions. She makes no reference at all to black elders or to black Christianity. Even with all the external constraints, her black youths almost play with identity. Ossie Stuart's focus is explicitly ludic, dealing as he does with Afro-Caribbean cricket. Admittedly, Stuart shows that it is mainly older blacks who keep cricket going. But it is significant that Stuart has to begin his chapter by arguing that 'the elder generation' has some role to play in the construction of black identity. It is the usual assumption, he tells us, that 'those symbols [of the black Diaspora] which have been identified as resource [to inform the identity of the Afro-Caribbean community] are in the main closely connected with black popular culture', and hence that 'those at the forefront of the imagination and recreation of African-Caribbean identity are black British youth'. Asians do indeed seem to have defining religious cultures while blacks - and black youth especially - are free to experiment with hybridity.

At the end of the conference, as at the end of this book, Stuart Hall looked back at the papers on black identity in particular and at the conference discussions in general. He emphasised that Claire Alexander was not 'talking about a kind of open-ended field where anybody could make up to be what they want: she wasn't talking about that kind of wild American post-modern version of identity, you know, like a smorgasbord, a super-market identity, where you go and choose up five, ten tins of whatever you feel like today. We're not talking about that. We're talking about operating a very constrained system, but nevertheless, even within those constraints, it is possible to use the identity question as a way of levering spaces open; even when that leverage doesn't put you in some new, wholly positive, wholly integrated situation - it simply wins you a bit of space'.

Hall was mainly concerned here to emphasise the serious limits on black freedom to exercise the 'art of being black'. Thus if Asian women are constrained by religious patriarchy, black women have to confront the way in which black youth masculinity is constructed - 'the way in which black men internalise the language of sexism, which is used about women in their own community. So they also talk about black women as "bitches" '. You can play with white stereotypes but they leave their mark. You can proclaim the cultural leadership of youth without freeing yourself by so doing from the constraints of the elders - whether the actual parenting elders or the imagined elders from an Afro-centric past. Perhaps future research should focus rather more upon these constraints as well upon the play of black youth identity.

Maybe future research on British Muslim and Hindu ethnicities ought to focus not so much upon the constraints as upon forms of youth and female dissidence. Yunas Samad's chapter is one indication of how that might be done. It contrasts British Muslims in Bradford and in Tower Hamlets. In Bradford 'leadership patterns, whether in the area of Pakistani, religious, mainstream or community politics were dominated by the first generation and these arenas gave them varying degrees of influence over subsequent generations'. The elders operated a patronage network legitimised by official recognition. They controlled mosques and religious institutions and hence the religious instruction of children. But in complete contrast to this apparently typical pattern of Muslim ethnicity, 'the various areas of influence in Tower Hamlets were dominated almost totally by the second generation'. It was they who controlled government sponsored community action programmes and who outflanked timid religious leadership by forming the Federation of Bangladeshi Youth Organisations.

This contrast in itself reveals that official multi-culturalism sometimes allows youth leadership to emerge. But Samad's argument is more far-reaching. Despite appearances, the reaction to Salman Rushdie and to the Gulf War was determined by youth radicalism in Bradford as well as in Tower Hamlets. In Tower Hamlets youth leadership of protest was obvious. In Bradford the Council of Mosques seemed to express an authoritative Islamic condemnation. But:

> The Council of Mosques was subjected to an intense push from the second and third generations who wanted them to take a strong stand. The youth stormed *en masse* Council of Mosques meetings, an arena where they never participated before, and demanded that the *fawta* should be adopted.

Few of these youth, says Samad, 'could be recognised by their religious behaviour'; indeed 'most of the discussions on Islam were taking place not in the mosques but in the pubs'. But that did not prevent pub Islam from being yet more essentialist than mosque Islam.

Another way of representing the generational balance within British Muslim ethnicity is developed in one of Pnina Werbner's papers, 'On Mosques and Cricket Teams', which makes a piquant comparison and contrast with Ossie Stuart's chapter. Here Werbner' s study of Manchester Pakistanis conveys a sense of ludic identity; they 'juggle social situations with the dexterity of a circus artiste', balancing religious transcendence with 'laughter, satire, fun'. They do this by balancing different symbolic domains. Religious institutions and Pakistani national communal associations 'are controlled by older men'. This is the realm of prestige in which male elders acquire honour and status. 'There is no room in this space for young upstarts [and] no room in it for women either'. It is these elders who have developed a Muslim ethnic identity. But 'if official religion, nationalism and economic production are the domain of male elders, then sports, entertainment and consumption are the domain of youth [and] women'. By contrast to Ossie Stuart's ageing black cricket teams, Pakistani cricket in Manchester is a young man's affair. But it is not only fun; it too is about nationalism and religiosity in another mode. Young British Muslims do not repudiate their ethnicity; in their activities 'an, old-new hybridism between Islam and popular culture is created' (Werbner 1992).

In this way Werbner runs the gamut from religious culture to hybridity. And yet another way of bridging the analytical gap between studies of Asian and black ethnicity is proposed in the recent *Routes and Beyond*, just published by the Centre for Bangladeshi Studies. A study of twenty young Bangladeshi men and women, it sounds from the advertising blurb to be an analogy to Claire Alexander's study:[17]

> *Routes and Beyond* moves us away from the familiar search for roots and follows journeys which cross numerous frontiers and lead in divergent directions. Rather than reinforcing popular stereotypes concerning ethnic minorities, our intention is to let the young Bangladeshis tell their own stories as far as possible. A vivid picture emerges of how the second generation are constructing diverse assertions of belonging within contemporary Britain which draw on multiple and dynamic identities (1994).

Conclusion

So we end up with black and Asian ethnicities not so different as they often seem. We can also break down other apparent polarities. Thus we end up with a renewed appreciation of the need to study white stereotyping, segregation, involution, identity-manipulation - the stuff of political tribalism. But we can also make a strong case for the special importance of understanding the debates about identity within moral ethnicity in this post-industrial, post-imperialist, post-modernist society where the politics of signification are so crucial. We can assert the need for a social and intellectual history of British moral ethnicity; at the same time we can put some confidence in an anthropology which moves away from benign imperial notions of ethnicity to place culture within its political and historical framework, and acknowledges the role of power in its imagination.

We can also begin to reconcile Aziz Al-Azmeh's Grand Narratives of universalism, modernisation, and the nation state with the free expression of post-modern heterogeneity. Stuart Hall's chapter makes this bid for a redefined combination of universalism and particularity. He speaks of a 'World music; the space of peoples that move their bodies in different ways; a space of peoples who will lay claim to universalism where citizenship rights are concerned, but who will not pay the price of universal citizenship by all becoming one, who insist that they have to be treated with respect ... in terms of a universal set of human rights, but who insist that they can look like Muslims and North Africans and Chinese, so long as they are prepared to pay the price of being part of a political collectivity'.

The great intellectual and political problem with which we are left is precisely this: what is the price of being part of a political collectivity? What do British Muslims have to invest in being British as well as being Muslim? What are the duties as well as the rights of universal citizenship? Hall insists that the price cannot be cultural - 'Let us be universal. Let us negotiate what the political price is, but after that, one has to take culture away from that'. Yet 'there is a trade off. Groups cannot be absolutely culturally different and want to claim the rights of society. You cannot say, 'It's my right to shoot Salman Rushdie, but tomorrow I'm going to show up at the DHSS and expect my handout just the same'. But what if proclaiming the right to shoot Salman Rushdie is one of the ways of proclaiming a Muslim youth identity?

The constraints on freedom of identity formation and expression, in other words, are not only structural and patriarchal but also part of the necessary price of combining universalism and difference. The conference left unresolved the key question of how to redefine and make operative Harry Goulbourne's project of the nation state and the project of being a citizen. This is, however, (to make a final St Antony's Ethnic Studies point) the critical necessity today in both Asia and Africa. It is also the critical necessity in multi-ethnic Britain.

Notes

1 This chapter quotes from the original versions of the papers presented at the Workshop.

2 There is probably a difference here between Al-Azmeh and Gilroy. Al-Azmeh indicts Romanticism and other irrationalist European thought, but wishes to reinstate the Grand Narrative of the Enlightenment. Gilroy is including Enlightenment ideas among those which have sustained racial typology and white supremacy.

3 Work on Kenyan ethnicity has become the most sophisticated in Africa (see also Spear and Waller 1993, Willis1993).

4 Atieno Odhiambo has written, with David Cohen, the most stimulating internalist account of Luo historical and social thought (1989).

5 Terence Ranger has recently been working on comparisons between the colonial invention of tribe in Africa and Soviet and Eastern European nationality theory. See his 'The Tribalization of Africa and the Retribalization of Europe' (1994). He is also working on 'Language, Empire and Identity', both in the imperial construction of the European nation states and in the colonial empires. Ossie Stuart has recently been working on a study of the history of the Afro-Caribbean community in Oxford - one product of which is his paper in this volume. He has also been working on ethnicity and physical handicap. See his ' Race and Disability: just a double oppression?', (1992) Yunas Samad has recently been working on British and European Muslim identity. See his 'Imagining a British Muslim Identification' (1993) and 'Book Burning and Race Relations: Political Mobilization of Bradford Muslims'. (1992) Tazeen Murshid is working on education, ethnicity and identity with particular reference to Asian pupils in London, and her book on these questions has been accepted by Trentham Books.

6 Brah remarks that Balibar's distinction between 'racism of the interior' and 'racism of the exterior' is not viable because imperial racism was part of the construction of Europe, and because many of those racialised outside Europe are now inside it. She also comments that the Irish have been positioned as simultaneously inferior and

superior - in the past, inferior within Britain but superior to natives in Africa and India; today, inferior to white Britons but superior to black and Asian ethnicities. Dr Brah presented a commentary on this text at a St Antony's Ethnic Studies seminar (Brah 1993).

7 Keith postulates some significant continuities, however. Thus for at least a century the East End has represented the exotic, civilisation's Other; contemporary Bangladeshi youth gangs are seen to fit into the tradition of East End gangs.

8 In 1993 there were two major conferences on ethnicity at South African universities.

9 The overwhelming majority of the chapters in the most significant recent study of Southern African ethnicity, Leroy Vail's edited collection, *The Creation of Tribalism in Southern Africa* (1989) are by historians rather than by anthropologists.

10 In his *An Anthropologist among the Historians and Other Essays* the American anthropologist Bernard Cohn has written splendidly on colonial constructions of identity in India, but he has focused on caste and communalism rather than on ethnicity. His 'African Models and Indian Histories' (1987, pp. 200-3) is a statement of the inapplicability of Africanist tribal anthropology to India.

11 While in African Studies the most influential social historical deconstructionist studies have focused on the invention of ethnicity, in India they have dealt with the creation of communalism or caste. The contrast is strikingly illustrated by an excellent recent collection - *Inventions and Boundaries: Historical and Anthropological Approaches to the Study of Ethnicity and Nationalism,* eds., P. Kaarsholm and J. Hultin, (1994). Africanist scholars - Ranger, Marks, Lonsdale, Baxter -write about the construction of ethnicity. (Lonsdale's 'Moral Ethnicity and Political Tribalism' is a particularly valuable development of his analysis). Indian scholars - Kaviraj, Chatterjee, Dhareswar - write about caste and communalism and make no mention of ethnicity. However, in a comment on a draft of this introduction, Yunas Samad has remarked that while it is true that communalism dominates the historical literature, ethnicity is very much used by students of contemporary affairs. This is not simply a division of labour between the disciplines of history and politics. It reflects a preoccupation with nationalism not only by academics and dominant groups but by the 'people'. Once independence is achieved the focus shifts and there is a significant upsurge in ethnicity, both in the academic world and in politics, such as Bengali linguistic politics, Sindhi nationalism, Sikh, and Tamil separatism, etc.

12 The interaction of slavery and ethnicity in Africa has been complex. The Nigerian scholar, Peter Ekeh, has argued that it was the rise of slave raiding and trading which made people rely on the moral kin-group rather than on the amoral state, and that colonialism then erected the edifice of invented tribes on the basis of the kin-group (Ekeh 1990). Afro-American attitudes towards the assumed tribal character of African society were also complex, but some black American modernisers took much the same attitude as Indians to tribal backwardness. When the Zimbabwean historian and novelist, Stanlake Samkange, married an Afro-American Ph.D. in 1958 in Indiana, the bride's local black newspaper described the hazards she would face in what was then Southern Rhodesia. There would be the Rhodesian colour bar. But above all, and this is what most negroes dread most she would have 'to accommodate the idea of belonging to a TRIBE' (Samkange Family Scrapbook, Harare).

13 Anthropological studies of the Caribbean are, of course, another matter. A figure like M.G. Smith, who wrote extensively both about Jamaican and Nigerian society, would merit a chapter of his own.

14 This argument reflects a similar debate within Africanist writing, where many scholars chose to emphasise African initiative and the African Voice rather than further to document colonial exploitation. I began my own career as an Africanist with precisely these emphases. See: Terence Ranger, (1969), *The Recovery of African Initiative in Tanzanian History,* (1970); *The African Voice in Southern Rhodesia, 1898-1930,* For

a structuralist critique of this position see A. Temu and B. Swai, (1981), *Historians and Africanist History: A Critique.*

15 For a summary of this African debate see, Terence Ranger, 'Introduction', (Ranger and Vaughan, 1993. pp. 12-5).

16 These quotations do not occur in Drury's chapter in this book.

17 The blurb in fact promises more than this rather unanalytical collection of interviews delivers. Claire Alexander is herself embarking on a post-doctoral study of Asian youth identities, with Stuart Hall at the Open University.

2 Racism and identity: Issues for the Irish in Britain

Mary Hickman

Stuart Hall makes the point that black people have been denied access to an English or British identity and as a consequence have had to discover who they are (Hall 1991). In contrast the Irish in Britain have had their identity absorbed within the British national collectivity and were forced to retrieve their identity at the public level. This extrusion of the Irish from public debate about ethnic minorities in Britain was necessary because of the historical strategies of incorporating Irish migrants and their descendants. These strategies, only to be understood in the context of anti-Irish racism, resulted in the silencing of the Irish and rendered them invisible as a minority.

The concept of incorporation refers to the processes by which the State actively attempts to regulate the expression and development of the separate and distinctive identities of, potentially, oppositional ethnic groups, in order to create and sustain a single nation-state. The crucial feature of incorporation was the strategies used by the state to achieve a centralised identity: Britishness. The point of interest was that the Irish first came in very large numbers to Britain during the 19th century a period most critical for the successful consolidation of national identity and culture in Britain (and by that means a class alliance).

In the 19th century both anti-Catholicism and anti-Irish hostility were significant factors that unified at important junctures different social classes and in this way helped in stabilising capitalist social relations and securing allegiance to a centralised national identity. Racist discourse about the Irish in the 19th century not only described the Irish as sub-humans but also as outsiders. Anti-Catholicism and anti-Irish racism projected the Irish as the antithesis of what was considered English/British. The Irish were Catholics, thus potentially traitorous, and racialised as possessing national characteristics that made them inherently prone to violence and uncivilised behaviour. Examining the documentary evidence of the 19th century reveals that both the type of jobs the Irish did in Britain and the conditions in which they were compelled to live were transmuted into corroborative evidence of their degenerative nature. Irish ghetto areas became synonymous with disorderly conduct. This was usually attributed to the ingrained Irish habits of drunkenness and faction fighting.[1]

A specific fear expressed in the 19th century about the settlement of large numbers of Irish in the new urban areas was of contamination. The attitude of many public officials was that, unless measures were taken to prevent it, the Irish would bring the indigenous working class down to their level. The Irish were deemed to monopolise a level of poverty and consequent barbarity unknown in the civilised world. The Commissioners conducting the 1836 Poor Law Inquiry (Ireland) concluded:

> Irish emigration into Britain is an example of a less civilised population spreading themselves, as a kind of substratum, beneath a more civilised community: and, without excelling in any branch of industry, obtaining possession of all the lowest departments of manual labour (cited in Jones, 1977, p. 48).

The health of the body politic was deemed to be endangered by the Irish. In 1943, *The Times* commented on the ease with which Daniel O'Connell was able to manipulate the Irish to support the repeal of the Union:

> A people of acute sensibilities and lively passions, more quick in feeling wrongs than rational in explaining or temperate in addressing them - as easily aroused into outrage by supposed oppression as subdued into docility by felicitous kindness - equally susceptible of gratitude for hypocritical sympathy as of indignation at unintentional or imaginary injury - no less impetuous in repaying the one than in avenging the other-such is the people whose virtues and vices... O'Connell has so fiendishly exploited (cited in Lebow, 1976, p. 56).

Here the characterisation was of the Irish being ruled by instinctual emotions, the implicit contrast was with the rationality of the English/British. This was a good example of an important feature of the Code of Breeding which underpinned the 19th century discourse of Anglo-Saxon racism (Cohen 1988). On many occasions in that period the Irish were explicitly contrasted with what it was to be English. For example, *The Times* in 1847 stated the following:

> To Englishmen a vigour beyond the constitution is an odious thing...it seems unkind and unjust to recommend for Irishmen a policy that would not be scouted for ourselves. But we must be ruled by circumstances. If crimes are unEnglish - if English means of detecting and punishing them fail, why should not an unEnglish power be exercised in districts where violence and murder stalk unavenged and unchecked (cited in Lebow, 1976, p. 67).

In these ways and in many other writings in the 19th century it was possible to detect the way in which Irish immigrants were depicted as both alien and inferior. This was also true of other colonised groups at the time but the difference was that the Irish were present in large numbers in the new urban industrial centres of 19th century Britain.

The presence of the Irish gave rise to other fears. For example, in 1848 during the last gasp of Chartism the government feared both an insurrection in Ireland and a combination of Irish nationalists and Chartists in Britain (Saville 1987). The Irish Confederates[2] in Liverpool and elsewhere in Britain worked in alliance with the Chartists and aimed to organise a sympathetic rebellion to detain the military in Britain. Borderline occupational groups such as shopkeepers and clerks hurried to enlist as Special Constables as the press highlighted the Irish threat. The press made much of the tensions between the Chartists and Confederates about the use of violence. By exploiting the emotive connotations of the term Irish, the press and the Establishment utilised a means of stigmatising Chartism and of fragmenting the working class (Belchem 1985). In the second half of the 19th century these divisions amongst the working class became consolidated and may partly account for the readiness of significant sections of the working class to vote Tory once the franchise was extended (Kirk 1980). Cedric Robinson has commented on this period in the following terms:

> most important to the understanding of the evolution of working-class nationalism in Britain ... is the formative role of another nationalism - Irish nationalism - played in the formative period of English working-class developments and its concomitant construction of English working-class culture (1983, p. 45).

In the case of the Irish we have the opportunity of tracing the history of the interrelationships of incorporation, segregation and differentiation and their implications for the identity of a large and significant migrant labour group over a period of 150 years. John Foster has described the existence of ghettoised Irish communities and anti-Irish hostility as a significant factor in the assertion of political and industrial authority over the indigenous working class in the mid-19th century (1974). Subsequent research has enabled the extension of Foster's analysis by demonstrating that segregation and differentiation of the Irish Catholic working class was even more widespread and systematic than he had outlined. Moves to segregate and differentiate the Irish were implemented by municipal government: for example, in the operation of the Poor Law and the development of policing practices.[3] However, no area was more important than education.

The impact of anti-Catholicism and anti-Irish prejudice on education debates in the 1830s and 1840s was such that a separate system of Catholic state schools were developed for the explicit purpose of educating the children of Irish migrants. This was a consequence of the fears of contagion. Even the most fierce anti-Catholic overcame their hostility to state funding of any Catholic enterprise in order to guarantee that Irish working class children were not educated with their own children in inter-denominational schools. For Irish children the consequences of government grants being extended to Catholic schools were that they were segregated and differentiated from the rest of the population. In other words, the Irish were integrated into a segregated system.

Catholic schools became the institutional structures for containing Irish children and the symbol of differentiation of Irish Catholics from the indigenous working class. The latter all of whom, whatever their other differences, shared Protestantism, and by the end of the 19th century, a national identity. The working class were not solely determined by their class experience, religion and national identity were also important. The Catholic Church and Catholic school were local symbols of an enemy within and were frequently attacked (Hickman 1990).

Anthony Archer in a study of the Catholic Church in the north-east of England, highlights the extent to which Catholics were viewed as a race apart, and the most obvious symbol of this to many non-Catholics was the Catholic school. In an interview with one non-Catholic who grew up between the two World Wars this century he elicited the following observations:

> we didn't mix you know really, you know at school or anything like this. They were very much at that time a separate community from non-Catholics. I suppose they had their affairs, like dances. I don't remember even mixing with them socially ... they were just a different type of people I think as far as I was concerned - like Jews you know (cited in Archer, 1986, p. 58).

Archer cites many other examples from both sides, of the perception of difference between Catholics and non-Catholics and of the means by which these differences were constantly regenerated. The separate institutions in the local neighbourhood, in particular the churches and the schools, were central to this.

It was left to the Catholic Church in Britain therefore to be the chief agency of incorporation of the Irish population. The long-term aim of the Catholic Church was to strengthen the Catholic identity of Irish migrants at the expense of weakening their national identity. Education thus, became a central element of this strategy (Hickman 1990). The aims of Catholic schools, as articulated by the Catholic Poor School Committee, were to transform the Irish into useful citizens, loyal subjects, respectable members of the working class and good Catholics. The interests of the government and the Church were consistently presented as mutually reinforcing. The expansion of Catholic education was carried out in a manner that ensured the control of the clergy over the schools.

It can be argued that a racist discourse of contamination, in the 19th century, ensured that Irish children were not educated with other working class children. An ethnically segregated education system was established with far reaching consequences for both the Irish Catholic children within Catholic schools and those educated in the rest of the state sector. One consequence was the masking of Irishness by Catholicism both within official discourse and for the children of working class Irish Catholic immigrants. Catholic schools held up a mirror to their pupils that reflected their Catholicity rather than their Irishness.

It was not surprising, therefore, that a contemporary account we have suggests the pressure experienced by the second generation to marginalise Irish identity. Tom Barclay, in his memoirs of a bottle washer, recounts his childhood in Leicester in the 1850s and 1860s. After describing his mother's recitation of old Irish legends and laments he continues:

> But what had I to do with all that? I was becoming English. I did not hate things Irish, but I began to feel that they must be put away; they were inferior to things English...Outside the house everything was English: my catechism, lessons, prayers, songs, tales, games...Presently I began to feel ashamed of the jeers and mockery and criticism (cited in Lees, 1979, p. 190).

This quotation indicates that becoming English was not based on an inevitable process of cultural assimilation but on acquiring a perception of the inferiority of Irishness compared with Englishness. The cultural pressures to become English and reject Irishness which Barclay cites, primarily emanated from the Catholic Church. His world outside the house was defined by the Church and the school. Those who struggled to retain this Irishness, were encouraged by their experience of Catholic schooling to maintain a low public profile for their identity.

When a further substantial phase of Irish migration to Britain took place in the post-war era these institutional processes of incorporation were an important factor in explaining the absence of the Irish in the 1960s and 1970s from discussions about racism and discrimination. Both visibility and invisibility were socially constructed and can change over time. In the 19th century the Irish were a highly visible group and subject to the racist practices described above. The fact that the arrival of hundreds of thousands of Irish people in the mid-20th century was barely officially acknowledged did not mean that a racist discourse or racist practices against the Irish no longer persisted.

On the contrary the invisibility of the Irish in official discourse (as opposed to popular discourse) about the newly emerged pluralism of British society reflected a number of factors. First the terms and conditions of the 1949 Ireland Act, which for security and labour supply reasons defined the Republic of Ireland as not a foreign country. This remains the legal position to this day and means that the Irish in this country were to be treated as British subjects; even whilst retaining Irish citizenship. The situation does not exist primarily because the Irish were white but because of the political and economic relationship of Ireland to the United Kingdom. Second, the successful defusing of the political threat of the Irish on the one hand by active incorporatist strategies and on the other hand by perpetuating racial stereotypes as found in Irish jokes. In the figure of Paddy racist theories of intelligence and moral degeneration were linked and relayed through poplar culture to become common sense, dangerousness was defused by turning it into social incompetence (Cohen 1988).

The fact that the Irish have been included within the boundaries of the British national collectivity does not necessarily represent either widespread acceptance of the Irish as English/British or the successful assimilation of the Irish and their descendants. It was arguable that this incorporation was more a reflection of attempts to preserve the British Isles as one labour pool and to lay a cultural claim to all of the Islands as single domain. Floya Anthias and Nira Yuval-Davis point out that racism remains fundamental to national identity in Britain and the foremost struggle about the boundaries of the United Kingdom was taking place in Northern Ireland (Anthias and Yuval-Davis 1992). Britain and Ireland form a free movement area. The movements of Irish people were not subject to formal British immigration control, rather it was the particular screening, harassment and detention mechanisms of the Prevention of Terrorism Act, which was used in the surveillance of the Irish population (Hillyard 1993).

In Britain the inclusion of the Irish within the category of White European does not protect them from various forms of racist discrimination and prejudice. Contemporary racist portrayal of the Irish focuses on various aspects of the Irish experience, culture and Irish politics. The racial stereotypes most commonly utilised depict the Irish as all: terrorists and inherently prone to violence, stupid, welfare scroungers, non-human (pigs); untrustworthy, unreliable, feckless, religious fanatics, culturally backward and drunken. For example, explanations of the present conflict in Northern Ireland were rooted in stereotypes that echo the rationality/irrationality divide of 19th century conceptions of the differences between the English and the Irish (Hickman 1980).

The stereotype of the welfare scrounger has also flourished. Terry Patterson in research about the access to social security benefits for Irish and other ethnic minorities argues that there was a contradiction at the heart of the treatment of Irish people by the British government and its social security and immigration agencies (1992). In law, there was the same access for all Irish people to Income Support, or to council housing when homeless, as for British citizens. This parity in law was contradicted by the institutionalised heavy policing of Irish claimants in Britain, and by the failure of benefit provisions or bilateral agreements to cover obvious contingencies, such as costs of attending family funerals in Ireland (Taylor 1992).

There is evidence available from a study 'Identity Crisis' undertaken by Central London Social Security Advisers Forum that Irish claimants receive a differential treatment to other claimants and part of that differential treatment constitutes discrimination. The Commission for Racial Equality (CRE) has issued a legal opinion that certain practices carried out by Social Security offices in relation to Irish claimants constitute racial discrimination (1992). Many other examples exist of discrimination experienced by the Irish in employment, housing and policing.

The majority of the Irish born living in Britain today emigrated between the late 1940s and the early 1960s and because of their absence from official discourse about ethnic minorities they remain almost entirely unresearched. A recent survey of the readership of the main Irish community newspaper in Britain, *The Irish Post,* revealed that the majority of its readers earns under £20,000 and were concentrated in manual and intermediate level jobs. Many indicated their continuing strong identification with Ireland and hoped to return to live there. Over fifty per cent said their response to Irish jokes was one of either anger, resentment or humiliation (only fifteen per cent were amused). Three quarters of the sample indicated that they would either never or rarely talk about Northern Ireland if there were British people present (Irish Post Survey 5 December 1992-23 January 1993).

The majority of the children of these migrants have attended Roman Catholic schools. What has been the impact of this on their identity compared with Tom Barclay's account a century earlier? Some Irish children in contemporary Roman Catholic schools would echo Barclay's words. Others resist the process of incorporation. For example, Philip Ullah's research, interviewing second generation Irish pupils in Catholic schools in London and Birmingham in the early 1980s demonstrated that the children of Irish migrants adopted a variety of responses to their situation. Just over a fifth claimed to be English, the rest to varying degrees chose an Irish identity. The single largest categories were the fifty-one per cent who said they were half Irish and half English. A sizeable section of the second generation were shown to have rejected assimilationist strategies (1985). However, the identity they adopted reflected the ambivalence which was contained in their every day lives. For example, subject to racist jeers yet living in a society which denies that anti-Irish sentiments were racist. Living in a family where their Irish heritage was taken for granted but perhaps going to a Catholic school which does not acknowledge the specificity of the background of the majority of its pupils.

Of the second generation pupils in Catholic schools (in London in the mid-1980s) who I interviewed eighty-one per cent gave their identity as Irish or Irish descent(1990).[4] Many of the second generation Irish in a London borough renowned for its anti-racist educational policies, complained about the absence of the Irish from such policies and stated that this denial undermined those anti-racist strategies in their eyes. For them it was hard to credit talking about racism and not refer to the operation of the *Prevention of Terrorism Act* or to the widespread tolerance of anti-Irish jokes.

Catholic schools continue to both directly and indirectly attempt to incorporate and denationalise the Irish in Britain and have taken few steps to challenge Irish stereotypes. The consequences for the identity of the Irish in Britain were complex. Children of Irish descent attending Catholic schools were, therefore, either, at risk of a crisis of identity, or become involved in processes of ethnic redefinition for example: London Irish. The analysis presented here broadly holds true for Scotland as well as England and Wales. However, the continuing significance of religious identity as a conduit for national expression in Scotland and the long term consequences of the 1918 Education Act (Scotland) requires an exploration for which there was not space here.[5]

The Irish exclusion from debates about racism and ethnic minorities was due to the dominance in Britain of a paradigm of racism that was primarily designed to explain patterns of racism and discrimination experienced by migrants from Britain's ex-colonies in Africa, the Caribbean and the Indian subcontinent. The main premise of this paradigm, stemming from the USA, was that racism was about colour. It was a paradigm which has never explained anti-semitism but nor does it explain, for example, contemporary practices in Germany for differentiating foreigners from the rest of the population. Rather as Philip Cohen has emphasised, racist discourses in pursuit of natural symbolism of inferiority have never confined themselves to body images, let alone just skin colour. Every kind of social behaviour and cultural practice has been utilised to signify this or that racial essence (1988). This was readily appreciated not only when the depiction of the Turks in Germany was considered but also when evidence about the Irish in Britain was examined.

The evidence of a racist discourse about and of discriminatory practices towards the Irish bears out what Dipankar Gupta has written in a study of the Quebecois (1983). Gupta outlines how Quebec offers the spectacle of a racist ideological discourse being activated in a situation where both the communities concerned, the dominated and the dominating, were European and white. His conclusion was that this reinforces the great truth that racism was the most comprehensive ideological weapon of domination and that it does not always obey the protocol of colour.

Identity remains an arena of contestation for Irish migrants and their descendants. Although Irish identity does weaken with generation, this was not the consequence of an inevitable process of assimilation to British society, rather the weakening of Irish identity, where it occurs, was the consequence of the pressures of specific strategies of incorporation. Social class, region and participation in Irish political and cultural practices were all significant factors both in the denationalisation of the Irish and in the resistance to incorporation. Thus the survival of Irish identity was more likely if the individual of Irish descent was of working class origins, lives in an Irish area, visits Ireland regularly and participates in Irish social and cultural activities. In these circumstances someone of Irish descent who was third - or fourth-generation Irish would select an Irish identity to describe himself or herself. The strategy of incorporation has had therefore varying degrees of success and further research would provide a fuller understanding of the basis of the contestation of Irish identity in Britain within the context of anti-Irish racism.

Notes

1 For further developments of the arguments in this paragraph see M.J. Hickman, 'A Study of the Incorporation of the Irish in Britain with Special Reference to Catholic State Education: Involving a Comparison of the Attitudes of Pupils and Teachers in SelectedCatholic Schools in London and Liverpool'.

2 The Irish Confederation broke away from Daniel O'Connell's National Repeal Association in 1847. The Irish Confederates shared the same goal of repealing the Union, but in contrast to O'Connell's constitutionalism they countenenced that freedom might have to be won by force of arms.

3 For example, see F. Finnegan, *Poverty and Prejudice: Irish Immigrants inYork 1840-1875* on the operation of the poor law. For discussion of the policing of Irish communities see W.R. Cockcroft, 'The Liverpool Police Force, 1836-1902'; D. Philips, 'Riotsand Public Order in he Black Country, 1835-1860 and R. Swift 'Another Stafford Street Row: Law, Order and the Irish Presence in Mid-Victorian Wolverhampton'.

4 Sixty-six pupils and thirty-nine teachers were interviewed.All respondents were asked this question: Which of the following terms would you use to describe yourself?
British
Irish
English
Of Irish Descent
Londoner
Liverpudlian
Other category

5 See the following for the specificity of Irish experience in Scotland: J. Bradley, 'Religious identity in modern Scotland: culture, politics and football'; J. Handley, *The Irish in Modern Scotland*; T. Gallagher, *The Uneasy Peace.*

3 Anti-racist strategies: National identity and French anti-racist discourses and movements

Cathie Lloyd

The growth of racism in contemporary Europe (Ford 1992) makes it important to study anti-racist movements in their political contexts, both national and international. France is an interesting example for several reasons. Like Britain, there is a long tradition of radical political opposition to racism stretching back in different forms to the Enlightenment. In France, issues of modernity were posed in a particularly insistent manner through the Revolution of 1789, which continues to have an important hold on the collective imagination. Three important themes are central to anti-racism: the Emancipation of the Jews (1791), the Ending of Slavery (1794-1802) and the Declaration of the Rights of Man (1789).

At the same time, the centralising impetus of Jacobinism runs counter to particularist demands that also inspired movements of liberation (Schnapper 1990). In France the issue of universalism/difference as a binary opposition is raised in an important way. Some of the most persuasive and illuminating analyses stress that although debates may be constructed in terms of universalism/difference they were however shot through with contradictions and exceptions (Balibar 1989, Silverman 1992). The theme of universalism/difference is, however, central to myth making about French national identity, thus binding anti-racism and national identity together in a complex way.

There is still considerable exchange between anti-racist associations and intellectuals, which facilitates quite wide discussion about the philosophy of anti-racism. Another specificity lies in the existence of several large national associations concerned with anti-racism more or less directly. These date back at least to the immediate post-war period and trace a lineage back to the period of the Enlightenment and the Revolution of 1789. I have called these traditional anti-racist organisations although this is not intended to imply that they were traditionalist or conservative.[1]

The way that traditional anti-racist movements interact with newer associations, particularly those that have developed in the past ten years, was of great interest because it illustrates how certain ideas persist and were partly transformed by the action of new participants. The discussions in France

(Galissot 1985, Taguieff 1991) about the limitation of anti-racist strategies against the rise of the racist-populist Front National (FN), involves wide ranging debates about the nature of national identity, the determinants of inclusion and exclusion, the internal limitations and contradictions of anti-racism and the way in which anti-racist strategy should be directed. The parameters of the debate are quite different to those in Britain, where discussion has focused on the adequacy of anti-discrimination measures, equal opportunities policies, the delimitation of ethnic identity and claims to representativity in anti-racist organisations. The French debate constantly addresses (mostly implicitly rather than explicitly) the themes of universalism and difference (Lloyd 1994), which relates strongly if obliquely to the debate in Britain.

This paper focuses on the nature of anti-racist organisations and their changing agendas in France. The discussion will examine the way in which the traditions of the Enlightenment have been selected and reinterpreted in the course of political struggles over the legitimacy of the Republic in France. Universalism/difference are central themes in definitions of French national identity but are also bound up with ideas of anti-racism. The Enlightenment still acts as a powerful magnet to all forms of progressive thought in France, although it has specific resonance for anti-racists.

In the first section, Enlightenment traditions of anti-racism[2] are examined. As a profoundly innovative movement, challenging the status quo, we cannot understand the Enlightenment without recognising its diversity. Spanning the eighteenth to reach out beyond the nineteenth century, the Enlightenment was an agglomeration of interests (Wuthnow 1989). The philosophes of the 18th century were in frequent disagreement, changed their views and expressed ideas which were often half-formulated. 'As a result we can find philosophes who argued both sides of almost any question' (Hankins 1970). One of the central themes of the period was enigma, and this was expressed in the diversity of genres used; travellers' stories, political treatises, polemics, epistolary novels, plays, poetry and so on. It was thought that the application of reason would literally throw light on any problem.

In order to interpret Enlightenment discourse today it helps to remember this open and ambiguous form of debate. At the same time, however, through the unrealised project of the French Revolution, the Enlightenment has a particular significance in France. Many contemporary debates make reference to the eighteenth century to justify their claims. There has been a continuous struggle to appropriate the ideas of the Enlightenment, which have a legitimating function for the French Republic. In particular the Third Republic called on these traditions while transforming them into a national myth, after the humiliating defeat of 1871 and the loss of Alsace-Lorraine. This was central to the building of a national, secular, public education system which even today is defended fiercely by the left (Citron 1991).

The philosophes were profoundly affected by the encounter with societies outside Europe, which tested and pushed their ideas often to their limits. They were often uncomfortable with the radical directions to which their ideas seemed to point (Jacob 1981). Fundamental questions were posed by the early forms of colonialism in the context of the slave trade. The nature of human society, the development of a 'science of man' and their relationship to the Other was central. Despite their radical challenge to the *ancien regime*, the philosophes did not fully transcend the assumptions of their time. As one writer points out: 'Despite a belief in human equality, eighteenth century thinkers, in their very eagerness to understand and classify people, developed a concept of human inequality based on climatic, cultural and racial criteria' (Cohen, 1981, p. 60). While broadly agreeing I would also stress the diversity of eighteenth century thought, which would serve both as a source of ideas of liberation and to justify colonialism and racism.

There were contradictions within Enlightenment thought. Profoundly moved by ideas of human equality and natural rights, yet unable to transcend certain forms of thought and the conviction of its enlightening mission so that it underpinned the civilising mission of France. This became more overt in the latter part of the nineteenth century in Third Republic's justifications of imperialism and the development of classificatory systems of racism (Said, 1993, p. 74).

Since 1945 official government discourse has involved evocation of the slogans Liberty, Equality and Fraternity. On occasion this was claimed to include anti-racism, although often in a contradictory way. Thus in 1973 after a series of racist murders President Pompidou stated:

> France is profoundly antiracist ... I think that the only solution is a common, real control of immigration (Wihtol de Wenden, 1988, p.162).

Contemporary anti-racists look back to the Enlightenment as the source of anti-racism.[3] The organisations also select their own cannon of privileged examples to legitimise their actions. This selection, aimed at highlighting the great and good among the philosophes fails to address the complexity and contradictions of anti-racist discourses. What this means is that we are given a wholly good or wholly bad picture, feeding into a polarised discourse which cannot effectively challenge official hypocrisy.

In France, the Enlightenment is the basis of a double claim: to be the source of anti-racist ideas and to provide a legitimacy for contemporary organisations who have (sometimes highly selectively) interpreted these ideas. Although the ideology of the Revolution is thought to be in crisis (Touraine 1988), it still has a powerful hold as the legitimating myth of the French state. Since 1984 the links between Government and some of the newer generation of anti-racist organisations[4] have given rise to considerable controversy. Popular anti-racism was thus caught between the need to base itself on official ideology and to mount an effective critique of government policies.

I will now turn to examine how these modern anti-racist organisations have used Enlightenment and other discourses. I outline the main organisations and indicate the challenges that have been posed by a new generation of anti-racists in the last ten years.

In France as in Britain, most support for anti-racism comes from the Left and progressive organisations, such as left-wing parties, trade unions and concerned groups in society. For the purposes of analysis I have divided these organisations into four categories: firstly, the traditional human rights organisation, second more explicitly anti-racist/anti-fascist organisations, third, immigrants and solidarity groups and finally the new generation of associations formed in the early 1980s.

The first two categories can be taken together to constitute a traditional set of anti-racist networks. The Ligue des Droits de l'Homme (LDH) belongs strictly to a human rights tradition and was profoundly involved with the Dreyfus affair. It was formed during the trial of Emile Zola for writing the pamphlet *J'Accuse* in which he denounced the conspiracy behind the Dreyfus affair (Zola 1988, Deljarre and Wallon 1988). Although it tended to be based on a Paris-based intellectual and political elite, the LDH quickly became broader setting up local committees.[5] The LDH set itself:

> the mission of taking up again the teaching of the Declaration of the Rights of Man and Citizen from which has come all the social evolution which France has accomplished since 1789 (Trarieux 1902)

The Ligue was mainly concerned about the separation of church and state, free education and trade union rights, although it also criticised the colonial situation in Algeria, thus linking human rights with racism, colonialism and opposition to anti-semitism. During the 1920s the LDH denounced conditions in New Caledonia, the growth of anti-semitism and fascism, and called for equal employment rights for Immigrant workers. The destruction of the Ligue's archives was one of the first tasks of the Germans when they arrived in Paris in 1940.[6]

Nazi ideologues, notably Arthur Rosenberg, wanted to destroy Enlightenment ideas. Ideas of human equality, universal natural human rights were negated by Nazism, posited as it was on man's fundamental inequality. In a speech on 28 November 1940 to the French Chamber of Deputies, Rosenberg attacked the ideas of 1789 (later published under the titles *Sang et Or* and *Reglement de Comptes avec les Idees de 1789*) intending to destroy the ideas of equality and advance the superior doctrine of Nazism in its place. The reply of George Politzer, in the clandestine press (1947), emphasised that Rosenberg's speech would have little impact due to the strong roots of the Enlightenment in France. This became the theme of many illegal Resistance publications such as *Le Patriote* published by the Ligue (Willard 1989).

After the war, the Revolutionary heritage remained an important aspect of anti-racist discourse. Articles were written about the ideas of the Enlightenment particularly those of universal human equality in a way that could be relevant to the contemporary reader.

Yet this tradition, as shown, was not monolithic. Because the republic was the site of daily political struggles throughout the nineteenth century. There were various interpretations and claims of legitimacy which arose from it. In particular this related to attitudes to the groups identified with different stages of the Revolution, particularly the Jacobins, Robespierre, and some of the most radical innovations and breaks with the *Ancien Regime*, including the Terror.

The MRAP was formed in 1949 as a regrouping of Jewish and other resistance groups initially concerned at the limitations of denazification and the continued instability of peace in the cold war period. Like its rival, the LICRA, it represented a realisation of the need for particularistic struggles within the universalistic framework of French political life. Its journal *Droit et*

Liberté was given to it by a Jewish resistance network.[7] Anti-racists of the 1950s and 1960s were concerned with classic notions of Nazi fascism, focusing on its violent and terroristic forms,[8] the inadequacy of denazification in Europe, fears of a German military renaissance and the rapid re-emergence of fascist organisations in France. Police raids against Algerians were compared to similar raids *au faciès* against Jews during the war (*Droit et Liberte*, 22-28 September 1950, No 42)

However the issue of racism in the colonial system and in a broader international context, became increasingly important, together with concerns about the treatment of Algerian immigrant workers in France (*Droit et Liberte*, December 1952, December 1954, July 1955). Both the LDH and the MRAP argued for a negotiated peace in Algeria and opposed the colonial regime there. Racism and fascism were seen as having a direct link, and fascism was clearly privileged in this discourse. During this time the treatment of North African workers was seen as reminiscent of racist practices during the occupation and under Vichy, and these issues were carefully reported by antiracist organisations for campaigning purposes (Lloyd 1993).

The campaign for a Law Against Racism began at this time, involving a wide range of participants especially lawyers and activists, to keep track of the kinds of discriminations which were taking place and to physically challenge discrimination in cafés and bars (MRAP 1984, LICRA/MRAP 1987 and 1989).

The transformations of the 1970s, together with the changing emphases on racial discrimination and racist violence against people of North African origin meant that the early emphasis of the MRAP on concern about the resurgence of fascism and anti-semitism was supplemented by a broader definition of the people threatened by racism and more social concern about the causes and expression of racism. As a body able to fight cases under the Law against Racism it operated a legal advice system and also lobbied for legislative and policy changes.

At the end of the 1970s in France, a ground-swell of activity against fascist groups and daily racism was also taking shape. The traditional organisations of anti-racism such as the MRAP retained considerable authority. Thus after the bombing of the synagogue of the rue Copernic on 7 October 1980 some 200,000 people demonstrated in response to a call for mobilisation on the streets of Paris.

However, different forms of anti-racist activity were also taking shape. For instance, the wave of protests and rent strikes against conditions in SONACOTRA housing between 1975 and 1980 mobilised many of the more traditional immigrants' organisations in protest at housing conditions and levels of rent in immigrant workers' hostels (*Liberation,* 10 November 1980). Comparisons were drawn between the activists in this dispute, mainly Algerian, and the underground leaders of the French Federation of the FLN during the 1950s and early 1960s, particularly when fifty-five of the activists had to go into hiding to avoid arrest.[9] The relations between the SONACOTRA strikers and the traditional sources of support, such as the trade unions were not good. They clashed with the Communist oriented trade union federation, the Conféderation Générale du Travail, (CGT) over tactics and found little more support from the Socialist Conféderation Français

Democratique du Travail (CFDT) who also feared that autonomous immigrant workers organisations might split the working class.

Much activity centred on housing, which had been hastily erected to replace the *bidonvilles* but they were little better than camps of prefabricated buildings. The inhabitants of the transit cities continued to protest against conditions, sometimes by burning them down. In many of these transit cities local residents' committees were formed to protest against conditions but also against police harassment, which had become worse with the tightening of identity checks. Young people who had been brought up in France felt particularly affected by these problems as their levels of expectation were rather higher than their parents. In the Paris and Lyon areas concerts were held to draw attention to racist murders and police harassment. Also a loose network of young people of immigrant origin was active and their existence was expressed by their publications, notably *IM'media* and *Sansfrontière*.

In the months leading up to the Presidential elections of 1981 there were hunger strikes protesting against deportations, the double penalty[10] and calling for civic rights for immigrants. These activities launched by Christian Delorme through the Comité intermouvements auprès des évacués (CIMADE) and the Mouvement pour une alternative non violente (MAN) mobilised massive support across France. The hunger strikes introduced a principle which was to become central to these early mobilisations, that of non-violent action (Jazouli, 1992, pp. 37-9). A manifesto saying 'No to Apartheid France' was launched (*Le Monde*, 17 April 1981, *Sansfrontières,* No 19 April).

This powerful moral crusade backed by religious authorities gained some concessions at the end of April from the Ministry of the Interior, delaying some deportations. One of the first acts of the new Ministry of the Interior, Deferre, was to issue a circular[11] announcing that no young person who was born in or who came to France at an early age should be deported.

The success of the hunger strikers took the initiative out of the hands of the more radical activists around Rock Against Police (RAP) and Za'ama Des Banlieues (ZAB), although they never entirely controlled suburban youth. Echoes of the uprising in Britain's inner cities were felt in French *banlieues* during 1981 and especially the summer of 1982. A series of racist killings and the experience of police harassment gave rise to considerable anger among young people. Outbreaks of lawlessness, particularly *rodeos* (stealing, driving and destroying high performance cars) were part of the cycle of violence.

Attempts were made by the youth of *banlieues* to organise a range of activities as a constructive response to the situation. At the Gutenberg transit city on the outskirts of Paris, an open door festival was organised in November 1983. The city, little more than a camp, was finally closed in early 1983. The Collectif pour le developpement des droits civique, established in the autumn of 1982, campaigned around the broken promises, the right to vote for immigrants settled in France, made by the Socialists by organising parallel and symbolic voting of immigrants in the local elections of March 1983.

In one Lyon housing estate, Les Minguettes, a spiral of police raids, confrontation with youths, and violent reprisals was halted by a group of young people, most with North African backgrounds, and led by Christian Delorme. Their aim was to transform anger into collective action by holding a hunger strike, from 28 March 1983, with several demands for the government.[12] The non-violent tactics were effective in drawing media support but failed to strike a chord with much of the French labour movement. The hunger strikers won pyrrhic victory. The wounding of Toumi Djaidja, one of the hunger strikers, by a shotgun on 17 June, was by mid-August followed by nine murders across the country. This led to serious talk among youth of Maghrebien origin about the possibility of self-defence. An alternative project was established to organise a non-violent march for equality and against racism, which was inspired by the great civil rights marches of the 1960s in the USA and the ideas of Martin Luther King.

The 1983 March for Equality was a founding act in many ways in the construction of collective action of suburban youth of immigrant origin. It represented their rejection of current stereotypes and their anonymity by going to parts of France they had never discussed their problems. It did however steal the limelight from organisations that had been more active at grass root's level for many years, some among disaffected and angry youth, but also the more traditional anti-racist organisations.

Many of the newer grass root organisations that proliferated around the *banlieues* of major French cities in the late 1960s and early 1970s were alarmed by the Minguettes initiative. Many of the young people who had initiated the March found it difficult to cope with the media attention and allowed the more seasoned organisers such as Delorme to act as spokesmen. The original organisation which spawned it, SOS-Avenir Minguettes did not survive the march.

The difficult decision reached by most of the existing associations was to support the march and particularly to make their resources available to it. Thus the local free radio stations, Radio Beur (in Paris), Radio Gazelle (Marseilles) and newspapers in particular *Sansfrontière* were opened up to the publicising of the march and their demands. The more experienced were concerned that some of the newer actors were allowing existing stereotypes to be perpetuated: hence Mogniss Abdullah in an interview with Bouzid Kara pointed out that the use of his first name only as author of his book *La Marche* perpetuated patronising treatment of North Africans in France treating them as children.

At the same time, a significant conflict had emerged between the marchers themselves and some of the support committees set up by the more traditional anti-racist networks. The effervescent atmosphere of total immersion in concrete action generated a strong sense of belonging among the young people who were part of the march. There was an almost inevitable clash with some of the older generation of anti-racist/anti-fascists who felt that they had 'seen it all before' and wanted to give advice to the new recruits to the movement.

Three logics of action in the March of 1983 can be identified (Jazouli, 1992, pp. 61-3). Firstly networks of Christian and Third World organisations such as CIMADE and MAN who were strongly committed to non-violence. Second the young activists who while they had not initiated the march saw it as a way of strengthening existing mobilisation and their own networks; Association de la Nouvelle Génération Immigrée (ANGI), the free radios and Sans Frontière. Third, some of the first two, particularly the activists around the Collectif pour les Droits Civiques and Sans Frontière, wanted to develop initiatives against violence. Also to build on the history of earlier struggles, to push the traditional organisations to re-evaluate their position and support them, and to make demands for civic action to oppose the institutional and political obstruction and discrimination which kept immigrant populations in a situation of insecurity.

The March arrived in Paris after a significant media build up. A Carnival spirit was engendered with the march carrying innovative banners, slogans linked into trendy youth culture, especially using slang. But at the same time deeply consensual with official recognition in the form of a reception at the Elysée by President Mitterand, who announced that some of the demands of the marchers were being met.[13]

The March was deeply consensual and the official spokesmen emphasised its universalism, stressing the links to Martin Luther King. Delorme said (quoted in Jazouli, 1992, p. 65).

> All the moral legitimacy of the March rests in this desire for fraternity and the wish for unanimity

It was a significant contrast to the Anti-Nazis League (ANL) carnivals that the 1983 March in France was experienced much more as a personal and moral renaissance, which rejected the presence of organised political groups and even trade unions.

The March for Equality of 1983 was disorganised but spontaneous, gathering momentum as it moved towards Paris. Young people were strongly involved in the March but their participation especially in dealing with the media was marked by uncertainty. Although the march presented a strong and positive image, it lacked a coherent programme. In fact it was an uneasy coalition of Delorme's ecumenical movement, traditional left anti-racist support and young people with different backgrounds from the *banlieues*, some organised, many not. Suspicion of established authority was widespread among the youth many of whom had experience of left-wing opportunism. The Socialist Government tried to remain connected to the new movements. While it supported a MRAP-led initiative at UNESCO, Assises pour l'Egalite in March 1984, it also began a dialogue with the *beurs*[14] with the reception of the marchers in December at the Elysee, although there was bitter controversy about which of them was acceptable enough to meet the President.

There was controversy among the youth organisations about the future direction of the movement. There was a strong trend in favour of identity politics, backed by their roots in the autonomous movement for self-representation. Another powerful current emphasised the dangers of a closed identity and the need to make links with broader forces in French society. A number of factors indicate that it was this trend, specifically the ascendancy of universalism over particularism, which progressively gained the upper hand.

During the summer of 1984, a convention of associations held in the Rhone-Alpes region expressed reservations about the humanist discourses of the previous year. The emphasis was much more on an autonomous expression of youth activity to prevent 'the reappropriation of their rights and their words'(*Liberation*, 9 June 1984).

A group of *beurs* developed a plan to retrace the previous march this time not on foot but on that symbol of working class French youth, the *mobylette*.

The plan was to end with another great anti-racist carnival in early December in Paris (*Liberation,* 8 October 1984). Again, this activity was intended to reinforce local campaigns which were mobilising against FN election meetings. However the continued marginalisation of youth of immigrant origin was shown when Toumi Djaidja, one of the original hunger strikers and marchers in 1983, was given an exemplary fourteen month sentence for a series of alleged thefts in Saint Etienne.

The divisions in the anti-racist movement were more evident in media representations. In some areas like Toulouse it was reported that the youths were amazed to be met by a traditional trade union demonstration of CGT members, including what would have been their fathers' generation of immigrant workers, with mint tea and loudspeakers emitting the songs of Jean Ferrat (*Liberation*, 5 November 1984). On other occasions there were more direct disagreements. One marcher, Mathilde told journalists:

> For us it was a shock. In the hall there were all the classical anti-racist organisations, MRAP, PC, PS, FASTI and all the rest. And then during the discussions we were face to face with people talking about police patrols, ethnic concentrations ... it was frightening! We felt that they saw us as emigres. And they separated us from the local youth (*Liberation*, 20 November 1984).[15]

There was an enormous misunderstanding. The left, traditional anti-racists, often expected their leadership credentials to be taken for granted. The youth saw little difference, and often collusion, between them and the authorities who oppressed them. This was shown in tricks they played on the organisers of reception committees. In one account of a repeated trick a marcher was said to have pretended to be an illegal immigrant in order to provoke the traditionalists to offer to help legalise his case. On revealing the trick, the response of the older activist was to angrily refer to their own credentials: as deportees to concentration camps during the war (*Liberation*, 2 December 1984).

Others saw the traditional organisations as doing excellent work in certain areas, such as literacy schemes or legal support work, but as far as youth was concerned they were out of their depth, sometimes paternalistic and often obstructing the creation of new more appropriate youth structures. One of the key problems, which the traditional organisations were forced to address by these new movements, was that the imperatives of anti-racism in the 1980s came less from the imperatives of immigration but were much more closely linked to the internal problems of French society. The new demands were about the need for citizenship (*Le Monde,* 1 December 1984). The roots of the new anti-racism within the problems of contemporary France was recognised by some commentators. Balibar wrote, on the demand for equality:

> It is said that its utopian! It would be if the youth of C84 (Convergence 84) didn't recognise the relation of forces and classes which exist in France today. But in denouncing the 'false problem' of immigration and in making the straightforward demand of equality the 'rouleurs' indicate the knot of real problems, that of racism, based in institutions before being in peoples

consciousness/unconsciousness and that of inequality, of wealth, employment, culture and power.
They can't transform this situation alone. It's clear that Immigrants and their children of 2nd, 3rd, etc. generation won't win effective equality of rights (right to live as full citizens of community to which they contribute without feeling perpetually threatened) if their cause isn't included in other social struggles and reciprocally , that these struggles will never surmount obstacles which they are encountering today if they don't make the fight against racism a priority so that they can take up the call for equality and civic rights without restrictions (Balibar 1984).

By the mid-1980s SOS Racisme and France Plus had emerged as the national forerunners among the new movements which had given rise to the March for Equality, Convergences 84 and 1985 (Jazouli, 1992, p. 101). The two organisations were composed of young people who were already involved in mainstream political parties. Many were members of the Socialist Party, or had graduated from student and lycee politics, although their initial impulse related directly to the imperatives of local associations, especially racial violence.

The arrival of Convergence 84 in Paris was less consensual and unanimous than the march of the previous year. Only 25,000 people, very young and ethnically mixed, were recorded as having turned out. In the press account there were references to the Notting Hill Carnival in London. The speech of one of the leading marchers, Farida Belghoul gave rise to an angry reaction in the more traditional MRAP. Belghoul dismissed the older anti-racists as unreliable and ambiguous in the support they offered.

They hold out their hands to us, but its partly because they are at a safe distance from our suffering. And the left? ... why don't they realise they are in the same boat as us? They are suggesting an integration which would mean the destruction of our integrity (*Liberation*, 3 December 1984).

The badge of SOS Racisme first appeared at the final demonstration of Convergence 84. The slogan 'hands off my mate' has an interesting resonance with Tom Robinson's slogan 'hands off our people' at the first ANL Carnival in Britain in May 1974. However, the difference between these two statements[16] points to an important distinction between the collectivism of the 1970s, 'our people', compared to, 'my mate', of the French youth movement of the 1980s. The initial position of SOS Racisme was that of a moral crusade with no political position. Julien Dray made this clear in a speech in June 1986:

The new generation is more generous than the old which pretended to openness but was dried up by ideology. Before, militants wanted to be hard, knowledgeable and aggressive. But Leninism is dead. The activists of today are more human, and they try especially to be effective

and Desir added:

> Our only ideological reference is to the Rights of Man. We have no motions or programmes or platform, hardly even a little charter. It would be a waste of time and an artificial way of creating divisions. Our philosophy is humanism (*Liberation* , 14 June 1986).[17]

After 1985, SOS Racisme organised annual mega-concerts with significant financial backing from the government. The organisation, however, could not hold back from politics. It was involved in organising opposition to proposed changes in the Nationality Code during the cohabitation period. In 1988 it announced a political programme, increasingly becoming concerned with the urban environment. In recent years it has distanced itself from the Socialists especially during the Gulf War. Given its earlier dependence on Government financial support (especially from President Mitterand) its activities have been curtailed.

During the debate about the Nationality Code in 1986 and 1987, new attitudes emerged among young French of North African origin, about the need to engage critically with French nationality, rather than to remain outside it (Hargreaves 1988, Silverman 1988). The mainstream *beur* associations stressed the need for a new synthesis of universalism which was not restricted to French values. Arezhi Dahmani of France Plus told the Long Commission:

> Our values are those of the French Revolution. Our values are secular and we support democracy completely. We support a system of values which is universal but which today is not the sole property of France.

Harlem Desir stressed:

> For us integration is primarily the rejection of exclusion, the rejection of the ghetto which includes the cultural ghetto (Long 1988).

The secondary school movement which led street protests against the introduction of selection procedures for University in December 1986, demonstrated the involvement of young people of immigrant origin in broader categories of French society, while at the same time retaining their collective references to their Islamic identity (Perotti, 1986-7, pp. 148-9).

The massive popular and euphoric mobilisations of the mid 1980s have proved difficult to sustain. The national demonstration on 6 February 1993[18] of about 50,000 people proved the continued existence of a broad base for such mobilisation, but the initial euphoria of the youth associations has given way to a more routine existence. The associations which took over the national scene after the second march (Convergence 84) have tended to orientate towards more characteristically French values with discursive references, especially, to secularism (Leveau and Wihtol de Wenden 1988). Universalist values, such as human rights, citizenship, symbols of the French revolution or even references to the philosophers of the Enlightenment were frequently made (Lloyd 1994) while other associations make important claims about their history and the contribution made by immigrants to the future of France. The regular commemoration of the massacre of Algerian demonstrators on 17

October 1961 was a clear example of the desire to link contemporary experience of racist violence to the life of the older generation (Guidice 1992, Lloyd 1993).

The accomplishments of the new movements can be seen as two-fold. Firstly, they mobilised a much more youthful population. In 1989 Harlem Desir claimed an average membership age of between fifteen and twenty-five with particular strength among secondary school pupils (Desir, 1989, p. 10). Thus anti-racism, in terms of a general identification and even a fashion with all the positive and negative aspects which that entails, rather than sustained activism, became commonplace among young people during the 1980s. Secondly, the new movements developed a new way of approaching anti-racism using a different range of resources, in particular music, film, comic strip and life-style activities (Mestiri 1987). The younger generation however, it has been argued, have a different political approach to the earlier youth movements which were inspired by the events of 1968. Motivated by equality, their orientation was more realistic seeking results in concrete actions rather than utopian dreams. Rather than opposing the system as an earlier generation had done in 1968, the youth generation of the late 1980s demanded that the system should at least observe its own rules (Desir 1989).

Initially the French grass roots' mobilisations were around violence, the police and immediate issues of bad housing. The 1983 March for Equality aimed to end the spiral of violence on housing estates, but by broadening out its aims the focus on immediate problems was blurred. Convergence 84 became broader quicker - with its demands for equality, although its participants were less ready to compromise. The appropriation of youth culture was important. The themes were urban rebellion, *intifada*, with particular reference to the struggle of the Palestinian youth and equality and universalism. French references to the Notting Hill Carnival, and Rock against Racism were not surprising given the link between French and British youth culture through the globalisation of popular music. They insisted on a different content to their universalistic appeals, one which claimed more of a place for more particularistic questions of identity and identification. So, while continuing to manipulate the ideas of the Enlightenment, contemporary French anti-racist organisations have been subtly shifting and manipulating its (already ambiguous) content. They have illustrated in a practical way that it is possible to construct new, more inclusive universalisms and that the prophets of doom who argue that the old narratives have come to an end, may have to think again.

Notes

1 The most obvious and active associations in this 'traditional' category were the Ligues des Droits de l'Homme (LDH) founded in 1989, the LICRA (Ligue International Contre le Racisme et l'Anti-semitisme) and Mouvement Contre le Racisme et Pour l'Amitié Entre les Peuples (MRAP), founded in 1949.

2 I have delineated 'anti-racism' here in parentheses to stress that I am not suggesting that an anti-racist discourse as such was possible at the time of the Enlightenment. This was prior to the enunciation of a coherent doctrine of 'racism'. Those elements of Enlightenment thought with which I am concerned here can best however be seen as

the antecedents of a body of thought posited on human equality, valuing aspects of different societies. It was opposed to what we might see as the antecedents of racism (theories of inequality, the devaluing of 'the other' and polygenism).

3 For instance the MRAP publication *Droit et Liberte* links the battle of the philosophes for rational knowledge to Diderot's opposition to anti-semitism, *Droit et Liberte*, 19-25 January 1951, No 59 (163). The Abbé Grégoire, active in both the struggle against slavery and for Jewish emancipation was frequently mentioned (*Droit et Liberte*, 24-30 November 1950, No 51 (155), *Droit et Liberte*, 22-28 December 1950, No 55 (159), *Droit et Liberte*, 29 December - 4 January 1951). Victor Schoelcher who organised the final abolition of slavery in 1848 was described as the first anti-racist of any consequence (*Droit et Liberte*, 12-18 January 1951, No 58 (162). There were many other examples.

4 In particular, SOS Racisme and France Plus.

5 By December 1899 it had 12,000 members and 70 local committees.

6 These archives were never recovered, although the Ligue was reestablished after the Liberation.

7 The group was the Union des Juifs de la Resistance et de l'Entre'aide, Interview with Albert Levy, ex-General Secretary of MRAP and editor of *Droit et Liberté*, 1 February 1993.

8 These themes continue to be present for example in relation to the bombings of the rue Copernic synagogue in 1980, the shootings at the Goldenberg restaurant in 1983, the firebombings of the SONACOTRA immigrant hostels in the South of France in 1989 and the desecration of the Carpentras Jewish cemetery in 1990.

9 This was later annuled by the Conseil d'Etat in March 1977, but writers such as J-L Hurst, *Liberation*, 10 May 1980 emphasised the similarities with the struggles of the Algerian war of liberation and saw the French solidarity network as similar to the *porteurs de valises* who had organised illegal support for the FLN.

10 Under the 'double penalty' foreigners convicted of quite minor crimes could be deported after serving a prison sentence. Several cases involved young people who had come to France at an early age and who had no connections with their parents' country of origin.

11 This was published on 26 May 1981.

12 An end to police raids, to stop the prosecution of youths who were involved in violence provoked by the police, moving of certain police officers and the establishment of rehabilitation projects on the estate to employ youths.

13 Notably a ten year resident card for settled immigrants, an enquiry into the legal provisions against racism and a further study of the need for the immigrants' right to vote.

14 *Beur* is Parisian backslang for Arab and this term was adopted by some youth of North African origins.

15 PC Parti Communiste, PS Parti Socialiste; FASTI Federation des Associations de Soutien des Travailleurs Immigrés.

16 It is not possible to say at present what, if any, connection there was between them.

17 Dray and Desir's speeches were reported on the eve of one of the big concerts at the Bastille in *Liberation*, 14 June 1986

18 The General Secretary of MRAP, Mouloud Aounit points out (*Differences*, March 1993) that the political content of the march (to commemorate the anti-fascist's defeat of the violent demonstrations and attempted coup by fascist leagues on 6 February 1934 (*Droit et Liberte*, 15 February 1952, No 107) was studiously ignored by the media.

4 Asians have culture, West Indians have problems: Discourses of race and ethnicity in and out of anthropology

Susan Benson

> Why this sudden bewilderment, this confusion? (How serious people's faces have become). Why are the streets and squares emptying so rapidly, everyone going home lost in thought?
> Because night has fallen and the barbarians haven't come. And some of our men just in from the border say there are no barbarians any longer.
> Now what's going to happen to us without barbarians? Those people were a kind of solution.
>
> From *Waiting for the Barbarians*, by Cavafy, C.P. translated by Edmund Keeley and Philip Sherrard, 1975.

This paper is concerned with social anthropological discourses about race, ethnicity and culture in Britain.[1] More specifically, I seek to explore the ways in which such discourses have served to construct Asian ethnic minorities in Britain as proper objects for anthropological study, and Afro-Caribbean ethnic minorities as, by contrast, problematic objects of investigation. For if Asian ethnic minorities have indeed been seen by anthropologists as a kind of solution to the disappearance or increasing inaccessibility of anthropology's traditional barbarians, the tribes and small-scale societies of the non-Western world, Afro-Caribbean ethnic minorities have proved singularly resistant to such an incorporation into the anthropological canon. Just why this should be so is a complex matter, and one that raises both intellectual and political considerations which anthropologists working in Britain have generally chosen to ignore. For beyond these particular concerns lies a broader issue: the ways in which ideas of community, culture, race and identity are deployed in the construction of ideas about the nation. In Britain, as in Cavafy's imperial city, discourses about barbarians may tell us as much about the problematic and unexamined nature of the Self as about imagined Others. While social anthropology certainly does not occupy the central position it once did in the construction of such discourses, its late twentieth century role is both a reflection of its history and a contributing factor to the politics of the present.

Anthropology, race and ethnicity

It is true to say, I think, that in general anthropologists working in Britain have proved to be rather uncomfortable with the idea of race and much happier with the concept of ethnicity. This is, at first sight, surprising: it was an anthropologist, Kenneth Little, followed by his colleagues and students at Edinburgh and elsewhere, who produced the first substantial body of empirical research on black and Asian communities in Britain in the post-war period; and in their work the focus is explicitly upon race and what were conceived of as the key social and political issues of the time, integration and assimilation (Little 1947, Collins 1952, 1957, Junod 1952, Ndem 1953, Garigue 1953, Banton 1955, Patterson 1963). These studies were pioneering in the developing field of race relations, but they were never incorporated into the anthropological canon, as taught in university departments or read as significant monographs. Indeed a close study of these texts reveals a sense of unease, of apology, which is both significant and interesting. This unease seems to turn on the absence from the communities studied of certain key features: an ordered kinship system, religious institutions, collective structures of social control. These communities are, in the eyes of their ethnographers, precisely not that, and ideas of race relations prove difficult to link to the kinds of concepts with which anthropologists in the immediate post-war period theorised the collectivity. In particular, the focus upon social problems, the process of absorption or the conditions for social assimilation transgresses the central assumption of structural-functionalist anthropology: that of functionally integrated, bounded units of study, to be understood in terms of their own coherent values and practices.

Banton and Patterson in particular went on to become influential figures in race relations research, but in many senses they left their anthropology behind as they did so. I would argue that it was only in the late 1970s, with a series of publications produced under the auspices of the SSRC Research Unit on Ethnic Relations at Bristol (Wallman 1979, Saifullah Khan 1979) and with the publication of James Watson's influential collection, *Between Two Cultures* that we can detect the emergence of a specifically anthropological voice within the race relations field. It is the nature and framing of this voice that I wish to consider in more detail.

The format of *Between Two Cultures* is, indeed, somewhat reminiscent of those other highly influential collections, *African Political Systems* and *African Systems of Kinship and Marriage,* both central teaching texts for classical British structural-functionalist anthropology. There is a series of chapters, each one having as its subject a different people or ethnic minority (Watson's terms): The Sikhs, The Jamaicans, The Greek Cypriots, and so on. There are other echoes, too, of those earlier anthropological texts: of the assertion of the anthropologist's privileged knowledge, able to provide 'reliable information' based upon 'field experience' in contrast to 'surveys undertaken by social scientists who had little, if any, knowledge of the migrants' backgrounds' (Watson, 1977, pp. 2-3). A double authenticity is asserted here. On the one hand, the authenticity of the anthropological account, and on the other, the authenticity of the experience of the migrants themselves, their particular 'cultural predispositions and personal attitudes' (Watson, 1977, pp. 2-3, 13) which are to be privileged over mere external accounts.

For Watson, as for most of his contributors, it is the theories of ethnicity then popular within anthropology (particularly the work of Abner Cohen on the positive functions of ethnic solidarity in urban situations (Cohen 1969, 1974) and Fredrik Barth on culture, identity and ethnic boundaries) (Barth 1969) that can best capture that authenticity. Indeed Watson is firmly opposed both to the 'excessive optimism of the race relations industry with its focus upon assimilation and to the polemical work of Marxist sociologists with their focus upon issues of exploitation and domination'. Castles and Kosack (1973) are singled out for special criticism. 'Their approach completely ignores the differences between groups ... it is a fallacy to argue that the migrants' own cultural predispositions and personal attitudes are irrelevant' (Watson, 1977, pp. 12-13).

The same note is sounded in Ballard and Driver's article published in the same year in *New Society* and entitled 'The Ethnic Approach'. Here, the authors describe the aims of the newly established Commission for Racial Equality as:

> laudable but inadequate. Above all, the central concept of racial equality seems likely to bypass the fact that we have ethnic, not just racial, diversity in Britain today. The minorities ... possess, in each case, a distinctive community and cultural life. These different lifestyles have now become as much a focus of so-called racial tensions and conflicts as their colour (Ballard and Driver 1977, p. 543).

Echoing the earlier classificatory framework of Michael Lyon (1972, 1973), Ballard and Driver go on to distinguish race as 'sets of individuals [my emphasis] sharing common physical characteristics' from ethnicity, which refers to 'the social group [my emphasis] to which an individual belongs' (ibid p. 544). This distinction between race and ethnicity, inauthentic and authentic social identities, exercises a powerful hold upon analyses from the 1970s onwards, both in and outside anthropology. Ballard and Driver are careful to assert that all ethnic minorities have ethnicity; other analysts, however, as we shall see, are not so sure.

The claim being made here, then, is that it is social anthropology that would make the most significant contribution to the uncovering and documenting of this previously neglected ethnic diversity. Ethnicity remains the dominant framework in most subsequent anthropological research, as may be seen from the review of the decade 1977-87 presented in *New Community* 1987 (Werbner 1987). In this respect this anthropological work plays a role in the construction of a broader liberal discursive formation developing in the 1970s. In which immigrants become ethnic minorities, ideas of assimilation into a homogenous British nation are replaced by ideas of multi-culturalism and a single British society is replaced by the idea of a 'mosaic of communities' living within the State. It also fits well with the discourses of ethnic essentialism to be found in the rhetorics of grant-aid as they developed in the late 1970s and early 1980s.[2]

Now, I do not wish to suggest that the development of a substantial body of research within this framework was a bad idea, or to deny the utility and desirability of the exploration of cultural pluralism and social differentiation among Britain's ethnic minorities. I would reject the idea, advanced by some radical critics, that the development of the ethnicity paradigm must be interpreted as a dark plot to divide and rule, to fragment and render invisible the unity of the black community (Bourne and Sivanandan 1980, Lawrence 1982). But it must be acknowledged that the anthropological silence in these texts on questions of racism, power and domination had some uncomfortable resemblance to that earlier silence on questions of racism, power and domination in the colonial encounter. By adopting the single ethnic minority as a focus for study, or by setting different ethnic minority communities side by side (The Pakistanis, The Italians) as analytical equivalents, these texts wrote across race, and privileged considerations of cultural diversity. Each people or minority is analysed in terms of a set of cultural practices and institutional arrangements proper to itself, or compared and contrasted in some particular respect with another people or minority. Thus even where the emphasis is upon the reworking of culture in the context of migration, the field within which this is held to occur is that of the collectivity, membership of which is taken as historically given. In this process, structural patterns of disadvantage are reduced to external constraints (Ballard and Ballard, 1977, p. 53) while considerations of race and racism become largely invisible. No dark plots, then, but a systematic preference for an analytical framework bearing significant implications for how to think about Britain's ethnic minorities.

Why ethnicity?

It is clear that in some ways anthropologists in the 1970s saw ethnicity as a bridging concept, one that might, as one enthusiast suggested, 'usher social anthropology into the systematic study of contemporary industrial society, without our discipline losing its identity' (Cohen, 1974, p. xxiii). Exactly why, however, requires some investigation. A charitable explanation has been offered by Chapman, McDonald and Tonkin (1989 p. 11):

> Ethnicity permits us as anthropologists to come close to home, as it is both cheap and fashionable to do. It also allows us ... having come close to home, to retain that grip on significant difference from ourselves (whoever we may be) that has been the moral and intellectual motor of the anthropological enterprise from the very first.

While I too would choose to emphasise the constraining force of both anthropology's past and its present, my interpretation would be decidedly less charitable. It is a truism to argue that British social anthropology developed its distinctive character in the context of imperialism and the colonial encounter, and its underlying structure as a discipline was inflected, perhaps indissolubly inflected, by that context. As a set of discourses, its conditions of possibility, (to borrow a phrase of Foucault's) were shaped by it; and its non-discursive structures (its ideas of good practice, of proper fieldwork, and so) on were defined there. Ethnographic narratives may change, theoretical fashions come and go, but discontinuities in British anthropological theory and practice (and there are many obvious instances of these) are superimposed upon a deeply embedded professional habitus.

At the centre of this habitus stands an idea of participant observation, fieldwork, in small and relatively bounded units of study. It is through fieldwork that individuals become anthropologists, have access to professional regard, jobs and publications. It is unsurprising, then, to find that when anthropologists turned their attention to working at home, as they increasingly began to do from the 1970s onwards as research funding dried up and countries overseas became less accommodating, they sought to replicate, at home, what they studied abroad. Just what might be considered to be proper objects of anthropological investigation becomes clear if we consider what contemporary (1990 and 1991) members of the Association of Social Anthropologists (ASA) working at home in the UK and Eire have chosen to study.[3] Two major areas of research predominate: firstly, the study of rural populations (generally communities), which comprises twenty-seven per cent of all fieldwork recorded; two-thirds of these are of populations in Celtic areas. Secondly, there are the tribes within: studies of ethnic minorities, which comprise twenty-nine per cent of the total. A poor third come studies of kinship, household and the domestic domain (ten per cent). The remaining thirty-four per cent consists of a diversity of less significant clusters of interests, none more than five per cent of the total, including the life-course, labour markets, work and unemployment, religion and health and illness. The general point is clear. Anthropologists working at home remained committed to the canons of their discipline. They sought out what they supposed to be bounded communities, be they rural or ethnic; and they continued to interest themselves in the exotic in the domestic, be it a Scottish crofting community or Gujaratis in Leicester. There are signs of more idiosyncratic choices being made in the 1980s, but even in the 1980s ethnic and community studies dominate the listings.

The deep structures of the discipline are inscribed not simply upon the choice of objects of study, but also upon the theoretical framework within which analysis proceeds. Issues of power, history and domination may have become fashionable questions in the post-colonial anthropology of outside and over there, but they are conspicuous by their absence from most (though not all) studies at home. Take, for example, the work of Anthony Cohen, one of the most influential of those seeking to expand the anthropological canon to include work done in Britain. Cohen's project - to link rural community studies to mainstream anthropological concerns - leads to a focus upon 'the contemporary sense of community in industrialised, mass societies' (Cohen 1986, p. 7), and to a concern with questions of identity, belonging and symbolic boundaries (Cohen 1982, 1983, 1986). Like Watson, there is a staking of claims here to a terrain overlooked by sociologists (Cohen 1983, pp. 17-18); like Watson, there is also the suggestion that this is a specifically anthropological terrain. And like Watson again, the very assertion of the central authenticity of actors' own experiences and concepts renders invisible the fine connections that run back and forth between agency and structure, representation of the self and representation by others. The 'greater realities of class and state' (ibid, p. 17) (or of inequalities and cultural hegemony) can be left to the sociologists.[4]

Working on the margins of their discipline, it is perhaps predictable that these anthropologists should be so concerned with finding authentically anthropological subject matter. Unlike those early race relations writers, they seek to remain firmly within the disciplinary fold.[5] In attempting to do so, and to define the nature of their project against that of sociology, I would argue that a particular kind of anthropology, one focused upon an organic view of culture, comes to stand for anthropology as a whole. And if ideas of race always imply questions of power and domination, ethnicity implies questions of culture, boundaries and identity, questions construed as lying at the heart of the anthropological project and at the heart of the authenticity of the anthropologist.

This preference, however, has serious and entirely unexpected implications. For if we look more closely at the research done on ethnic minorities by anthropologists in Britain, there is a curious and striking imbalance: an abundance of work on Asian ethnic minorities and very little on African-Caribbean groups. In the period up to 1970 only six studies are listed for current ASA members, and five of these concern African-Caribbean populations. In the period after 1970 there are thirty-six studies, of which over half are on Asian communities (fifteen from the Indian sub-continent, four from elsewhere), four on Mediterranean populations, two on Gypsies, two on Jews, one on Ireland and four on African-Caribbeans (the remaining four resist straightforward classification). If Britain's black and Asian population can be described as a congerie of ethnic minorities, then clearly some are more ethnic than others. How do we account for this?

Divisions of labour and fictions of community

Most straightforwardly, this pattern could be read as a reflection of a pragmatic academic division of labour between sociologists and anthropologists. Since most sociological research from the 1950s onwards were concerned with race and with the African-Caribbean population, anthropological research simply moved into the vacuum. But there is a more worrying division of labour in play here. It hints at a shared assumption that in some important respects Asian groups and African-Caribbean groups are different. Putting it crudely, that if the researcher's interest is in political issues and responses to racism, or problems and social disadvantage (that is, if s/he is a sociologist) s/he studies West Indians; and if s/he is interested in religion, ritual, culture and ethnicity (that is, if s/he is an anthropologist), she studies Asians. An offensively crude characterisation, perhaps, but one which is given some support if we consider, for example, the articles published over the past fourteen years or so in *New Community*, the journal of Commission for Racial Equality. If an issue is focused upon race or social problems, research on African-Caribbeans appears. If it is focused upon ethnicity or culture, Asians predominate.[6] If Asians have culture, then, West Indians have problems: an opposition which denies both the vitality and interest of Afro-Caribbean cultural practices and the impact of racism upon the lives of Asian populations.

The weighting of anthropological research towards the apparently culture-rich ethnic minorities may be seen as both a reflection of broader stereotypes concerning strong Asian cultures and weak African-Caribbean ones (Lawrence 1982, p. 99) and as playing an active part in the construction of these offensive dichotomies.

It is relatively easy to pick out and to confront the most obvious writing of this kind (for example, Lyon 1972, p. 257, 1973, p. 337-9, Mason 1974, p. 288, Rex 1979, pp. 226-232), both in and out of anthropology. But it is less easy to confront or even to recognise the assumptions which, I have tried to argue, are woven into the fabric of academic enquiry and continue to underpin apparently very diverse kinds of arguments. When Modood, for example, rejects the term black as a description of Asian ethnic minorities (1988) or, in a later paper (1990a) argues that anti-racist thinking cannot adequately account for the Rushdie affair, his assumption is that race is about oppression and African-Caribbeans, ethnicity about autonomously generated culture and Asians.

> most ordinary people wish to be defined in terms of a historically received identity ... they wish to be known for what they are, not for what others find problematic about them (1988, p. 398).

> Muslims are wiser here than anti-racists: in locating oneself in a hostile society one must begin with one's mode of being [ethnicity] not one's mode of oppression [race] for one's strength flows from one's mode of being. British thinking on race ... has regarded the descendants of African slaves in the New World as the paradigm of a racial group. The historical oppression of this group, however, has been such that its mode of being has become virtually identical to its mode of oppression ... the materialist's claim that they are what white society has made them achieves some surface plausibility (1990a, p. 92).

Similarly Ballard in a recent article argued for the limitations of 'deprivationism' and in favour of 'An ethnic perspective'. His general concerns (to explore the role of culture in the political strategies through which ethnic minorities in Britain negotiate the terms of their existence) are admirable. But when Ballard moves on to discuss just what this culture might be, we find the old dichotomies creeping back in, South Asian settlers 'have access to a heritage on which imperial hegemony had relatively limited impact' while 'Afro-Caribbeans are generally much more weakly organised in institutional terms; they excel instead in terms of their skills in personal survival and dignity-maintenance' (Ballard 1992, p. 489).

These dichotomies map out a distinctive space within which ethnic minorities can be thought or think themselves. I do not wish to suggest that ethnic minority populations themselves have played no part in the construction of these discourses. This is indeed a crucial issue, but one which cannot be included in this paper.[7] But what I would insist upon is the historical longevity of divisions between too much culture and too little culture in the construction of ideas of the Other in English culture: nineteenth century discourses on Jews and the Irish are a case in point. And the ways in which, at different historical moments, too much or too little culture might have very different implications for ideas of belonging to the nation. In multi-cultural Britain, a nation of diverse communities, each with their cultural heritage, what place can be offered to a community without culture? If ethnicity is a question of the documenting and celebration of relations of cultural difference, how can a culture defined in terms of negatives define itself? And within the superficially very different discourse of the New Right (Barker 1981), where again we find ideas of culture and community intertwined but here linked firmly to ideas of a one race and one nation politics, it is not at all clear whether no culture is better or worse than a culture non-negotiably different. As others have pointed out (Duffield 1984, Eade 1990), there is considerable common ground here between apparently very different political positions. This common ground consists of shared ideas concerning the necessary relationship between culture, identity and the collectivity. The specific contribution of anthropology here is the strengthening of this assumed necessary relationship.

I doubt, therefore, that it is simply enough to suggest that anthropologists should redress the balance, and conduct more research on black-dominated Pentecostal churches or African Caribbean youth groups. In some ways the problem for anthropological research is a more intractable one, and concerns the nature of African-Caribbean cultural practices as they can be thought within social anthropology. As I have tried to suggest, anthropologists working on ethnic minorities in Britain have tended to make use of an organic view of culture. The assumptions of boundedness and of the possibilities of mapping predictable patterns of institutional connection fit well with questions of caste, religion, marriage systems and so on. They do not fit with what is generally understood to be the shape of African-Caribbean cultural practices. All too frequently, these practices are described in the literature in terms of negatives - what is not present (distinctive religious identities, for example) or what is seen to be fragmented or disordered (family structures, for example). How can the anthropologist write about a culture of negativities, of absences, of fluidity? There are no firm cultural boundaries, no exclusive institutional arrangements. Rather a number of possible positions held and reworked through an awareness of a common situation of exclusion, of a historical identity and its meaning in the present. That historical identity is not to be understood as represented though any fixed corpus of custom or in any agreed set of institutions; nor can it be limited to the cultures of disaffection that mesmerised sociological researchers in the 1980s. Rather it must be approached through an understanding of the fragmentations and solidarities of the African diaspora: bodily practices, cultural dispositions, partial engagements with contradictory and shifting political and economic contexts. As Afro-Caribbean intellectuals are aware, this is a culture that makes itself up, and in some important respects knows that it makes itself up.[8] What is needed, then, is a rethinking of ideas of culture, identity and collectivity in social anthropology, a destabilisation of some of the fundamental assumptions which I have argued, underpin much research at home.

This leads me to my final point. One of the potential strengths of theories of ethnicity in social anthropology is their critical purchase upon assumptions of authentic and primordial identities. It is necessary to reject absolutely the idea that what we have are authentic Asian cultures and identities and constructed or invented Afro-Caribbean ones. Rather I would agree with Benedict Anderson (1983) that all communities (and identities) are imagined. What we need to ask is in what manner and by whom they are imagined. As historians of tribal identities in Africa know (Peel 1989, Vail 1989, Lonsdale 1990, Ranger 1993) this process of imagining involves cultural work, and develops on the contested and fragmented terrain of representation. Nor can communities be imagined freely, but only, as Marx said of the making of history, under circumstances directly encountered, given and transmitted from the past. The past of Asians in Britain includes a history of imperialism and of cultural transformation in the context of imperialism; the past of African-Caribbeans cannot simply be reduced to a history of oppression. Equally, as Eade's work on the Bangladeshi community in the East End demonstrates, current conditions constantly transform the ways in which particular populations may imagine themselves. Thus far, in contemporary Britain, it seems to be the case that Asian communities have been imagined, by their members as well as by others, through ideas of authenticity and tradition. This is not a position open to African-Caribbeans: the history of the African diaspora insists upon a knowing gaze. Yet, as feminism has discovered to its cost, a politics founded upon ideas of authenticity and non-negotiable identity can prove a serious liability perhaps, its loss in the context of ethnic minority politics might be no bad thing.

Notes

1 Earlier versions of this paper were given at social anthropology seminars at Cambridge and the London School of Economics, and at Terence Ranger's seminar at St Antony's, Oxford. I'm grateful to all those who made comments there.

2 The role of grant-aid in constructing the communities it purports to serve and in offering a space within which claims to the leadership of discrete ethnic communities might be contested is discussed, for example, in Eade (1990, 1991) and by various contributors to Werbner and Anwar (1991).

3 It proved difficult, without extensive research, to discover exactly what anthropologists who had worked at home did. The Aslib listings were unhelpful, as were departmental lists; and in the end I decided to make use of the 1990 and 1991 *Annals of the Association of Social Anthropologists of the Commonwealth and Directory of Members*. The great majority of those who would consider themselves to be professional social anthropologists trained or working in British institutions are included here; and while the coding of fieldwork listed was sometimes difficult, I have where possible drawn upon the theoretical interests listed to clarify the matter. Where a single anthropologist has conducted more than one piece of research at home on different topics I have enumerated them separately. A small number of those who had worked at home now hold posts abroad; and a few holding posts in the UK were in fact born elsewhere. I have not excluded these since all shared a commitment to the discipline and their pattern of research was identical to others on the list.

4 Cohen has recently (1990, p. 204) acknowledged some of the limitations of his own early work and that of his contemporaries. And there are, of course, exceptions: in very different ways, for example, Ennew's work (1980) on the Hebrides or Chapman's account (1978) of the construction of Scottish identity demonstrate a concern with issues of dependency and representation.

5 That marginalisation is a real issue can be seen very clearly in the proportion of papers based upon anthropology at home published in *Man* since 1970: a dozen out of some four hundred, five on rural communities, four on ethnic minorities.

6 See, for example, *New Community* Vols 2 and 3, 1972, 1972-3: both with sections on Ethnic minorities in Britain - fifteen papers, of which two were general, one on African-Caribbeans, ten on Asians, one on the Welsh and one on Romanies; or Vol. 6 1978: 'Youth and the Second Generation' - three papers on Asians (arranged marriages; marriage, family and ethnic identity; needs and problems), three papers on African-Caribbeans (life-styles; self-esteem and control; educationally subnormal schooling); or Vol. 15 1989: 'Race and the Health Service' - two on the Asian elderly, two on black adoption and fostering, three on African-Caribbeans (schizophrenia; compulsory detention under the mental health act; cannabis psychosis). There is one significant exception to this tendency in anthropological research: Abner Cohen's attempt (1980) to interpret Carnival in Notting Hill in terms of the changing politics of culture, community and identity.

7 For recent anthropological attempts to explore this issue see Eade 1989, 1990; Werbner and Anwar, 1991.

8 See, for example, Brathwaite's recognition of the contested cultural work that must go into the construction of 'peoplehood' in the Caribbean (1974, p. 244), or Gilroy (1987) or Hall (1992a) on race, identity and cultural politics in Britain.

5 Ethnicity and the politics of cultural difference: An agenda for the 1990s?

John Eade

Deprivationism and culture

The early 1990s appear to be a testing time for established positions within the 'race relations industry'. Cross, for example, has recently detected three major weaknesses within the literature on Britain's ethnic minorities:- a pre-occupation with 'simple verities' such as the 'black experience', a discounting of culture and an assumption among researchers and policy makers that they knew what the real issues were without listening to 'the voices of the minorities themselves' (1991, p. 311). Cross concludes that

> If the agenda for research and action is to the relevant for the 1990's, then it has to be one which is proclaimed by minorities. To those who wish to hear, there are many articulate voices pressing the claims of a myriad of new concerns. It will be our job to listen (ibid.).

The challenge laid down by Cross has been vigorously taken up by Ballard in an assault on what he regards as the conventional wisdom within the literature. A deprivationist perspective which concentrates upon racial discrimination and racial disadvantage as forms of exclusion. He contends that:

> Although an assessment of the exclusionism encountered in any given context is undoubtedly a necessary component of an analysis of the minority experience, it is never a *sufficient* basis for doing so. And for a simple reason: an analysis which limits itself to an exploration of deprivation will inexorably suggest that the victims of exclusionism lack the capacity to take charge of their own destiny (Ballard, 1992, p. 485).

Ballard calls for an alternative perspective which examines the diverse ways in which different ethnic minorities have resisted these forms of exclusions mentally, physically and culturally. Members of these minority communities must be seen as active subjects rather than as passive victims of oppressive structures. Theoretically attention turns towards ethnicity and culture so that analysts can properly understand the minority 'rejection of the conventions of the dominant majority' and their 'skilled and creative redeployment - both individually and collectively - of the alternative resources of their imported cultural traditions', which enables them to start circumventing racial exclusion 'with ever increasing success' (ibid., p. 487).

Ethnicity: the emergence of a concept

The model presented by these recent interventions suggests that members of ethnic minorities were drawing on internal resources which enable them to resist in highly creative and diverse ways the external constraints of racial discrimination, structural inequalities and state actions. Listening to the voices of ethnic minorities entails both a model of society that fully acknowledges the ability of minority groups to resist modes of oppression, exclusion and deprivation through the mobilisation of internal cultural resources. It also requires research techniques which enable internal voices to be heard properly. Championing the cause of ethnicity requires us to reassess the claims of anthropologists like Ballard to understand the dynamics of ethnic minority groups more deeply than those operating within the race and racism problematic.

The development of anthropological discourse concerning ethnicity and ethnic group relations has to be understood in the wider context of anthropological theoretical movements during the 1950s and 1960s. Structural-functional models of social solidarity were being revised during that period partly in response to changing political, economic and social conditions in sub-Saharan Africa where the British School had a major investment. Migration from the countryside to Africa's rapidly expanding urban centres was leading to the creation of heterogeneous urban communities, which were not readily analysable in terms of the analytical categories and fieldwork methods devised for villages and tribal units. Models of social cohesion were developed that highlighted the issues of social and cultural change as well as the emergence of new forms of social and political solidarity.

Ethnicity was an analytical category which was elaborated to make sense of the emergent social and cultural formations within Africa and other parts of the Third World. In an influential collection on *Urban Ethnicity* Abner Cohen, one of the doyens of British anthropology in sub-Saharan Africa, defines an ethnic group:

> as a collectivity of people who (a) share some patterns of normative behaviour and (b) form a part of a larger population, interacting with people from other collectivities within the framework of a social system (Cohen, 1974, p. ix).

Ethnicity, he proceeds to explain, 'refers to the degree of conformity by members of the collectivity to these shared norms in the course of social interaction' (ibid.). The research task of the urban anthropologist is, therefore, to examine 'the symbolic formations and activities found in such contexts as kinship and marriage, friendship, ritual, and other types of ceremonial' performance that collectively was called culture (ibid., pp. ix-x).

Cohen provides a future programme for social anthropology faced with the demise of what had been assumed to be relatively isolated, homogeneous communities. Although ethnicity is to be found particularly within the city, the latter was 'part of the national state' and urban anthropology was 'the anthropology of the complex structure of the new national state' (ibid., p. xi).

Cohen's formulation of ethnicity did not mark a radical break with Durkheimian notion of collective representation, which lay at the basis of British anthropology's long standing preoccupation with social structure and social function. He warns of a tendency to define ethnicity as an epistemological device to make sense of 'the bewildering complexity and heterogeneity of urban society' (ibid., p. xii). He criticises Barth in particular for stressing the varying relevance of ethnic categories to people's behaviour and argues that:

> Norms, beliefs and values are effective and have their own constraining power only because they are the collective representations of a group and are backed by the pressure of that group (ibid., p. xiii).

The study of urban ethnicity and ethnic minorities in Britain

Since Sue Benson considers the development of anthropological discourse concerning ethnicity generally within Britain elsewhere in this volume I will limit myself to a brief sketch of developments within the study of Britain's ethnic minorities. The interpretation of ethnicity developed by British anthropologists such as Saifullah Khan and Wallman during the 1970s drew heavily on the model developed by Barth. What particularly impressed them was Barth's insistence that study should focus on 'the ethnic boundary that defines the group, not the cultural stuff that it encloses' (1969, p. 15). Ethnic groups were sustained through social differences between insiders and outsiders expressed through people's perceptions and interaction.

The relevance or irrelevance of ethnicity depended upon the social situation, which was determined by structural constraints and the perceptions of social actors. Wallman acknowledges the element of change in the following terms:

> no ethnic boundary can remain static throughout history or for every situation. Both 'our' ethnicity and 'theirs' are processes which respond to other things happening, other boundaries, other options pertaining at the time (Wallman, 1979, p. 5).

The dynamic and changing significance of the ethnic boundary is related to the variable use of cultural traditions by members of ethnic groups:

> Nor will two sets of people with common cultural origins placed in similar minority positions necessarily use the same elements of their traditional culture to mark themselves off from non-member 'others'. What they do use will depend on the resources they have, on what they hope to achieve

(whether conscious or not) and on the range of options available to them at the time (ibid., pp. 5-6).

Wallman's highly influential discussion of ethnicity reveals a concern with structural constraints, perceptions of social actors, change and the situational context of social transactions. Similar preoccupations can be seen in the writing of another senior anthropologist, Banton (Jenkins 1986). A programme was established for an anthropological study of Britain's ethnic minorities which insulated researchers from the general movement among their colleagues from functionalism and interactionism towards structuralism and Marxism. Research concentrated on the empirical investigation of immigrant communities within a pluralist framework where attention was focused on the social solidarity and cultural cohesion of ethnic groups and their relations with outsiders, whether that be other minority groups or the indigenous majority (Saifullah Khan 1976, 1979a, 1979b, Jeffery 1976). While the dynamic, flexible and situational character of the ethnic boundaries between these groups was acknowledged there remained a preoccupation with certain fundamental social and cultural institutions; the family, kinship group, language, religion and place of origin.

During the 1980s ethnographic studies of local ethnic minority communities continued the preoccupation with what were assumed to be fundamental social and cultural institutions. The investigations by Werbner (1985, 1990), Bhachu (1985) and Shaw (1988) of Pakistani Muslims and East African Sikhs in Manchester, Southall and Oxford pursued well worn tracks of household composition, marriage regulations, rituals of gift-giving and social solidarities of a caste-like character.

Ethnicity was intimately associated with these fundamental social and cultural institutions. Werbner provides the most detailed discussion of ethnicity, which has to be understood as a process:

> located in a primary sense in the domestic and inter-domestic domains which determine the social reproduction of a group over time. In these domains ethnic group reproduction is achieved...through a culturally distinctive system of gifts and services which are extended on ritual and ceremonial occasions (Werbner, 1990, p. 2).

Werbner, Bhachu and Shaw share a mutual interest in examining the maintenance of ethnic boundaries between insiders and (predominantly white English) outsiders. They acknowledge the changing character of ethnic group relations as perceptions on both sides are transformed by political and social developments that include racism and the emergence of a second generation. Werbner takes the most daring theoretical step by criticising Barth's insistence on the ethnic group boundary rather than 'the cultural stuff that it encloses' as 'simplistic' and 'theoretically misguided'. 'Boundary interaction', according to Werbner, 'continually reflects or highlights internal divisions, both within the state and within the immigrant group itself' (Werbner, 1991b, p. 141).

By the end of the 1980s Barth's earlier emphasis on boundary maintenance was being revised along with a greater sensitivity to issues emphasised by the critics of the ethnicity perspective. The tendency to reify ethnic groups, inadequate attention to racial differentiation and conflict, power imbalances and class, as well as a tendency to blame the victim (Jenkins, 1986, pp. 176-7). In a collection of papers on *Black and Ethnic Leaderships in Britain* many of these issues are addressed by anthropologists and the relevance of other perspectives is carefully explored. Werbner in her editorial introduction acknowledges Marxist explorations of urban struggles around race, class and the operations of the state and referred to the path-breaking volume - *The Empire Strikes Back* - and its Marxist challenge to 'simplistic "culturalist" approaches to the study of ethnic groups'. Gilroy's typification of community as 'the locus of cultural resistance to the domination of a wider society' is commended in spite of its utopian picture of community unity (Werbner, 1991b, p. 114).

The current position: ethnicity rampant?

The anthropological perspective towards ethnicity would appear to be well placed to carry out the agenda outlined by Cross and Ballard for the 1990s. A model of cultural pluralism which incorporates issues of power, resistance, conflict and change could possibly provide the basis for what Donald and Rattansi were looking for: a 'critical reappropriation of the concept of culture' which was based around 'cultural authority and individual agency' and requires 'a careful analysis of contemporary political struggles over representation, symbolic boundary formation, and identification'. A 'conflictual dialogue' where 'the meanings of "race", racism and antiracism are forged, broken and remade' (Donald and Rattansi, 1992, p.4). Perhaps ethnicity could establish the context for an understanding of a recent 'rethinking of culture' which:

> undermines the claims and comforts of community understood in terms of a normative identity and tradition whether that of nation, religion, ethnicity or 'the black experience'. It emphasises the contingency of any instituted cultural authority. It insists that 'race' and identity are inherently contestable social and political categories: that is why it calls into question multi-cultural and antiracist paradigms, as well as the logic of assimilation (ibid., p. 5).

However, before we accept the revised anthropological version of ethnicity we need to consider the limitations imposed by its essentialist and primordialist assumptions. Ethnic minority communities are distinguished by a social and cultural essence which was available for empirical investigation by the outside observer. The essential characteristics of ethnic groups are revealed in their social and cultural institutions which were seen as primordial. Fundamental in terms of providing a structural foundation upon which other institutions rest and requiring intense loyalty. For an understanding of the changes which occur within ethnic groups and their modes of cultural expression we need to reach down to the family and inter-familial networks. As Werbner explains:

> Ethnicity as process is thus located in a primary sense in the domestic and inter-domestic domain which determines the social reproduction of a group over time (Werbner, 1991b, p. 117).

Political representation is ultimately determined by these social and cultural institutions. Ethnic group 'centres' can be detected according to Werbner because they are 'the locus of high economic or cultural value and of dense networks of intense interaction'. These centres 'provide both a social base and a cultural *raison d'etre* for political struggles'. Peripheral political activists are those who operate at some distance from these primordial institutions and who 'have forged social and cultural links across the ethnic boundary', especially with state agencies (ibid, p. 119).

The problem with this essentialist and primordialist project is its failure to think through the implications of social and political processes for its model of society. There was a recognition of the changing formation of fundamental and determining social and cultural institutions but the only way Werbner, for example, can explain these changes was by recourse to the long-standing anthropological principle of segmentation (ibid, p. 118). Why groups should segment remains unexplained but her model depends ultimately, it seems, on an assumption that social actors were inherently competitive (some may be more competitive than others).

Towards other models: the politics of prioritisation

Although the agonistic model of social structure informing ethnic group analysis has a long tradition within British social anthropology, many anthropologists have moved on to other models of structure and some, more recently, have been influenced by post-structuralist developments. Post-structuralist writings reveal the refreshing ways in which people can work across disciplinary boundaries to explore the implications for an analysis of ethnic or race relations of a decentred human subject. Their investigations share an emphasis upon the social construction of individuals and groups through discursive narratives and practices, a relational, de-centred and non-possessive approach towards power and resistance and an insistence on discontinuity, divergence and heterogeneity. They have directed attention towards the more complex process within the politics of representation which involves the construction of 'new ethnicities' through diverse discourses and practices (Hall, 1992a, p. 257).

Hall celebrates the emergence of 'new ethnicities' which challenge the hegemonic, racialised ethnic identity of the English. He perceives a 'new politics of representation' which 'has to do with an awareness of the black experience as a diaspora experience and the consequences which this has for the process of unsettling, recombination, hybridization and cut-and-mix' (1992a, p. 258). Against the dominant images of Englishness the new politics operates 'on new and quite distinct ground - specifically, contestation over what it means to be British where there was 'no simple "return" or "recovery" of the ancestral past which is not experienced through the categories of the present' (ibid.).

The strength of Hall's approach is its sensitivity to post-structuralist themes and to new modes of ethnic representation which even the revamped anthropological model of ethnic groups has paid scant attention. Moreover, he demonstrates his openness to diverse ways in which those on the margins, as Ballard puts it, were taking 'charge of their own destiny'. However, in prioritising discourses around the black experience Hall lays himself open to the charge made by Cross that he is still preoccupied with 'simple verities'. Modood, in particular, has pointed to the dangers of anti-racist usages of the blanket term black when applied to the specific needs of South Asians in Britain (1988, 1990b). He spells out the implications for policy making of the anthropological research discussed above with its detailed description of the manifold social and cultural identities generated among South Asian settlers. His prioritisation of a particular identity entails the replacement of the term black with the competing claims of these constituencies based on cultural traditions associated with an area of origin - Asian (1988) - or religion -Muslim (1990b). Black is a term which may be used by South Asian activists operating within local political arenas (Werbner 1990, Eade 1991), by Afro-Caribbeans and anti-racist policy makers whatever their colour, but it has little or no meaning, according to Modood, for the majority of South Asians in Britain.

Hall's appeal to 'the black experience' and the advocacy by Modood, Werbner and Ballard of different levels of social incorporation among Asians reveals more than theoretical disagreements over models of society and an involvement in different communities. Their construction of rival unitary constituencies, however sensitive to processes of differentiation occurring within those constituencies, entails a political manoeuvre whereby a particular social or cultural identity is prioritised. The prioritising of a particular constituency is underpinned by a claim to authentic knowledge by the academic commentator and/or by those she or he represents to others through the mediums of writing and film. These constructions of authentic communities can be used in the formation of public policy concerning the distribution of state resources and become the basis for rival claims to those resources. Not surprisingly the construction of unitary constituencies in the context of multi-cultural and anti-racist strategies during the last ten years, for example, has not been confined to the totalities already described - blacks, Afro-Caribbeans, Asians, Pakistanis, Muslims. Others have merged at local and more global levels located around territory, religion, class or gender partly encouraged by state policies and practices which led to the funding of specific organisations on an extensive scale during the 1980s.

Deconstruction and specific engagements

Cross has urged us to listen to 'the claims of a myriad of new concerns' presented by the minorities themselves. Yet listening does not solve the problem raised by the politics of prioritisation - how to decide between competing claims to knowledge and rival modes of resistance?

This problem has been confronted to an illuminating way by Knowles and Mercer in their discussion of the relationship between feminism and anti-racism (Knowles and Mercer 1990). They acknowledge that the differing constructions of women and black people leads to a politics of prioritisation which presents a dilemma for black feminists. How to reconcile the imaginings of community and the contesting of meanings, which Donald and Rattansi claim to be such a striking feature of current developments? How can they be analysed with these post-structuralist approaches firmly in mind but without pursuing 'a naive postmodern embrace of an endless multiplication of cultural identities' (Donald and Rattansi, 1992, p. 6)?

Black feminists have attempted to resolve their dilemma through the construction of a 'black female constituency as an object of political analysis' which 'is demarcated by the experience of race and gender oppression, a common history of revolt and its analytical distinctiveness in feminist discourse organised around the family, patriarchy and reproduction' (Knowles and Mercer, 1990, p. 65).

Against monocausal and homogenising constructions of racism and gender Knowles and Mercer propose a deconstruction of the constituencies black people and women (ibid., p. 79). Deconstruction is 'not an arbitrary process, neither is it guided by an understanding of cultural difference (Asian, Afro-Caribbean, and so on)' (ibid.). Their alternative is to examine the specificities of political struggles:

> instead of a parallel existence of subjects and claimed interests, we see constituencies as organised by specific issues as they arise on the political agenda. In other words groups of subjects (constituencies) are created in terms of a commonality of interests around the specifics of policies. Hence a recognised category such like black women is unlikely to be constructed by an issue such as the deportation of widows whose citizenship is gained through marriage (ibid., p. 83).

The effect of their approach is to displace 'political alignments built around qualifications for membership of antiracist and antisexist struggles'. However:

> It deconstructs commonly accepted political constituencies and the generalised political objectives with which they are associated. It offers in its place a mode of engagement with specific incidents, practices and actions which have the effect of generating various forms of race and gender disadvantages (ibid., p. 84).

Since 'there is no general relationship between race and gender as forms of social division' Knowles and Mercer propose a situational analysis which only 'postulates temporary links between groups of subjects with interests and positions' and 'involves the construction and reconstruction of political constituencies in struggle' (ibid.).

The perspective adopted by Knowles and Mercer offers a way out of the problems inherent within Hall's exploration of the political and ideological construction of difference or the situational analysis of ethnic processes developed by Werbner, Ballard, Wallman and others. The ambitious theorising of the 'black experience' or ethnic minority communities is replaced by a more modest examination of how power, resistance and knowledge operate in the construction of constituencies within the context of specific struggles involving policy makers, community and political representatives and those they claim to represent.

The perspective has informed other contributions to Cambridge and Feuchtwang (1990) as well as Feutchwang elsewhere (1980, 1992) and Eade's writing about Bangladeshi community representation and politics in Tower Hamlets (1989, 1990, 1991, 1992). The perspective can be used to investigate the emergence of constituencies such as the Muslim community in Britain through local political struggles over public resources in a way that can reveal the diversity and sometimes contradictory character of Islamic constructions without recourse to the social reductionism of the ethnicity school. There was no need to suggest the presence of an essential and primordial unity embodied in the term Muslim community and necessitating the satisfaction of certain interests or needs. An Islamic communality need not be invoked to explain similarities in the construction of those interests and needs between different locales within the country. Rather attention can be directed towards the possible similarity between political discourses and practices involved in the construction of those interests and needs especially by community activists, political representatives and state agencies.

Conclusion

This chapter began with Cross's appeal for an agenda for research and action relevant to the 1990s and 'proclaimed by minorities'. Despite Ballard's assertion that the ethnicity perspective could provide the academic basis for such an agenda the abiding problems within ethnicity's framework of cultural pluralism seriously undermine such a claim despite valiant efforts to incorporate the issues of power, resistance, conflict and change.

Other approaches towards the study of race, racism and ethnicity could have been considered (the major contribution by Rex and his collaborators (1986), for instance) but I chose by way of contrast the recent reworkings by Hall of the Marxist perspective which offered a radical critique of these approaches during the late 1970s and 1980s. Hall leads the discussion of ethnicity into a consideration of the politics of representation where new ethnicities have been generated by those on the margins of British society through resistance to the dominant, racialised constructions of English ethnicity. He also shows an appreciation of the heterogeneity and complexity of contested meanings around belonging and identity but he still posits a black experience which prevents us from moving beyond the 'simple verities' criticised by Cross. We are still enclosed within an anti-racist discourse which fails to answer the issues raised by Modood, for example, concerning the specificity of Asian or Muslim needs.

Revised versions of ethnicity or revamped Marxist interpretations of the 'black experience' establish rival priorities and unitary constituencies. In order to resolve the problems presented by these ambitious theoretical schemes. I have welcomed the approach outlined by Knowles and Mercer among others, which examines the specificity of political struggles through a deconstruction of constituencies such as women and black people. Rather than looking for a general relationship between gender and race they investigate the temporary links forged between constituencies in the context of power, resistance and knowledge. This method enables us to interrogate assertions of social and cultural commonality in the context of local struggles over public resources without assuming a more general oppression or concerted resistance to dominant groups. Where similarities appear between different locales and constituencies explanations can proceed through an initial investigation of the political discourses and practices involved in the sites of struggle.

My emphasis on the role of political understanding and procedures was intended to counteract the preoccupation among anthropologists with social and cultural formations. I also hope that my support for investigations of specific struggles in locales will encourage others to be wary of claims made on behalf of such unitary constituencies as Britain's Muslim or Asian community and generalisations about the success or failure of ethnic minorities. In listening to the voices of different constituencies and their diverse explorations of cultural identity and belonging we must interrogate claims to authenticity and primordiality upon which their prioritising projects frequently rest and which have been used in academic studies of ethnicity, race and racism.

6 Essentialising the Other: A critical response

Pnina Werbner

> In their uncondition of being strangers men seek one another. No one is at home. The memory of this servitude assembles humanity
> ('No-Identity', Levinas, 1987, p. 149).

Whether it was Foucault, Derrida or Said who triggered the crisis of representation in anthropology, the very foundations of the discipline's taken-for-granted assumptions about how we know the Other have been undermined by deconstructive critiques of ethnographic writing and authorial authority. One resolution to the resulting impasse has been to shift the focus from a study of the Other to a study of ourselves, of Western colonial and post-colonial discursive practices and fictions of alterity. Anthropology's object of study, in the words, became the works of other anthropologists - their rhetorical anthropology, we find that this option - of studying our own Western discursive practices as a way to knowledge has itself been subjected to a crisis of representation. In Britain, for example, anti-racism as a mode of correcting false fictions of Otherness has recently been acknowledged as a devastating failure by radical activists, as well as by more conservative critics (Cohen 1988, Murphy 1987, Modood 1988, Ali 1992). More seriously, even, the radical camp has come to question its own taken-for-granted representations of the authentic realities of class, race and nation (Hall 1991). Instead, multiculturalism as an expression of authentic voices of Otherness has made an uneasy comeback through a refocusing on identity and the politics of representation. Yet multiculturalism lends itself easily to charges of cultural essentialism, and the counter attack has already begun, this time from the feminist camp (Murphy 1987, Yuval-Davis 1992, Ali 1992).

Among the fictions of representation created by anthropological deconstructivists have been real fictions of classic anthropological texts, representing a new mythology of the history of the subject. As the present subject/victim of such a fiction of representation by fellow anthropologists, I am grateful to the editors of this volume for allowing me space to reflect upon my own work and its implications. The present response argues for a theoretical perspective that shifts attention from text to practice as an essential detour to understanding representation. In the face of the present volume's dual critique, by Eade and Benson, I hope to show that this approach is not an essentialist one, even when the object of research is a community, or communities.

The challenge has forced me to reflect seriously on my recent monograph (Werbner 1990), and why I believe it represents a departure from earlier anthropological community studies. Put simply, I tried in my study to say something about friendship. More specifically, I tried to say something about friendship between people who start off as strangers. Let me explain this statement a little more fully because it has bearings on how we understand such representations as community, identity, culture, ethnicity, or race - and all the different acts and gestures of identification these concepts imply.

The point about friendship is that it isn't a given - it is a voluntary act of identification, of reaching out, of proximity in Levinas's terms. It is a recognition of oneself in the Other, of the Other in his/her difference and resemblance to oneself; of one's ultimate responsibility for the Other; it is the creation of a trace which endures.

So when I wrote about Pakistani immigrants to Britain, what I wanted to understand is how they, who came as strangers to each other (all those myths about reconstituted Punjabi kin groups and villages notwithstanding) chose to make gestures of identification and proximity. Let me make this quite clear, because this matter is very widely misunderstood. The people I knew - and I explain this in great detail in my monograph - came from different parts of Pakistan, which is a very big country with a population of one hundred million people. They came from different towns and villages. They came from different caste groups. They came from different class backgrounds. At most, with them some introductory letters. But they made friends, lots and lots of friends. They could have made friends with their English neighbours. They could have made friends with their Indian or Afro-Caribbean workmates. To some extent, they did that too. But they created the most enduring and powerful bonds of friendship with other Pakistanis who spoke the same language, told the same jokes, ate (or refused to eat) the same foods, listened (or refused to listen) to the same music, practiced the same rituals and festivals, donated money to the same causes, cried over the same tragic events, shared the same sort of nostalgia for a lost home, carried gifts for friends when they went back home. I did not invent this pattern of friendship or its contents. I simply observed and wanted to understand it. One of the finest monographs on black people in Britain, Roger Hewitt's *Black Talk, White Talk* (Hewitt 1986), is also a book about the ways in which people choose their friends and create powerful bonds, which exclude outsiders.

This brings me to structural functionalism, the villain of anthropological deconstructivism. Structural functionalism was a holistic theory, which tried to theorise the interdependencies between politics, law, production, consumption, reproduction, kinship, ritual, religion and so forth. It tried to understand what happens when relationships between people are multiplex, not compartmentalised. How are such relationships managed? What makes them endure? What undermines them? My approach is different. In my book, when I try to understand friendships forged between stranger migrants (immigrants, sojourners), I invert the structural functionalist approach. I turn it, as it were, upside down and back to front. This approach started from a heuristic postulation of a given whole. I start from the assumption of a void - from strangerhood, non-relationship. So when I find that these strangers - let us be quite clear about this: they do not know each other, they have never met before - when I find that these strangers create, generate, make multiple identifications with one another, then that is a process (not a pre-given static condition) which I find interesting. I find it interesting, perhaps, because it tells me something about my own family who have been immigrants and sojourners for three generations on three continents; it tells me something about my grandparents and parents and about myself.

When these strangers make friends, I found, they don't keep those friends apart from their businesses, their workmates, their political battles or their family rituals. They don't compartmentalise their friends, they don't erect spatial and temporal barriers between them. They mix them all together. And they also mix up the things they do with them, and the loyalties and help they expect from them. In other words, they create multiplex relationships out of that void, that initial emptiness. They do so voluntarily, through a myriad of different acts of identification.

But this also creates complications for them. Because friends, like family, make demands. They set standards of behaviour. They gossip. And sometimes they are disloyal. Friends have other friends who may be disliked. Friends may not be all they seem: they originate from different class backgrounds, or castes. A person suddenly discovers that her/his best friend won't agree to let her/his daugher marry his/her son because s/he comes from a different/higher Muslim caste (which shouldn't exist in the first place, but does). So how can s/he be a friend? Once the void has been bridged, it is not only supportive but powerfully coercive, disturbing, conflictual.

It is these cumulative changes that I refer to when I talk about ethnicity as a process located in a primary sense in the domestic and inter-domestic domain. As postmodernist theorists have recognised, cultural objects, practices, lifestyles and desires are the very medium of competition for power and status. The game of consumption, production and reproduction is a game of practical knowledge constituted by cultural aesthetic forms and moral convictions. We are not dealing here with a field of persuasive rhetorical representations within the political arena, but, quite to the contrary, with the taken-for-grantedness of the quotidian, of everyday life, the lived in world, the commonsensical, unexamined assumptions which, as such, are the locus of implicit, and thus doubly powerful, affective commitments. In other words, we are dealing with identity as an implicit reality.

The cumulative effect of productive/consumptive household strategies also has implications for inter-racial and inter-ethnic relations: residential expansion and economic encroachment into new, more lucrative economic enclaves are mediated by cultural understandings. Hence, these effect the long term material basis of ethnic groups and the way they represent themselves to Others or defend themselves against racist violations of their personhood and sacred symbols.

This process of ethnicity or of community formation is not a once-and-for-all, single event: it is a continuous, unfolding process of discovery and argument. There is no assumption of a fixed, holistic community, out of time and space. For a younger generation of Pakistanis, or for women, the sociality which their parents forged in bridging the void of strangerhood may be very oppressive. Those former young, adventurous migrant strangers have now become conservative male and female elders who take it for granted that their worldview is the right one, which should therefore be accepted by young people whose life experiences have been quite different. In this respect Sue Benson is right: the initial migration process which resulted in a holistic conflation of domains is over. The process is now one of inter-generational and gendered struggle and negotiation, of forging new kinds of friendships across differents sorts of voids and fighting new anti-racist battles. But those struggles are only comprehensible if we recognise that the beliefs of that older generation are powerful forces to be contended with, precisely because they are embedded in multiplex relationships and in processes of consumptive production and reproduction.

When Pakistanis/Punjabis/Muslims/Asian migrants first came to Manchester, they were few in number. In 1951 there were 200 hundred Pakistanis in Manchester. By 1991 there were 20,000 Pakistanis in the city and its southern suburbs. The change is a radical one: from a time when all Pakistanis were, in Alfred Schutz's terms, consociates, to the present situation when they are merely contemporaries (Geertz, 1973, p. 365). This radical transformation changed what community as an analytic representation has come to mean. Because, as the number of Pakistanis grew, people became more selective in choosing their friends. They tended to make friends with people from the same sort of class background, or the same region of origin; they chose friends with the same political commitments, or the same sectarian religious beliefs. So the social field of Pakistani contemporaries in Manchester came to consist of dense friendship knots, or clusters, with voids between them, bridged by ramifying acquaintancy networks. Some of these friends formed voluntary associations articulating their interests. Friendships were, by now, stratified by class and occupation, and this was publicly objectified at weddings and religious festivals. Members of the ethnic elite lived in certain neighbourhoods, and ethnic businesses clustered in specific industrial and commercial districts of the city. Working class people formed region-of-origin friendship networks and lived in inner city ghettoes.

From an analytic perspective, then, community was by now no longer a group of consociates who lived together. Community had become, in effect, a kind of argument through practice: an argument of images between those different knots of friends with their different life styles, consumption patterns and visions of what their community should be like, by comparison to other communities, seen from a particular vantage point.

Community was nevertheless constituted as practice by the traces of localised discourses and interactions taking place in a myriad of public events: at weddings and funerals, fund raising drives, mosque elections, factional struggles, public protests, religious festivals, national and religious celebrations and ceremonies, as well as in multi-cultural or multi-racial or multi-religious forums and arenas created by the state and local state.

John Eade has written very perceptively about how the ambiguities inherent in the term community are utilised rhetorically in the public sphere, in order to appeal to different constituencies simultaneously during local election campaigns. I like his arguments and I think he has givem us valuable insight into the powerful connotations of the word community for English people. But community is not simply a rhetorical trope. It is a network of moral proximities and shared aesthetic participations constituted symbolically, and it is also a useful analytic term.

The term community, like nation or caste, is one of those words that make sense systemically, as part of a semantic field of differences. It is a relational word. A nation only exists in a family of nations. A caste only exists in a hierarchy of castes. An ethnic community as a localised collectivity sharing a common identity, only exists as part of a multi-ethnic segmentary system of ethnic communities - on the tremendous complexity of overlapping and nesting relations of identity among British Asians (Werbner 1991a, 1991b). Terms such as nation or community simply don't make sense outside such semantic, taxonomic and relational fields.

John Eade appears to assume that primordiality equals essentialism. The identification is a false one. I use the notion of primordial attachments, following Geertz, to refer to the empirical fact that people in many different parts of the world often mobilise to defend their language, their religion, their nation and their culture if and when these implicit, taken-for-granted modes of living and communication are silenced or violated. Identity seems rooted in these sentimental attachments because personhood and value are constituted through relationships mediated everywhere by symbolic modes of interaction. In Manchester people who have overlapping identities - who are Pakistanis (co-nationals), Punjabis (speakers of the same language), aficionados of Urdu poetry, Asian music and the fragrance of *mhendi* (lovers of the same culture) and pious Muslims (co-religionists) have powerful relational bonds of identification with one another. But people also mobilise as citizens; the identity of citizenship is a powerful one (Rex 1992, Werbner 1993). And, of course, they mobilise as racial victims, whether of discrimination and industrial restructuring or of physical and symbolic violations: of violence directed against their body, property, sacred symbols and personal or public face, in the sense used by Levinas.

To essentialise is to obscure the relational aspects of identity, experience or collective representations, to valorise, as it were, the thing in itself, as being autonomous and separate, cut off from ongoing relationships (Strathern in press). This applies equally to tradition (a past cut off from the present), custom (a rule set apart from practice), gender (woman or man unto her/himself) and community (a collectivity unto itself).

Segmentary systems are built around the intersection of space, time, social scale and lived identity. Each inclusive term (e.g. South Asian) encompasses oppositions (Pakistani and Indian) at a less inclusive social scale. This is the primary principle of segmentary systems.

'Why do groups segment'? Eade asks disarmingly. There is, of course, no simple answer to this question. Complex historical processes led to the partition of Pakistan and India or to the emergence of the division between the Deobandi and Barelwi Islamic movements in South Asia. So too, there are complex material and organisational reasons which lead to the recurrent splitting of joint families at certain points in the domestic life cycle, or to the segmentation of Punjabi burial societies when the number of their members increases beyond an optimum size. Once groups segment, they are no longer the same, identical, they now have distinct names or representations; yet they also bear the trace of their common origin: Deobandis and Barelwis are both

Sunni Muslims ; Sunnis and Shias are both Muslim; Muslims, Jews and Christians are all people of the book.

Stuart Hall's recent discussion (1991) provides, in effect, if unwittingly, a disclosure of the ontological and phenomenological dimensions of this segmentary principle of fission and fusion, of the inverted segementary tree so familiar to anthropologists. Opposites not only repel, but are also attracted to one another, they bear the trace of their resemblance, articulated in an encompassing term of identification which, in turn, silences those differences. The relationship between communal representations or identities, seen thus, is inherently dynamic and positional. Its further complexity lies in the way multiphrenic, overlapping identities are managed in practice, or singular identities highlighted in political contestations.

Such silences, the silences of ethnicity, are quite different from the silences of racism as violation. Ethnicity does not deny proximity and alterity, it merely highlights difference, while recognising a common humanity. It acknwledges opinion and argument. The violent silences of suppressed voices denied a political presence in the public sphere are generated by a denial of Otherness, a denial of face in Levinas's terms. The two silences, of ethnicity and racism, are thus quite different, indeed, opposed. There is no becoming in the silence of racism because no proximity or commonality is acknowledged. Such a silence is the silence of tyranny (Levinas, 1987, pp. 18-23, 47-53) of absolute I-ness or ipseity.

There is also a third type of silence, which I shall call a methodological silence, of the type discussed by Strathern (1991) in her application of Chaos theory and fractal graphics to problems of social scale. Methodological silences are constituted by the gaps created by our scientific discourses, the remainder these discourses generate. As Strathern points out, no representation, however complex and apparently exhaustive, is ever complete; there are always, in principle, further gaps to be filled, described or explained. In this sense all knowledge is partial and replete with silences. As we produce knowledge, 'we become aware of creating more and more gaps' (Strathern, 1991, p. 119). Discussing black people, we become aware of ignoring Asians, discussing Asians, we ignore Muslims, and so forth, right down to the individual, the self, and the divided self.

There are, then, at least three types of silence, which differ, in principle, from each other. The voices of ethnic and sub-ethnic groups, like the voices of individuals, are not necessarily silenced by violent suppression; they are given expression at different scales of action, in particular contexts, in front of different audiences. By contrast, minorities who are oppressed, marginalised and silenced, seek to make their voices heard in the widest public spheres: on the national media, as part of a national high culture, and in economic and political debating forums. It is in these contexts that national images and public agendas are formulated which affect the destiny of these groups.

Which communities will be given public expression in this widest arena depends not simply on situational factors, as John Eade rightly argues, but on the commitment of those knots of friends sharing identical worldviews and common agendas. The moral community is not a unity. It is full of conflict, of internal debate about moral values and the relationship to Others. It involves fierce competition for leadership. It also involves competition for the right to name: Who are we? What do we stand for? What are we to be called? Are we Muslims? Democrats? Pakistanis? Socialists? black? Asian? The power to name, to inscribe, to describe, implies a power to invoke a world of moral relationships. Naming is a forceful act of leadership. Thus I agree with John Eade that the people who create agendas for action must be studied if we are to understand the public face of community.

Seen, then, from the viewpoint of a public rhetorical struggle for rights, face or jobs, it is evident that processes of social exclusion and incorporation which sustain cultural boundaries are less critical to the public objectification of ethnic communities than the rhetorical tropes produced by cadres of ethnic activists and intellectuals in an explicit ideologising of taken-for-granted values and practices. This is why I have argued that modern day ethnic groups in capitalist societies are defined publicly by their centre or centres rather than by their peripheries. At the centre are the cultural experts and communal activists, the organic intellectuals who compete among themselves for moral, aesthetic or religious hegemony. The periphery consists of ethnic consumers who often straddle ambiguous boundaries. Some of these ethnic cosmopolitans create bridging associations which also claim to speak for the whole community, glossing over - like the organic leaders - its internal divisions.

Such a view explains why ethnic solidarities are achievements, usually ephemeral. Permanent settlement brings fragmentation as numbers increase and associations multiply. At the same time the efflorescence of associations creates an institutional network which allows for the social reproduction of cultural and ideological diversity, leading to a process of increasing communal incorporation and institutional completeness, an elaboration of the moral, aesthetic and interpretive community in all its argumentative complexity.

My response to John Eade's critique is, then, that it reduces community to a rhetorical trope. It thus fails to conceive of community as a symbolic, relational field, objectified in quotidian, taken-for-granted, implicit practices. Eade, in other words, textualises community as a public trope.

Turning to Sue Benson's critique, I find it somewhat ironic that her article should appear just as Abner Cohen's *Masquerade Politics*, an anthropological study of the development of the Notting Hill Carnival, is published (Cohen 1993). Against her critique, that book discloses the rich and evolving cultures of British Caribbeans; it addresses the issues of changing public representations, the struggle against racism and economic subordination, the politicisation of culture and cultural politics, while arguing for the irreducibility of cultural forms as aesthetic genres. Carnival as a cultural and social movement has evolved dialectically in political and cultural contestation, and is thus an historically changing, dialogically engaged creation of local groups and social networks, celebrating local knowledge and engaging with local predicaments in the context of the nation-state.

Like Eade, Benson prefers to textualise community and identity. Ignoring the realities of moral proximity, unilateral giving and competitive consumption as these objectify relational practices, she argues that since communities are imagined, we need to ask by whom and in what manner this cultural work of imagining is done. Of course, this is precisely what a number of anthropologists have recently attempted to do (Werbner and Anwar 1991), but Benson does not engage with their contributions, as Eade, a contributor himself, does. To understand why she doesn't, we need to place her critique of ethnicity studies within the broader context of the contemporary anthropological critique of an orientalist, colonial anthropology and its discursive practices.

In its thrust to create new paradigmatic truths, the recent deconstructive critique of anthropology has created new representational fictions. It has done so by choosing to deliberately ignore or obscure the works of earlier and contemporary anthropologists devoted to the study of race, colonialism and postcolonialism: Evans-Pritchard's study of the Sanusiya order's anti-colonial struggle in Cyrenaica, the Manchester School's studies of labour migration and the colonial encounter in South-Central Africa, Levi-Strauss's documentation of the racist destruction of Brazilian Indians in *Triste Tropique*, Geertz's studies of the emergent ethnicities in new nations, and a host of recent anthropological accounts of violence and terror in the Third World.

In the same spirit, Benson glosses over the fact that most ethnographic monographs on ethnic minorities in Britain were written by members of the communities themselves, or by incorporated members (Pryce, Wallman, Desai, Benson herself, Saifullah Khan, Bhachu, Dahya, Anwar, Mascarinas-Keyes, Barot, Josephides, to name a few), by anthropologists with long-term field experience in Africa, Asia or the West Indies, and by recent immigrants from the Middle East and Africa (including myself), with only a few anthropologists (Jeffery, Banks and Shaw spring to mind) apparently choosing their fieldwork subject (or is it object?) free of prior dialogic engagements. This, above all, explains the choices of fieldwork site, not notions of strong Asian and weak black cultures, an absurd imputation, given the importance in the discipline - or at least in urban anthropology - of urban black ghetto studies by such distinguished anthropologists as Lewis, Hannerz or Leibow.

The strong-weak cultural dichotomy is more likely to be perpetrated by sociologists seeking broad explanatory frameworks, but it is, above all, the kind of commonsensical fallacy employed by laypersons and policy makers. To accuse anthropologists of this particular bias seems perverse, and Benson's reading of Ballard's article, for example, can only be understood in the light of her own political perspective as a feminist, a claim I shall explicate more fully below.

From imaginary anthropologists to imagined communities, it can be argued that in discursive terms, the concept of the imagined is useful but inadequate for a proper analysis of racism and ethnicity. We need to formulate more subtle concepts to highlight the nature of the moral proximities which generate communities imaginatively. Thus, I have suggested (Werbner 1990, 1991a, 1991b) that ethnic communities are moral communities, engaged in unilateral giving, fund raising and self help, and that they evolve, in response to racist violations, into communities of suffering. These may well encompass Asians, Caribbeans, Africans and others in shared local action, transcendent self-representations, and original cultural creativity. The suffering of oppression has been, historically, not only a degrading but also a culturally creative force, shaping powerful mythologies: Judaism, Christianity, Islam as well black diasporic cultures all arose in response to common experiences of suffering by imagined communities.

To understand who imagines in relation to which hegemonic violations requires localised knowledge. And it is precisely in the study of the local that anthropological strengths are most evident. Immigrants turned sojourners create their own symbolic spaces which empower collective action. Local practices, local self representations and discourses, local contestations, both empower and delineate identity. Nor is the local limited territorially: increasingly the interest is in translocal and transnational communities, constituting new localisms. Whereas sociologists tend to limit their subject of study to significant texts (mainly the press and media), supported by surveys or interviews with strategic personalities (both victims and oppressors), anthropologists hang around with ordinary people, record ordinary discourses and unspectacular rituals and celebrations. It is these which constitute the everyday taken-for-grantedness of culture, community and identity. To the extent that these ordinary people studied feel threatened - physically or symbolically - or subordinated economically, to that extent anthropologists observe and try to understand these phenomena.

There is also, however, a public sphere in which public representations, whether ethnic or racial, are struggled over. When Modood argues that foisting a black identity on Asians disempowers and marginalises them, it should be quite clear that what is at stake is not merely psychological empowerment or collective mobilisation, but economic and political power: job allocations, group representation, resource distribution, public office (1992a, 1992b). Against him it can be argued that there is no particular reason why an Asian identity should be privileged - it too is open to being challenged in the public sphere where, as we argue in our collection, administrative fictions of community are a necessary addendum to equitable redistributive policies.

So while Hall revises an earlier anti-ethnicity position and invokes cultural modes of resistance, other academic activists, this time feminists, including Sue Benson herself as she reveals in her concluding paragraph, challenge this new-old multicultural model as currently espoused in somewhat different terms by Modood, Ballard, and even Hall. The feminists argue that to endorse communal autonomy is to promote patriarchal values which deny women the equality due to them as British citizens (Murphy 1987, Yuval-Davis 1992, Ali 1992, Goering 1993). I agree with this view in the double sense that I believe, as a citizen, that women as citizens have the right to decide for themselves, and also as a student of ethnicity because I know that any fixed communal label is necessarily fictitious, ignoring as it does the internal differentiations and segmentations implicit at any particular level of inclusiveness, and the multiple, overlapping, and often contradictory, ethnic identifications of its members. To legally or financially empower specific named collectivities at the expense of others is to privilege a particular, situationally defined, collectivity as an essentialised whole unto itself (Samad 1992).

As a final point, then, it is not we (the anthropologists) who essentialise and reify community. First, the state reifies community unavoidably, for inescapable adminstrative reasons. Second, and more importantly, the people we study have multiple, complex identities, and we try to understand the different spaces and contexts, the symbols and rituals, the ideologies and beliefs, the passions and rationalities which move them. It is they who draw on the past to think about the future and mobilise for action; it is they who network, fund-raise, build and work to reproduce their culture and their communities.

While I agree with Benson that culture is always a contested terrain, anthropologists, more than others, are conscious of the situational and changing scale of that contestation - from the domestic and interdomestic to neighbourhood, urban, diasporic or national politics. If we are to take culture seriously, and explore the rich intricacy of cultural or religious practices and transformations, we need to engage with the specificities of anthropological work beyond Britain, and draw upon anthropological tools which allow us, as anthropologists, to understand that intricacy systematically. We need to locate our analyses - whether of social power, ethnic representation, racial violence, economic commodification, gender relations or urban ritual - explicitly within contemporary cross-cultural theoretical debates.

7 On the reproduction and representation of Hinduism in Britain

Steve Vertovec

The large scale, post-Second World War migration of South Asians profoundly changed the religious, as well as ethnic and racial, landscape of Britain. Temples, mosques and gurdwaras were now commonplace in most large British cities, and Hindu, Muslim and Sikh festivals and holy days were acknowledged in schools and other public spaces.

The religious traditions themselves have proceeded along differential trajectories of development in the country (Badham 1989, Knott 1991, Vertovec in press). Yet central to all of the myriad developments affecting South Asian religions and their practitioners were processes of identity formation, consolidation and institutionalisation through which religion and ethnicity come to be fused in ways new and unique to the post-migration context. An examination of such processes regarding these religious minorities can help us understand the ethnic phenomena generally (Hall, 1992a, p. 254).

Much recent scholarship on Hinduism in the subcontinent has come to emphasise the historical ways and means by which this religious rubric has been rather artificially constructed - by foreign Orientalists, indigenous sages, and nationalist organisations - particularly since the nineteenth century (Frykenberg 1989, Thapar 1989, Hardy 1990). In the following essay, similar and subsequent ways and means were traced, indicating how Indian traditions have been re-constructed, reproduced or transformed and how settlement and institutional change in Britain has fostered and reified notions of Hinduism and Hindu community as *ethnic* phenomena.

The Hindu population of Britain: background and breadth

The immigration of South Asians in the 1950s and early 1960s was one almost wholly undertaken by men (most of whom were in their 20s to 40s). Systems of recruitment and patterns of chain migration led to the establishment of, in various locations throughout Britain, pockets of men largely from the same kinship groups, villages, districts or regions of India mainly Gujarat and the Punjab. By the late 1960s and early 1970s, wives and dependants of the men migrated. At the same time there was an increasing movement of South Asians from territories in East Africa (Kenya, Uganda, Tanzania, Zambia, Malawi). Holding British passports, great numbers came to Britain in the late 1960s; in 1972, the wholesale expulsion of Asians from Uganda saw tens of thousands arriving *en masse* in Britain. The British Asian population therefore developed by way of contrasting modes of migration and from diverse socio-cultural and economic backgrounds.

Table 1 provides an approximate breakdown of the British Asian population by area of origin and religion within Britain's total population of over 54 million in 1984.

Table 1
Hindu segments within the total Asian population of Britain

1,271,000 Asians (about 2% of the total population), of which
- 807,000 Indians (1.4% of total pop., 63% of Asians[1]), of which
  - 48% Hindu[2] (.6% of total pop., 30% of Asians), of which
    - 70% Gujarati-speaking, of which
      63% East African Gujarati (44% of total Hindus)
      37% Indian Gujarati (26% of total Hindus); and
    - 15% Punjabi-speaking, of which
      20% East African Punjabi (3% of total Hindus)
      80% Indian Punjabi (12% of total Hindus); and
    - 15% Other Indian

Source: Knott and Toon 1982, Peach et al. 1988, Knott 1991

(Due to the limitations of survey and census categories, this breakdown obscures the presence of Indians from other parts of the global Indian diaspora - particularly the Caribbean [especially Guyana, Trinidad and Jamaica], Fiji, Mauritius, and South Africa - whose numbers in Britain likely amount to tens of thousands (see Vertovec, in press)

It was important to underscore the geographical variance of British Hindu origins, for provenance has played a fundamental role in determining patterns of post-migration settlement, social institutions, religious practices, and identity formation. And with regard to such developments, distinctions of provenance were by no means limited to general regions (Punjab, Gujarat, East Africa), but extend to particular provinces and districts, even towns and villages therein. This was so because each level of provenance can be associated with salient differences of language and dialect, socio-economic bases, caste composition, kinship and domestic structures, and - as stressed earlier - specific religious traditions. Accordingly, in a context of diaspora, levels of provenance may become the central reference points for the establishment of segmentary identities and social networks (Crissman 1967).

On perhaps the most obvious, broad level, distinctions between Punjabis and Gujaratis were marked. In addition to major language differences (the former speaking Punjabi, Hindi and some Urdu, the latter, Gujarati, Cutchi and Hindi), a host of overt and subtle social and cultural differences abound. In Britain these were characterised in stereotypes which Punjabis and Gujaratis have of themselves and each other such as, that Punjabis were more prone to drinking and smoking openly in pubs, eating meat, having less regard for certain religious observance, Gujaratis being associated with the opposite of these behaviours (Knott 1986, Nesbitt 1987).

While most British Punjabis were from the adjacent areas of Jullunder and Ludhiana their composition includes various caste groups (including Jats, Khatris, Brahmins, Chuhras and Chamars). However, the overall salience of caste distinctions among Punjabis in Britain, and in India itself, was arguably less marked than those associated with other regional social structures (Sharma 1969, Vertovec 1992b).

Among British Gujaratis, in contrast, there were many significant levels or spheres of differentiation, 'which make co-operation between them minimal or difficult to achieve' (Michaelson, 1984, p. 2). British Gujaratis hail from parts of Surat and Charottar (Kaira) on the mainland, and from Saurashtra (Kathiawad) and Kutch further West. Linked to a large extent with linguistic traits (given over twenty varieties of Gujarati language), there was often considerable social differentiation among Gujaratis, such as that between Kathiawadis and Surtis (Knott 1994) and between Kutchis and mainland Gujaratis (Logan, 1988, pp. 9-10). Kutchis, for example, purposefully utilise their language 'to distinguish themselves as a category apart from other Gujarati groups' (Barot, 1981, p. 124).

Also amongst British Gujaratis, there exist important characteristics and developments with regard to East Africans *vis-a-vis* Indians. One consequential source of difference arose through the migration process itself. The East Africans, who were essentially refugees, arrived as complete multi-generational family units. Not only has this meant that the age structure of the two groups varies considerably, but 'The presence of elders and an accepted authority structure among the "Africans" has led to greater cohesion and a greater acceptance of traditional Indian values' (Michaelson, 1983, p. 31).

With regard to their social identities, too, stereotypes among and between the groups persist. East Africans were usually associated with higher educational and occupational backgrounds than Indians and their supposed longer and deeper acquaintance with the English language and with urban, middle class European (albeit colonial) lifestyles has connoted a better preparation for successful living in Britain. Though it would be difficult to prove the validity of all such traits, they remain common stereotypes which determine much by way of attitudes and social formations.

Yet East African can be quite a misnomer when one considers the fact that large numbers of Gujaratis migrated to Kenya, Uganda and elsewhere in the region only after the Second World War: thus their Indian roots were as strong as those who came to Britain directly, yet they share experiences with those who were settled in East Africa for generations (Erikson 1984). The nineteenth century and post-Second World War migrations to East Africa, however, were largely by persons from different areas of Gujarat (the former mainly from Saurasthra and Kutch, the latter from Churottar and Surat), which had an important bearing on their linguistic and caste makeup, cultural practices and social institutions both in East African and, now, in Britain. The same must be recognised for Punjabis as well (Ballard 1986). Moreover, a number of those born and raised in East Africa were educated in India, and among most Asians in East Africa - regardless of actual place of birth and upbringing - many pervasive ties of religion, kinship, caste and economy were maintained with India.

Gujarat is well known in the subcontinent for the number, complexity and distinctiveness of caste and sub-caste groups, and the same can be said for Gujarati caste phenomena in Britain. Michaelson (1983) notes the presence of at least thirty distinct Gujarati castes in Britain, each with a specific provenance in India. These prominently include Patidars from Surat and Charottar, Lohanas and Visa Halari Oshwals from Kathiawad, Bhattias and Leva Kanbi Patels from Kutch (Pocock 1976, Barot 1981). Although in East Africa and in Britain - as throughout the South Asian diaspora (Schwartz 1967) - a caste system could no longer govern social, economic, ritual, or other relationships, caste identities among Gujaratis have continued to be of considerable importance with regard to status, marriage, social networks and formal institutions. Caste has also played a large role in differentially reproducing and transforming socio-religious phenomena in Britain.

Disparate religious traditions among British Hindus derive from diverse regional, caste and sectarian origins. Differences of religious heritage between regions in India reflect varying histories involving the presence of certain *sampradayas* (traditions focused on a set of beliefs transmitted through a line of teachers), revivalist or reformist movements, contact with Islam and with other major religious traditions (including Buddhism, Jainism, Sikhism). This was compounded, in addition, by the local or provincial prevalence of certain castes and sub-castes, sometimes holding their own unique beliefs, practices, or sectarian attachments. Such diversity was reproduced in several ways within Britain.

Although most persons in Britain who regard themselves as Hindu recognise many of the same special days in an All-India Hindu calendar, several festivals, periods of fasting, and other times of religious significance were additionally prescribed given one's place of origin (Nesbitt, 1987, McDonald 1987, Logan 1988, Vertovec 1992b). Modes of celebrating such holy days or periods vary by region and district of origin, but some are recognised across much of India such as Diwali, Navratri, Janashtami.

The presence of identifiable doctrinal or devotional traditions (again, many of which having regional and caste-based affiliations) further complicates the British Hindu makeup. These include three rival sects of Swaminarayanis, Arya Samajis, Radhasoamis, Pushtimargis (Vallabhacharyas), and people with special devotion towards the Mother Goddess, Sathya Sai Baba, Shirdi Sai Baba, Santoshi Ma, Baba Balak Nath, or Jalaram Bapa. What were sometimes called neo-Hindu movements were also prevalent in Britain, having both South Asian and indigenous British membership; these include the Ramakrishna Mission, Brahma Kumaris, Brahmo Samaj, various yoga and meditation associations, and, importantly, the International Society for Krishna Consciousness (ISKCON) better known as Hare Krishnas. There were also what might be called regional-minority communities (especially Bengalis, Tamils and Telugus, Indo-Caribbeans, Indo-Mauritians, Indo-Fijians) with their own styles and focuses of worship. Further, in Britain there were South Asian religious communities or local populations which blur the boundaries (Nesbitt 1987, p. 4) between what were often commonly thought to be discrete traditions, particularly between Jains-Hindus (Michaelson 1984) and Sikhs-Hindus (notably represented by Valmikis and Ravidasis; Nesbitt 1989). And even though generally both Punjabi and Gujarati religious cultures at large were steeped in Vaishnavism, one can witness a greater emphasis on Rama and the Ramayana in the former, and on Krishna and the Bhagavata Purana in the latter. It was the presence of such varied religious traditions and orientations which give rise to questions regarding reproduction and representation.

Facets of reproduction

Here, I use reproduction in referring to two identifiable, but not necessarily unconnected, cultural processes among migrant or diaspora communities. The first was that of cultural transmission between generations, whereby, through 'messages sent and received at different levels of consciousness' (Nesbitt, 1987, p. 8), children and young people learn and gain competence in manifold kinds of group-specific knowledge, action, and disposition.[3] The second was that of institutionalisation,[4] or the organisation and of certain roles, relationships, meanings and symbols stemming from a desire to ensure their continuity.

It might be said that the foremost environment for cultural transmission in any social group was the domestic sphere, and this was no different concerning religious nurture among British Hindus (Jackson 1985, Nesbitt 1987). Women were the main agents of religious transmission. The child's mother was the most significant figure in this process, but other women, such as the paternal grandmother or aunt, may also be important, especially if they live in the household or nearby. It was they who show the children how to perform *puja* or let them learn by participating; teach them prayers; explain what to eat and how to fast; tell or read them stories of the deities and show them how to celebrate festivals. It also tends to be women who answer children's questions and decide that they should attend *satsangs* (religious gatherings), discourses, cultural performances and the temple. (Logan, 1988, p. 122).

Logan (Ibid., p. 8) concludes that 'most children gain the bulk of their knowledge of Hinduism at home, from women, particularly through observation of and participation in ritual. Their knowledge of myths and theological concepts, however, was much weaker. (Ibid., pp. 123-4)

It was the traditions associated with provenance, sect, and social group or caste which essentially condition these popular, domestic forms of practice; therefore, at present, Hindu reproduction by way of cultural transmission or religious nurture in Britain was dominated by widely varying features reflecting the diverse social and geographic origins of the South Asians.

Regarding reproduction by institutionalisation, a more complicated pattern was emerging which, as described in the next section, has much to do with processes of representation as well. Bowen (1987) has outlined three phases of institutional development among British Hindus which, although initially intended to describe the evolution of the Gujarati population in Bradford, may serve to characterise processes on the national scale. Taken together he (Ibid.,

p. 15) writes, 'the phases entail a dialectic between homogeneity and heterogeneity, unity and diversity'.[5]

The first phase pertains especially to the period in which the British Asian population was comprised predominantly of young male migrants. In the late 1950s and early 1960s, some loosely-knit associations or committees were formed locally in various cities around Britain, particularly functioning to organise for all - regardless of area, sect or social group/caste of origin - modest celebrations of important All-India Hindu holy days.

The second phase witnessed the growth of diverse regional-linguistic, sectarian, and caste associations. Toward the end of the 1960s there had been a marked growth in the number of persons from distinct regions, sects and castes in each locale around Britain. This growth in numbers was also marked by much secondary migration within Britain, leading to geographically self-segregated groups within the British Asian populations, particularly regional ones (Jackson and Smith 1981, Robinson 1986). The growth of regional, sectarian and caste communities in given locales combined importantly with individuals' concerns about social, cultural, and religious provisions for their newly established families. These factors led directly to the establishment of numerous, group-specific associations and institutions. Also, many people arriving from East Africa in the late 1960s and early 1970s had gained considerable experience there in and maintaining caste, sectarian, and other communal organisations (Morris 1968); such experience was quickly utilised to create or expand similar associations after settlement in Britain. This phase of particularistic institutionalisation has continued with momentum through the present day: from but a handful of Hindu associations dotting the map of Britain in the early 1960s, there were currently some 737 Hindu organisations of many kinds spread over at least 146 British towns and cities and boroughs of Greater London.[6]

Many associations were set up with a view to providing or coordinating religious activity - ideally and ultimately, to raise funds toward, to establish, and to manage a temple or centre which could also function as a place of worship. Initially, specific devotional groups met in private homes, 'serving in a sense as congregations without temples' (Burghart, 1987a, p. 9). A house in Leicester, remodelled as a temple in 1969, was reputed to be Britain's first formal place of Hindu worship; the Multifaith Directory Research Project (see note 6) now lists 303 places of Hindu worship across the country.

The establishment of temples in Britain has been a major source of social, cultural and religious reproduction, yet it has also entailed many significant kinds of change as well. This has included fundamental changes in the role and status of priests (Barot 1987), and in the frequency and procedure of key rituals - especially in temples which have arisen through negotiation among people from different regional origins (Knott 1986, 1987, Nye 1991). Temples in Britain were valued by their users not only for providing a source for the accumulation of spiritual merit (*punya*) through devotional worship and service (*puja*, *seva*), but they also may be the arenas for enacting more secular aspects of communal compliance and status acquisition, the latter particularly by way of publicly presented donations (Barot 1973, 1987). Temples were also significant contexts for the reproduction of religious practices, especially as this was where children learn many basic ritual acts and modes of behaviour. Although a number of generalised Hindu temples and associations exist, the great majority were characterised by regional,[7] and sectarian/devotional[8] orientations.

In addition to the large number of associations organised for specifically religious purposes, the number of caste associations have proliferated dramatically since the 1960s. It was particularly in East Africa where, for a number of reasons, a process of 'communal crystallisation' (Morris, 1968, p. 34) took place through which mainly Gujarati caste groups created and elaborated formal caste associations to oversee collective social and political, as well as religious, interests. It was especially such East African Gujarati-derived caste associations which currently abound in Britain (Michaelson 1979, 1983). Of the 737 existing associations among British Hindus mentioned previously, no less than 90 were specifically caste-based in name (and doubtless more were assumed under other, more general Hindu or Gujarati appellations; see note 9, below). Caste associations in Britain were organised on both a local and national scale in order to hold regular or annual gatherings, to celebrate religious festivals, and to produce detailed directories of members.[9] Further, the workings of caste associations assist in the arrangement of marriages and act to maintain links of many kinds with villages and regions in the subcontinent.

The third phase characterising institutional development was that marked by the formation of umbrella organisations. Thus far little actually exists, on either national or local levels, which operates very effectively to undertake or to coordinate Hindu activities, or to express and to safeguard common interests, across the board of regional, sectarian and caste groups. The National Council of Hindu Temples (UK) was at present the body which comes closest to this ideal. Over thirty temples and societies were directly affiliated to the Council. Among its endeavours, the Council has been known to use its network to raise funds in one city so as to help found a temple in another (Barot 1987). It also publishes a quarterly newsletter and sponsors large scale weekend Hindu Youth Festivals, drawing young people from around the country. Despite its broad network, however, some Punjabis complain that the Council appears Gujarati dominated, that it seems to favour Gujarati temples and organisations, and that, therefore, its name should be changed to reflect a regional bias.

Such problems were found locally as well. Bowen (1981, p. 45-7) observes that within Bradford's Hindu Cultural Society, the office-bearers hail from all over India; moreover, it 'does not set out to cater exclusively for any particular section of Bradford's Hindu community' and therefore 'has articulated its own view of itself as an "umbrella association" for all the Hindus in the area.' Nevertheless, the Gujarati community does not support it because of linguistic differences. A final facet of reproduction that of religious education is described in the following section.

Facets of representation

In Britain there were a host of individual and institutional agents, both within and outside the South Asian community, who - although involved in varying discourses - assume or propound certain unitary representations of

Hinduism. Each of these operate in different ways, but all have effects on the nature and content of identity in relation to symbolic boundary formation, social interaction, community relations, and resource allocation.

Formal organisations promulgate the most clearly defined representations of Hinduism in Britain. The National Council of Hindu Temples (UK), in virtually everything it does, assumes or declares Hindu commonalty. Suggesting what 'all Hindus' believe, understand, and do, the Council offers its pamphlet entitled *Hinduism: An Introduction to the World's Oldest Living Religion* as 'the authoritative statement on the tenets of the Hindu religion'. Though well meaning, and containing many statements which few believers would dispute, the booklet propounds a wholly Krishnaite orientation (Burghart, 1987b, pp. 231-2).

The Vishwa Hindu Parishad - which has emerged as a prominent force of right-wing Hindu nationalism in India (van der Veer, in press) - was now well established in the UK, with at least fifteen reported branches across Britain. By far its most significant impact in this country has been by way of sponsoring the Virat Hindu Sammelan (Great Hindu Gathering), attended by tens of thousands, at the Milton Keynes Bowl in 1989. This event, together with its large souvenir booklet, promoted the kind of understanding of Hinduism and Hindu community one would associate with the VHP. In one article in the booklet (Ibid, p. 94), we read of the 'Hindu race', and that the word 'Hindu ought to be understood in the context of the nationhood sense and not in the limited religious sense'.

In 1985, a comparable event called the Cultural Festival of India was held over the course of one month at the Alexandra Palace in north London. It was organised by the Bochasanwasi Shree Akshar Purushottam Sanstha, a branch of the Swaminarayan *sampradaya*. According to the Festival Guide, 'The objective was, firstly, to present the glory of India in its pristine purity to the new generation of Asians and to the British People'; it was, secondly, an attempt to create cultural understanding and harmony' (Brear, 1986, p. 23). The 'general motive, however, was crystallised into the particular one of showing how the religion of Lord Swaminarayan (who was "the Supreme God Himself") inherits this ancient richness and focuses it' (Ibid., p. 24). Similarly, Logan (1988, p. 74) concluded that 'the exhibition had a distinct bias towards Gujarati Vaishnavism.'

The International Society for Krishna Consciousness (ISKCON) has assumed an exceptional place among British Hindus, particularly the majority East African Gujaratis (Carey 1983). Although the prime movers of ISKCON were white (especially American) converts, British Asians usually show great respect for the strength of ISKCON members' devotion, their knowledge of Sanskrit, their strict vegetarianism, and their elaborate, detailed rituals. ISKCON's magazine, *'Back to Godhead'* was widely read by Indians, and their *Bhagavad-gita As It Is* - a translation and commentary on the Bhagavad-gita written by the movement's founder, Bhaktivedanta Swami Prabhupada - was perhaps the most common translation of this key text found in Britain. It was likely that ISKCON's greatest impact will continue to be on Asians born and raised in this country. Carey (Ibid., p. 481) foresees this because

> ...the enthusiastic preaching of the devotees, backed up by an abundance of pamphlets outlining the need for vegetarianism and the perils of drink,

and good English-language translation of classical texts, all go a long way in providing a clear set of moral and ethical directives and a robust religious sensibility.

Such a development underscores the importance of representations directed particularly at young people.

It was estimated that thirty-five per cent of Indians in Britain were UK-born (Robinson 1990, p. 274). Because they were growing-up in Britain, instead of in an Indian context steeped in their religious traditions,

> ...many Hindu youngsters are confused because they lack an adequate conceptual framework within which to set their practical knowledge and experience in such a way that they can make sense of Hinduism both to themselves and to outsiders. This state of affairs partly explains the rise of more formal methods of transmitting Hindu values and ideas which have emerged in recent years among various Hindu organisations including caste and sectarian associations (Jackson, 1985, p.71).

Heightened awareness of this situation has led, at one point, to (unsuccessful) moves among some British Asians to establish their own, state-supported, Hindu school (Kanitkar 1979). Yet supplementary courses, offered -with diverse styles and contents - by numerous organisations, have become the major source of formal religious nurture among Hindus (Jackson and Nesbitt 1986, Jackson 1987). While regional, sectarian, and caste traditions were being reproduced through informal nurture at home,

> ...some of those communities which provide formal Hindu nurture for children - whether they are conscious of it or not - seem to be presenting young people with a more conceptual and unitary view of Hinduism than that gained less formally. Sometimes this view seems to sit uncomfortably with the picture of the tradition gained elsewhere. Other times the two pictures appear complementary...

Young British Asians, together with their white peers, were also influenced by the picture of Hinduism taught within Religious Education courses in state schools. Since the mid 1970s, most Local Education Authority (LEA) Agreed Syllabuses for Religious Education have come to place a strong emphasis on increasing pupils' knowledge and understanding of several world faiths, including Hinduism (Jackson 1987). Although in many cases somewhat ill-conceived at first, by the mid 1980s considerable thought had gone into sensitively portraying Hinduism in the classroom: this has included efforts to recognise the great variety of traditions within the rubric, as well as to be aware of the fact that the version of Hinduism taught at school may differ significantly from the regional, sectarian and caste traditions in which Asian children participate at home and at the temple (Jackson 1984, Killingley *et al.* 1984). Nevertheless, differences among and between LEAs, schools and teachers has meant that, across the country, R.E. teaching was very uneven; the result was often a picture of Hinduism which was over-simplified, over-generalised, and riddled with factual errors.

A singular and rather stereotyped view of Hinduism and Hindus in British society was found, with a range of consequences, in other spheres as well. For example, Knott (1986, p. 53) points out:

> The South Asian population in this country is generally identified in two ways by the government, the press, the Church and community relations bodies. One is as 'Indians, Pakistanis and Bangladeshis' (commonly called 'Asians'), and the other is as 'Hindus, Sikhs and Muslims'. In Leeds, local bodies use this second system of classification for their interactions with the South Asian population, and as a result it is the representative religious bodies which have been authorised to receive local government urban aid and deprivation grants for the ethnic groups.

Such an assumption, by state administrations, of communal unity among ethnic groups has been seen to generate a host of conflicts which can be ultimately dysfunctional for a group in terms of the use of resources, leadership, and collective mobilisation (Kalka 1991).

Yet it was largely simplified and generalised representations of Hinduism which were formulated and promoted by many British Asian organisations themselves. These representations were often symbolised in the names of institutions themselves: of the 737 associations reported, 105 (fourteen per cent) have generalised Hindu names[10] (which, of course, may mask the actual regional-linguistic or caste composition of an association;[11] nonetheless, the choice of such a name remains significant with regard to how they choose to see themselves and/or depict themselves to others, Asian and white).

In addition, many organisations (even those with clearly regional or sectarian orientations) publish circulars, newsletters, pamphlets and booklets which were filled with articles and statements regarding what Hinduism is and what Hindus believe. Virtually all of these were drawn from, or were reformations of Hindu ideologies which emerged in the nineteenth and early twentieth centuries (including its rationalisation, neo-Vedanta combined with Puranic understandings, Sanskritic deities - with an emphasis on Vaishnavism - approached through *bhakti* yet linked with monotheism, historicisation, and so on). This was also evident in the common use, interchangeably with Hinduism, of Sanatan Dharm - in this context stripped of its original socio-political connotations and employed as a wholly neutral term (Knott, 1986, p. 78). Knott's (1987, pp. 163-4) study in Leeds exemplifies much regarding processes of representation throughout Britain:

> In the temple 'Sanatana Dharma' is held to be a system which incorporates all Hindus, irrespective of ethnic or sectarian divisions. It symbolizes temple religion: it is hailed in one of the final verses of the *arti* service with the phrase 'Sanatana Dharma *ki jay*'; it is the focus of dialogue with other faiths. ...The content of those religious practices which take place in the temple - which form a part of 'Sanatana Dharma' - reveals the dynamics of this process, the development towards this new and standardized form of Hinduism.

The growing prominence of a generalised Hinduism or Sanatan Dharm was found throughout the diaspora. In a survey of overseas Indian communities, Jayawardena (1968, p. 444) found evidence of general trends leading 'from village and caste beliefs and practices to wider, more universalistic definitions of Hinduism that cut across local and caste differences.' The trend leads toward the creation of what may be called an ecumenical Hinduism (Williams 1988, pp. 40-41).

Like the Hinduism which emerged in India, that of Indians in diaspora settings such as Britain has been formulated and utilised *vis-a-vis* an Other - or more correctly, in the latter case, Others. It was this development in contexts abroad which has accented the emergent Hinduism as an ethnic phenomenon (Jayawardena 1980, van der Veer and Vertovec 1991, Vertovec 1992a).

Conclusion: Ethnic Hinduism in diaspora

The identifications, status attributions, and practices of groups *vis-a-vis* one another, by way of both self- and other-ascribed criteria, essentially amounts to what we often mean as ethnic dynamics. By its nature, the *vis-a-vis* process entails an increasing collective self-consciousness, as members of groups grow aware of how others see them, and as they come to realise and to articulate how they wish to see themselves in new or changing contexts. As we have seen in both the Indian and British contexts, notions of Hinduism and Hindu community have arisen through such dynamics and their stimulation of collective self-consciousness.

Throughout most daily interactions with whites in Britain, the *vis-a-vis* dynamics usually entail self-consciousness in terms of black and Asian criteria (while within the Asian populations, their *vis-a-vis* dynamics relate to a host of segmentary identities surrounding region, caste, family, village, and so forth). Yet among Hindus (and other Asian peoples) with devout religious inclinations in Britain, there was a further, important *vis-a-vis*: that within facets of an environment at once oddly both religiously plural by way of harbouring numerous religious communities, and overwhelmingly secular in terms of its public institutions, culture and ethos.

Thus in the course of Logan's (1988, p. 124) research many adults reported that they had become more aware of their religion in Britain, as a result of belonging to a minority group in a predominantly irreligious society. They could no longer take their religion and their children's assumption of it for granted. Their collective *vis-a-vis* Christianity and secularism, as it were, takes precedence over their regional, sectarian and caste *vis-a-vis* dynamics. Therefore, 'In becoming a self-conscious tradition in a new location,' Knott (1987, p. 165) writes, 'the vernacular has given way to the pan-Indian, diversity has given way to a unified system of belief and practice, and ethnic [regional] identity has given way to "community".' It was a process compounded through being approached as a single community, by various state, educational, religious (Christian and inter-faith) and other public bodies - and by common understandings of white British. British Hindus were being represented, and were increasingly representing themselves, as a single faith: at the same time they were moving (albeit at differential paces) towards reproducing themselves as a community. Hence, Burghart (1987b, p. 233) concludes, 'the cultural awareness of Hindus has been sharpened in an alien cultural milieu, and they were ready to believe - as many non-Hindus do - that Hinduism was an ethnic religion'. Still, however, it was regional, sectarian and caste-specific traditions which were continuing to be reproduced in domestic and local community spheres: therefore, conflict and confusion persist. This will likely give way as new generations were inculcated with the generalised representations of Hinduism promulgated by broad-based associations and state schools.

With regard to some of the *vis-a-vis* dynamics specifically affecting the dynamic of religion and ethnicity, I think it was important to bear in mind that,

> Religion is fundamental to the ways in which people often identify themselves not only in relation to others and to historical circumstances, but also in relation to some deeply believed transcendent reality, ordained code of conduct, and sacred symbols. This-worldly and other-worldly points of reference, as it were, are interposed (Vertovec 1990, p. 247).

Religion supplies criteria which were wholly unlike other criteria (social actions, cultural forms, economic activities) to which groups refer by way of positioning themselves in relation to one another. For the social scientist, religious phenomena were approached as historically conditioned socio-cultural constructs open to re-definition, re-configuration, and re-institutionalisation of symbols and social forms in light of shifting contexts. For the religious adherents, transcendent, sacred notions concerning cosmology and soteriology were regarded as a-historical in content and ultimate in authority. Therefore we should not lose sight of the fact that although Hinduism appears largely to be a relatively recent construct in India and Britain, for those who regard themselves as Hindus this by no means diminishes any of its personal and collective power; its reformulated symbols and institutions have taken on new roles, in different times and places, as ultimate reference points for identity.

Notes

1 The balance of the recorded British Asian population is comprised of twenty-nine per cent Pakistanis and seven per cent Bangladeshis, the overwhelming majority of both of whom are Muslim.

2 The balance of the Indian population is forty-one per cent Sikh (of which fourteen per cent 'East African'-Punjabi/ eight-five per cent Indian-Punjabi) and eleven per cent Muslim (of which thirty-eight per cent 'East African'-Gujarati/ twenty-three per cent Indian-Gujarati/ thirty-eight per cent Indian-Other).

3 After Bourdieu (1977, p. 214), 'The word *disposition* seems particularly suited to express what is covered by the concept of habitus (defined as a system of dispositions). It expresses first the *result of an organising action*, with a meaning close to that of words such as structure; it also designates a *way of being*, a *habitual state* (especially of the body) and, in particular, a *predisposition*, *tendency*, *propensity*, of *inclination*' (italics in original).

4 This notion is employed in its Weberian sense, which Eisenstadt (1968, p. xxxix) summarises, in part, as 'the capacity to create and crystallise ... broader symbolic

orientations and norms, to articulate various goals, to establish organisational frameworks, and to mobilise the resources necessary for all these purposes ...'.

5 Bowen's model is similar to Dahya's (1974) stages concerning the 'fusion' of 'ethnic/sectarian/national groups' and the subsequent 'fission and segmentation' of sub-groups among Pakistanis in Bradford and Birmingham.

6 Information regarding 'Hindu' organisations is derived from materials of the Multifaith Directory Research Project based at the Religious Resource and Research Centre, University of Derby (in conjunction with the Inter-Faith Network for the United Kingdom). My thanks to Paul Weller and Rachelle Castle of the Centre, and to Brian Pearce of the Inter-Faith Network, for their kind help and assistance.

7 Major regional orientations (by way of distinctions concerning both language and specific traditions surrounding a focus of worship) are reflected in the names of organisations such as: the Bharata Mandal - Gujarati Samaj, Surrey Gujarati Hindu Society, Punjabi Hindu Society, Panduranga Hindu Temple, and Ram Nivas - Gujrat Vaishnav Mandal (and similarly for the non-Gujarati/Punjabi, 'regional minority' populations; for example, the Maharashtra Mandal, London Tamil Society, Caribbean Hindu Society, and Fiji Sanatan Dharam Ramayan Mandli Leeds). Other regional orientations are not so clear, although the names may suggest such: for example, one may associate names like Shree Vishwa Hindu Mandir and Shri Ram Mandir as reflecting a largely Punjabi membership, and Radha-Krishna Temple, Shri Krishna Mandir, and Shri Gita Bhavan Mandir to be largely Gujarati.

8 *Sampradayas* and other particularistic devotional traditions are evident in names like: Sri Sathya Sai Centre, Shri Nathji Temple, Vedic Mission Arya Samaj, Jalaram Prathna Mandal, and Balmiki Adi Bir Vir Mahasabha (further, region and *sampradaya* may even be combined, such as with the Shree Kutch Satsang Swaminarayan Temple).

9 Local caste associations have names such as: the Shri Gurjar Kshatriya Gnati Mandal, the Charotar Patidar Samaj, Chovis Gam Patidar Samaj, Shree Bardai Brahman Samaj, Jansari Gnati Mandal, Shrimali Soni Samaj Leicester, and Shree Lohana Mohajan. Some examples of U.K.-wide bodies linking such local associations are: the National Council of Vanik Associations, the National Association of Patidar Samaj, the Shree Sorathia Prajapati Community, the Saree Limbachia Hittechhu Mandal, the Leuva [sic] Patidar Samaj (SNB) of UK, and the Federation of Anavil Samajes (UK).

10 These include local names such as: Sanatan Mandal, Shree Sanatan Dharma Sabha, Bhakti Mandal, Bharat Sevashram Sangha, Bharat Hindu Samaj, Hindu Religious and Cultural Society, or simply Hindu Temple, Hindu Society, or Hindu Centre.

11 For instance, Bowen (1987, p. 24) notes that Bradford's Shree Hindu Temple was founded and largely maintained by Gujarati Prajapatis.

8 The politics of Islamic identity among Bangladeshis and Pakistanis in Britain[1]

Yunas Samad

The collapse of the Soviet Union and the demise of the cold war has led some analysts to debate whether the next arena of global confrontation would be between the Islam and West (Akhtar, 1989, p. 7-8, Buzon, 1991, p. 441). It has been argued that the potential for cataclysmic conflict was discernible in events taking place in the Middle East such as Iran's opposition to the West and the Gulf War. In this scenario Muslims in Europe were viewed as potential fifth columnists. The fact that the controversy over *The Satanic Verses*, opposition to the Gulf War and the head scarves affair in France were led by umbrella organisations that, at least initially, were funded by Middle Eastern and North African powers was considered as evidence for supporting this view. This argument, however, is profoundly flawed as Islam is deeply divided and this was apparent in the behaviour of the religious groups that were active in the opposition to Salman Rushdie and the Gulf War. There was intense rivalry between groups who allied themselves with either Saudi Arabia or Iran which suggests that Islamic solidarity was a notion that has little substance in the political arena. Equally it would be simplistic to conclude from the above that these powers, instead of ideology, used petro-dollars to buy the support of British Muslims.

The history-from-below school shows that popular assertion has a dynamic and independence that troubles elite leaders who claim to represent it (Rude 1959, Thompson, 1963, pp. 77-85, Ghua, 1982, pp. 1-8). In the Rushdie controversy the UK Action Committee on Islamic Affairs that led the campaign was dominated by the pro-Saudi lobby. This group's initial popularity diminished for two reasons. First they refused to support the *fatwa* and later they refused to criticise the Saudi government for supporting military operations against Iraq. The main beneficiary was the, pro-Iranian, Kalim Siddiqui (Samad, 1992, p. 516). The swings in popular support suggest that they were subject to pressure from below. Even this push from below, however, was heterogeneous in character and there was considerable differentiation between the responses of the largely Sylheti population of Tower Hamlets and the largely Mirpuri population of Bradford. The Mirpuris of Bradford established themselves at the head of the anti-Rushdie campaign, not only nationally, but internationally. In contrast was the muted response of the Sylhetis of Tower Hamlets.

In the fervour accompanying these controversies a new term gained popular currency; British Muslim. The appropriation and usage of this term was an implicit recognition that religious identification was the major characteristics of British people originating from South Asia. British Pakistanis or British Bangladeshis as alternative categories were pushed aside as politicians and the press quickly jump on the bandwagon. However to accept this assumption and to focus on Islamic identity, only, would be a Whig interpretation of history. This paper will elaborate an ensemble of cultural identities and analyses the various combinations that emerge in different generations. On this basis it will become possible to understand why religious identification becomes politicised at a particular juncture.

The Pakistanis of Bradford and Bangladeshis of Tower Hamlets have in general terms many similarities yet their specific features were different. They were concentrated in inner city areas and were the largest ethnic minority in their respective locations. Both of these factors promoted community networks that replicated most of the cultural distinctiveness of their regions of origin. Towards wider society both the Bangladeshis in Tower Hamlets and the Pakistanis in Bradford highlight a national identity. National identification, however, consists of two main characteristics. One that emphasises the Muslim identity and the other highlights the regional cultural side. These broad brush strokes are fluid, overlap and weave. Furthermore neither Islam nor regional culture were homogenous but internally differentiated. Islam was divided along doctrinal lines and cultural identity was informed by locality of origin, dialects, village-kin networks and social stratification.

An important feature influencing the identity patterns of these communities was the districts they originated from. In Bradford the overwhelming number of settlers of Pakistani origin can be broadly divided along cultural lines between Pakhtuns and Punjabis. However out of the 44,000 or so who were from Pakistan about 40,000 were from the district of Mirpur. Similarly of Tower Hamlets' 25,000 Bangladeshis ninety-five per cent originated from the Sylhet district (Bradford Heritage Recording Unit, 1987, p. 14, Eade, 1993, p. 28). These loyalties based on localities were reinforced by differences in dialects that separate Mirpuris form other Punjabis and Sylhetis from other Bangladeshis.

Identification based on locality was reinforced by village-kin networks. These primary blocks were brought together into alliances consisting of extended families. Among the Mirpuris, *biraderis*, (endogamous groupings claiming patrilineal descent) formalises relations within kin groupings. This was reinforced in turn by, *vartan bhanj*, the institutionalisation of gift exchanges at specific ritual moments in the life cycle. Village-kin networks played an important role in the process of chain migration. Initially young men were sent to be cared by relatives and as a result village and district ties were established in Britain. These relations were reinforced by arranged marriages operating within these networks and by the formation of graveyard committees, which finance burial in the villages of origin. These loyalties were the basis for factional politics both in Tower Hamlets and Bradford (Carey and Shukur, 1985, p. 413, Werbner, 1990, pp. 96-104, 131).

These various solidarities were consolidated by social stratification based on castes of high and low status. Practically speaking most the Sylhetis population, with few exceptions, belong to low status castes and originally were small holding farmers. Caste stratification was also found among the Mirpuris with a small number of high status groups represented by Rajputs and Jats but low status groups were predominant such as *kamins* who were craftsmen; carpenters, potters, barbers, etc.

Another set of identities based on Islam also plays an important role in forming the world view of the Mirpuri and Sylheti population. Religious identification subsumes sectional interests based on region, language, village-kin relations and class. However even Islam was far from being monolithic and there were doctrinal divisions. Both among the Sylhetis and the Mirpuris the Barelwis sect was overwhelmingly dominant and Deobandis, Jamat-i-Islami and Tablighi Jamat were also present.

However these cultural and religious identities were reformulated within the class context that informs the Mirpuris and the Sylhetis responses to various issues. Up to the 1970s both groups were working in semi-skilled and unskilled positions. The Pakistanis were working in heavy engineering and textiles while Bangladeshis were concentrated in the garment sector and catering. They were located, despite their geographical differences, precisely in those sectors of the economy that were in the shadow of post-industrial Britain. Sectors that have been subjected, in some cases, to savage economic restructuring and deep recession. Many middle-aged Bangladeshis and Pakistanis were long term unemployed and this has been compounded by high unemployment among the young. Both communities were near the bottom of the social hierarchy and have done much worse than Gujaratis; both Muslims and Hindus, Sikhs, and East African Asians (Ballard, 1990, pp. 227-8, Robinson, 1990, pp. 293-4).

The Sylheti and Mirpuri communities exhibit similar features concerning class, religious sect, village-kin network (with *biraderis* playing a modifying role among Mirpuris) and a core identity that was linguistically defined. All these various cultural, religious and class identifications come into play in the political arena and were reformulated by the local and national political landscape (Ben-Tovin et al 1986). This becomes apparent when the reactions of Pakistanis in Bradford and Bangladeshis in Tower Hamlets were examined. The two communities show quite different responses even at the juncture when they briefly identified with a general Islamic standpoint such as the opposition to *The Satanic Verses* and the Gulf War. One thing that was clear from the evidence of the fieldwork was that there has been no an increase of religiosity. Instead three substantive points emerge from the comparison between the communities, which explain the various responses to the Rushdie affair and the Gulf Crisis.

The first prominent feature was that different generations were influential in the two areas. In Bradford the leadership patterns, whether in the arena of Pakistani, religious, mainstream or community politics were dominated by the first generation and these arenas gave them varying degree of influence over subsequent generations. The first generation generally operated a clientele system based on patronage and village-kin network, which was legitimised by the recognition they received from the authorities. The Mirpuri interest in Pakistani politics decreased as the community became more permanent. Hence the activities of the Peoples Party of Pakistan and the Islamic Democratic Alliance, which claims to have support in the city, were more ceremonial than substantive. Generally these were groups directed at the first generation. However there were also two Kashmiri groups, one pro-Tory and the other headed by a Labour councillor Amin Qureshi, which were undergoing a revival of interest that cuts across the generations; due to the political upheavals taking place at present in Kashmir.

The first generation leadership pattern was also prevalent in the mosques and religious institutions. This arena was transformed by the formation of the Bradford Council of Mosques, which acts as the collective spokesman for twenty-two out of the twenty-six mosques and eighteen other Muslim organisations. Half the Mosques were Deobandi and ten were Barelwi (Ruthven 1990, pp. 81-2). A Deobandi-Barelwi alliance dominates the council with the chair and secretaryship rotating between them. The two dominant characters in the organisation were Sher Azam, a trans-border Pakhtun, and Pir Maroof Shah who was the most important of the Barelwi *pirs*. The religious arena, however, overlaps with the political sphere. Pir Maroof Shah instructs his followers to vote labour. But it should be noted that his Rajput supporters support the Tories which serves to underline the fact that only some followers were influenced by their *pirs*. The other link with the Labour Party was through the community action programmes, which were based in the Bradford Council of Mosques. Councillor Mohammad Ajeeb was instrumental in setting up various initiatives located in the Council of Mosques. Initially he acted as the manager of the advice centre, located in their offices and coordinated substantial number of Manpower Services Commission projects that were based there. Approximately over 5000 school children were being imparted religious instructions by the Barelwi mosques and an equal number were passing through Deobandi institutions. Consequently the influence of this group encompassed young Muslims as well as first generation settlers.

In mainstream politics the Pakistani community became increasingly involved and all the political parties were sensitive to the ethnic minority vote. Three marginal seats, Bradford North, Bradford South and Keighly were sensitive to the Pakistani vote and in Bradford West a third of the electorate were Muslim. Labour claims that the Mirpuris vote for them because they were disadvantaged and discriminated against and that their policies target these very areas. This was not, however, the only factor influencing the Mirpuri electorate, as was demonstrated by Edward Lyons' defection to the Social Democratic Party in 1983. Lyons had formed good relations with clan leaders and was able to take a number of them with him. The result was that it split the Labour vote allowing Geff Lawler winning the seat for the Tories (LeLohe, 1990, pp. 63-6).

In contradistinction the various arenas of influence in Tower Hamlets were dominated almost totally by the second generation. The first generation leadership was generally businessmen operating a clientele system and their influence was limited to certain arenas. While the second generation leadership emerged out of the various community action programmes sponsored by central government under Section 11. These developments, however, were not mutually exclusive and first generation leadership has been involved in community action programmes and vice versa (Joly 1987).

The first generation was restricted to the political parties orientated to Bangladesh, mosques and to the Bangladesh Welfare Association. The Awami League and the Bangladesh National Party have adherents in Tower Hamlets, restricted mainly to the first generation, and were based on district and village-kin allegiances. The other arena where the first generation were influential were the mosques and religious institutions. But this influence was divided into two currents. The Barelwis main mosque was the Jamia Masjid in Brick Lane and the reformist sects congregated around the East London Mosque. This Deobandi institution, recipient of Saudi largesse, had close links with Tablighi Jamat, Dawat-ul Islam and its youth wing the Young Muslim Organisation. The Barelwi leadership in the Brick Lane mosque, on the other hand, was intimately associated with the Bangladesh Welfare Association. Leading members were also important figures in the mosque. The significance of this was that it allowed this group to wear two hats simultaneously; one nationalist and the other Islamic. Through the activities of the Bangladesh Welfare Association the mosque was also closely linked with the High Commission in London, the Awami League and later with the military authorities in Bangladesh. However on religious issues such as the Rushdie controversy the Bangladesh Welfare Association was silent and the Brick Lane mosque was very active. This flexibility allowed them to emphasise a particular identification when it suited them.

The first generation became isolated from subsequent generations due to their response to racial violence. The East End of London has a history of racist and fascist organisations dating back to the turn of the century. In the late 1970s and early 1980s Bangladeshis were targeted by the National Front. The death of two garment workers in 1978 triggered of a wave of protest and the second generation began to pressurise the leadership on taking a strong stand on the issue. The Bangladesh Welfare Association's role, however, had been limited to acting as intermediaries between the community and the authorities and were quite unprepared in dealing with street violence. Consequently their pusillanimous response led to the second generation to challenge, unsuccessfully, the leadership of the Bangladesh Welfare Association. Defeat led to them breaking away. Unrestrained by the first generation they reacted strongly to racial violence, which rewarded them with greater credibility in the community. They formed several territorial based youth organisations such as the Progressive Youth Organisation, Bangladeshi Youth Organisation and the Young Muslim Organisation. These local groups coalesced to form the Federation of Bangladeshi Youth Organisation (Carey and Shukur, 1985, pp. 413-4).

The second point of difference between Pakistanis of Bradford and the Bangladeshis of Tower Hamlets was the question of institutionalisation of leadership and its effects. In Yorkshire the formation of the Bradford Council of Mosques led to the co-opting of religious leaders along side 'secular' leaders by the local authorities. While in the East End of London it was only the 'secular' leadership that was co-opted. Why the Bradford Metropolitan Council institutionalised the religious leaders? They feared, in the early 1980s, that the city would be convulsed by riots as in Brixton, Liverpool and Birmingham. The trial of the Bradford Twelve was a good example of the tension that existed particularly among the youths. The Metropolitan Council wanted a tame Council of Mosques to control the discontented youth and for this end urged the various religious institutions to join the Council of Mosques and arranged for funding from the Manpower Services Commission. The result was it unified and institutionalised the religious leadership and increased their influence in the community.

The real breakthrough, however, for the religious leadership came with the Honeyford affair. The opposition to Honeyford was dominated by the Asian Youth Movement, a collection of left-wing groups such as the Socialist Workers Party and the Bradford Council of Mosques. The middle ground dominated by mainstream parties were squeezed from both sides. Although the Labour Party backed the opposition to Honeyford some Labour councillors rebuked Mayor Mohammad Ajeeb for speaking up on the issue. The importance was that this arena allowed the religious leaders, who up to then had played a subsidiary role, to establish their credibility with the Mirpuri community and particularly with the youth. The other important factor was that the Mirpuri community was left with a lingering sense of injury. Pakistan, Islam and the honour of the Mirpuri *biraderis* had been insulted and these were the same substantive issues which were raised in *The Satanic Verses* agitation (Halstead, 1988, pp. 74-111, Murphy, 1987, pp. 109, 141, Samad 1992).

In the case of Tower Hamlets the Federation of Bangladeshi Youth Organisations and its affiliates turned its attention from racial violence to institutional racism. Their involvement in community action programmes led to the second generation leadership being institutionalised at the expense of the first. The widening of their world view brought them into co-operation with the Labour Party, the Greater London Council (GLC) and Inner London Education Authority (ILEA), which funded youth groups, mother-tongue and religious classes and welfare rights activities. However the political fortunes of the second generation was closely linked to the Labour Party and the GLC and ILEA. With the abolition of these authorities and the emergence of a Liberal/SDP Alliance controlling the council the fortunes of the 'secular' leadership went into decline. This combination of events led to the termination of funding for an array of Bangladeshi organisations (Eade, 1990, pp. 494-5). The collapse of the Federation of Bangladeshi Youth Organisations, due to internal rivalry, only accelerated the decline and the 'secular' leadership, based in the Labour Party, were left in disarray. These developments, however, were in part compensated by some second generation leaders joining, what was now, the Liberal Democrat council.

The cutting of funds exacerbated the problems of the third generation. Youth clubs were closed and young Bangladeshis ended up on the streets alienated from society and their families. The combined effect of all these factors was that second generation leadership lost influence over the third generation, which began to develop independently. Only recently have attempts been made to address specifically the problems concerning the youth.

The third factor that needs to be considered was the local political developments and how they influenced young Bangladeshis and Pakistanis. The response to *The Satanic Verses* by Mirpuris was vigorous, particularly among the youth, because these issues conflated with the internal dynamics of Bradfordian politics. Before the anti-Rushdie campaign the question of identity, whether Muslim, Pakistani or Mirpuri, had become an impassioned issue. The legacy of the Honeyford altercation explains the sensitivity of

Bradford's Muslim population to *The Satanic Verses* controversy and the Gulf Crisis.

The developments taking place among Bangladeshi youth were different and these campaigns could not connect with ongoing issues. A particularly East London characteristic was the emergence of territorial gangs that were involved in potentially serious conflicts. These groupings were also involved in drugs; splif and ecstasy, petty crimes, mainly against their own community, and attacks on the white community. All these factors led to increasing tensions with the police and the young Bangladeshis were complaining of being harassed. The criminalisation of the young by the police has its parallels in the Afro-Caribbean community that was an important reason for social unrest.

These three factors, generational control, institutionalisation and local issues, informed the response of the Bangladeshis and the Pakistani communities to the Rushdie controversy and the Gulf crisis. In Bradford when the Rushdie agitation exploded the Mirpuri community took it as an insult to injury. The Honeyford affair had left the whole question of identity a highly sensitive issue and here was a fellow South Asian insulting their honour. The Bradford Council of Mosques' prestige among the youth rose substantially because no one else took a stand on the issue. However the Council of Mosques was subjected to an intense push factor from the second and third generations who wanted them to take a strong stand. It was highly significant that the youth stormed *en masse* Council of Mosques meetings, an arena where they had never participated in before, and demanded that the *fatwa* should be adopted. The Council of Mosques refusal to do so resulted in intense criticism and many young Pakistanis became disillusioned by the weak response. Some became involved with a pro-Iranian splinter group, Al-Mujhaid, and its youth wing the Muslim Youth Movement. Today there was little evidence to suggest that any of these groups have anything but a minority following. Most of the youth who participated in the agitation could not be recognised by their religious behaviour either before or after the campaign. As one observer commented that most of the discussions on Islam were taking place not in the mosques but in the pubs.

Similarly the Council of Mosques came under strong pressure from the youth to take a strong stand on the war in the Gulf. The moderate leadership, led by Sher Azam, came under intense pressure to declare *jihad* from Bradford. This response was modified by the intervention of Councillor Mohammad Ajeeb who argued that the opposition should be channelled through the Peace Committee organised by Bernie Grant. Basically the youth's response was anti-establishment in character. Main stream issues such as jobs, housing, education, and the lack of opportunities compounded with the feeling that they were not getting a fair deal made them search for an alternative identity. The political posturing of Tehran and Baghdad gave the youth a sense of solidarity with the oppressed of the world.

In Tower Hamlets the picture was quite different. The Rushdie controversy was a low key affair in comparison to Bradford where there was innumerable numbers of demonstrations and even conflicts with the police. In Tower Hamlets there were only two large demonstrations to Hyde Park and several meetings. The question raised was how even this limited activity was possible considering the deep cleavages in the community along generational lines.

Was there an outburst of Islamic renewal that united the Bangladeshis community on this issue? Certainly religiosity was a factor but this was restricted to the first generation and to a few from the subsequent generations. The UK Action Committee and the Islamic Solidarity Committee, later joined by the pro-Iranian Kalim Siddiqui, were active in organising meetings in both the reformist and Barelwi mosques. Thus they were able to draw the Bangladeshi community into the campaign. Friday prayers and the family networks were the main ways that religious Sylhetis were drawn into the opposition to *The Satanic Verses*. It should be also noted that some Bangladeshis were senior members of the pro-Saudi lobby and were very much involved not just locally but nationally in the various campaigns.

This fails, however, to explain how the controversy spread to the wider community particularly to the youth. One partial explanation was the ambivalent response of the 'secular' leadership. On one hand representatives of this group gave early warning that the book would cause trouble in the community. On the other hand it towed the party line and a resolution supporting Salman Rushdie was passed by the local Labour Party. Here the indications were that Islamic identity was externally imposed by wider society. The decisive factor that tipped the majority of the Bangladeshis, particularly the youth, in supporting the opposition was the reaction of the Establishment. The role of the media, government and the political parties was crucial. The tabloid press' portrayal of Muslims as raving fundamentalist and heathen savages angered many Bangladeshis, of all political persuasion, and confirmed a perception that the community was deliberately targeted. Educational establishments, schools and colleges discussed and debated the issues around the book. This alerted the youth who up to then were marginal to the issue and they were forced to take a stand on the issue. The Establishment's unequivocal stand combined with the dramatic increase in racial tension forced the community to close ranks. The anger generated by the negative stereotyping of Muslims was an important factor that was responsible for younger Bangladeshis in joining the protest. One woman, a Labour Party activist, described the need to demonstrate community solidarity by wearing a head scarf and openly showing her Muslim identity, not as an act of religiosity, but as act of defiance.

The Gulf Crisis also showed similar developments. Here the religious leadership adopted an ambiguous stance and were divided. They could not condone the annexation of Kuwait or US' involvement in the region but the reformist mosques closely associated with the pro-Saudi lobby were more muted in their reactions than their Barelwi counterparts. However among the second and third generations there was some support for Saddam Hussain as he was seen to be standing up to the West. Again the decisive factor was the media that was responsible for the creation of a highly polarised debate on the issue, which was brought to the attention of Bangladeshi youth by being reenacted in the educational institutions in the borough. However the channelling of the opposition through the Peace Committee organised by Bernie Grant defused tensions that were building up. The feature common to both the Rushdie controversy and the Gulf crisis was that for most Bangladeshis Muslims political identity was being foisted upon them by wider society. Once stereotyped the community's response was to solidarise as Muslims but this was a passing phenomenon and as yet an Islamic political identification was not an influential force among Sylhetis.

In Bradford, for young Pakistanis in particular, the issue of identity, whether Pakistani, Mirpuri or Muslim, was an impassioned issue before *The Satanic Verses* was published. The controversy over the book conflated with local issues resulting in social protest. Deploying religious metaphors and symbols to express their discontent which was structural in origins. In Tower Hamlets, however, the opposition to Rushdie did not interact with the issue of criminalisation of young Bangladeshis. Consequently the response was not of the same magnitude as their counterparts in Bradford. In both areas the younger generation were angry and the discontent was fed by discrimination in employment, housing, education and the general lack of opportunity. While in Bradford the situation has cooled, for the moment, however in Tower Hamlets tensions were climaxing.

Notes

1 I wish to thank the Wingate Foundation, the Nuffield Foundation and Rhodes Chair of Race Relations, Oxford University, for supporting this research.

9 The impact of religion, culture, racism and politics on the multiple identities of Sikh girls

Beatrice Drury

Introduction

This article was based on research conducted on young Sikh women in Nottingham during the early 1980s, with a follow up study in the mid 1980s.[1] This period was of significant importance to all Sikhs. It was during this period that events in the Punjab culminated in, Operation Blue Star, the dramatic storming of the Sikhs' Holy Temple in Amritsar in 1984. The subsequent assassination of the then Prime Minister, Mrs Indira Gandhi, and the communal violence that followed focused world attention on the position of Sikhism in India.

During this time, one of the most significant questions for those studying the Sikh Diaspora and indeed for members of this Diaspora themselves, was what were the likely effects of Operation Blue Star on their emergent identities? I was able to compare the multiple identities of young Sikh women before and after the conflict and to examine how and why identities derived largely from religious and socio-cultural criteria may be transformed into ones which are given political meaning in Britain.

By exploring my respondents self-ascribed identities, I wanted to know whether they considered themselves to be Sikh and their reasons for either rejecting or subscribing to such an identity. Furthermore, I was particularly interested in examining their perceptions of difference between themselves (as Sikhs) and Others, specifically looking at the characteristics which they believed distinguished Sikhs from non-Sikhs (white people, Afro-Caribbeans, other Asians - Pakistanis, Gujaratis, Bangladeshis, Hindu Punjabis etc.). I also examined the extent to which their identities were multiple, flexible and situational, in other words, the extent to which being a Sikh was one of several identity options available to these young women. Some of these alternative self-defined identities included being Indian, Asian, English and black British (Drury 1988, 1990, 1991).

Characteristics of Sikh identity

First, it was important to point out that when asked whether they considered themselves to be Sikh, all my respondents replied positively. In exploring why they considered themselves to be Sikhs and the diacritica that they themselves employed to distinguish Sikhs from non-Sikhs, I was able to identify three major criteria: the ancestral, religious and socio-cultural, which were deemed necessary by the vast majority of these young women.

In explaining what distinguished a Sikh from a non-Sikh, the majority of these young women attempted to draw upon the history of Sikhism and its religious beliefs and prescriptions. They were able to refer to its founder, Guru Nanak and to some of the events in the lives of other Gurus, especially Guru Gobind Singh. For instance, the majority referred to the Sikhs' long and bloody struggle (from 16th to 18th centuries) against Mughal hegemony. The most common example given was that of Guru Gobind Singh whose leadership in the war against Mughal oppression led to greater cohesion amongst the Sikhs but at enormous personal sacrifice (he and his sons lost their lives). This historical feature of Sikhism was considered to be one of the factors which helped to distinguish Sikhs from Others, especially, Muslims.

Guru Gobind Singh was also known for his success in infusing cohesion and ensuring a distinct identity among his followers by establishing the Sikh Code of Conduct. For those who underwent the initiation ceremony (Khande-di-pahul) at which Amrit (nectar) was given to signify membership of the Sikh brotherhood (Khalsa).Today, as in Guru Gobind Singh's time, the Code of Conduct was only obligatory for those who have chosen to be officially initiated. Sahj-dharis (those Sikhs who have not been initiated) may adhere to the Code, if they so wish, but are not obliged to do so.[2] Only a very small minority of my respondents had taken Amrit and were therefore expected to keep the rules set down by Guru Gobind Singh. Although the vast majority were not formally initiated, however, there were specific sections of the Code that were considered by these young Sikhs to be salient characteristics, which distinguished Sikhs from Others.

For instance, the five Ks especially Kesh (hair) and Kara (bangle) were named by the vast majority (ninety-seven per cent) as a specific religious requirements for all Sikhs. When applied to themselves, seventy-five per cent observed Kesh and seventy-three per cent wore the Kara. The majority of these young women expressed positive attitudes towards maintaining these traditions.

Some young woman, however, wished to be more like the twenty-five per cent of respondents who did not have long hair (kesh) and the twenty-seven per cent who did not wear the Kara. Only a minority of these respondents had overtly challenged parental expectations, whilst the vast majority said that their parents had not expected them to keep these religious requirements, especially since they had not taken Amrit. Although these young women did not observe Kesh and Kara, it was evident that the majority, nevertheless, believed that such traits distinguished Sikhs and thus themselves from non-Sikhs.

With regard to the question of covering one's head, ninety per cent of all respondents thought that men, should, if possible wear the turban especially in the gurdwara. And ninety-two per cent believed that women were obliged to cover their heads with a *chuni* when in the presence of the Holy Book and often when in the company of older relatives. Indeed the vast majority followed this custom whenever they went to functions at the gurdwara.

The Sikh temples provided these young females with yet another criterion with which to enhance their identities as Sikhs. Forty-eight per cent went to the gurdwaras regularly (at least once a week) to participate in the services and other ceremonies, and to meet their friends. Forty-four per cent attended less frequently, predominantly at weddings and festivals and the remaining minority of eight per cent did not go to the gurdwaras at all. Despite these variations the vast majority referred to them as our temples. No matter how often they went to the Sikh temples they were all critical of inadequate resources (including religious education) for young people. Most believed that the gurdwaras provided an important cultural and social space for Sikhs in general, and for women in particular.

In addition to the gurdwaras, the existence of the Guru Granth Sahib (the Holy Book) helped to reinforce a distinct identity amongst these young Sikhs. Although the majority admitted that their knowledge and understanding of the Granth Sahib was somewhat deficient, they nevertheless referred to it as our Bible and tried to compare and contrast it with the teachings of Christianity.

Other Sikh characteristics that were considered important were related to smoking and drinking alcohol. When asked whether Sikhs were permitted to smoke, all 102 respondents replied that the Sikh religion did not allow smoking but the majority thought that whilst the vast majority of women adhered to this requirement, most men disregarded it. None of the girls smoked and indeed their views on this matter revealed that they disapproved of smoking not just for reasons of good health but also because they were not in favour of Sikh women smoking.

Similarly, a strong majority (eighty-one per cent) of the young women thought that Sikhs in general were not allowed to drink alcohol but that this rule was mainly observed by women rather than by men. Sixty per cent said that they did not drink alcohol at all. Forty per cent said that they did so but the majority of these said that they drank moderately and mainly at home within the family for special occasions. Sikh norms relating to alcohol were contrasted with those in the wider society, thus once more, a feature of Sikhism was highlighted to enhance a sense of being Sikh and therefore of being somewhat different.

In explaining why Sikhs in general and they in particular were distinct in some ways to Others, the vast majority of the girls in my study also employed cultural markers which were not religious *per se*. For instance, the arranged marriage was cited as a major distinguishing feature, especially *vis-a-vis* white people (to whom the majority referred as the English) and Afro-Caribbeans. Ninety-two per cent expected to have an arranged and only eight per cent thought that they would have a love marriage. The majority (sixty-six per cent) contrasted themselves unfavourably with their white and West Indian peers who were perceived to enjoy greater choice and face fewer constraints in the marriage stakes. The remaining thirty-four per cent also drew distinctions between themselves and their white and West Indian peers, but, they pointed to the advantages of having a traditional marriage as opposed to the disadvantages of love marriages in the wider society. Here, perceived differences acted to enhance a positive Sikh identity.

The vast majority of my respondents did recognise that the arranged marriage is a common feature amongst Asians in general. However, they also demonstrated an awareness of the requirements of endogamy, that was, ninety-eight per cent stated that Sikhs are expected to marry within the group and that this applied even with regard to love marriages.

When they were asked whether they themselves would be prepared to marry other Asians (Hindus and Muslims) and Afro-Caribbeans and white people, eighty per cent declared that they would only consider marrying a Sikh husband. Within the context of marriage, differences of culture, religion and race were employed in defining and maintaining clearly marked boundaries between Sikhs and non-Sikhs. Whilst recognising that they shared some cultural traditions with non-Sikh Asians, the majority thought that religious differences were important enough to decline the possibility of marriage with a Hindu or Muslim. Pakistanis, in particular, were singled out as members of an out group who were highly unsuitable as prospective marriage partners due religious and historical factors. Punjabi Muslims were seen to be historically antagonistic towards Sikhs and their religion and references were often made to Sikh struggles during Mughal times and to communal violence during the partition of India.

In discussing their views on intermarriage between Sikhs and white people and West Indians, eighty per cent of my respondents referred to cultural differences and to racial criteria when justifying why they themselves would not be willing to make such a marriage. Additionally, they emphasised the importance to them of internal constraints (mainly in the form of gossip, family ostracism and loss of community support) and of the existence of external constraints. The latter referred mainly to the possibility that an Indian who marries a white spouse may be rejected by the latter's family due to racial discrimination and prejudice.

In contrast to the above, a minority of twenty per cent said that they would be willing to marry a non-Sikh if given the opportunity. Most, however, also thought that it was unlikely to happen and the majority demonstrated an awareness of the obstacles and possible pitfalls of mixed marriages. Primary concerns were over family and community reaction. Thus, the views of the majority of eighty per cent as well as those of the minority of twenty per cent of all respondents, indicated that the boundaries between us and them were clearly marked with regard to marriage and that this was an area in which a Sikh identity was paramount.

The Punjabi language was another feature which according to these young Sikhs, distinguished them from Others. Although seventy-nine per cent stated that they were not very proficient in it, as they had not learned to read and write it and were often obliged to use English words when conversing in Punjabi due to lack of vocabulary, it was evident that having an additional language to English was seen to be of positive value. Forty-five per cent spoke mainly Punjabi with both parents; thirty per cent spoke Punjabi with their mothers and Punjabi and English with their fathers; twenty per cent spoke both languages with both parents and only three per cent spoke only English.

The majority (seventy-two per cent) would have liked to have studied Punjabi at school and ninety-six per cent intended to pass it on to their children. Forty-four per cent thought that mother tongue classes at school would improve intergenerational communication and help maintain Sikh traditions. A further forty-eight per cent also gave these reasons but, in addition, believed that formal lessons in Punjabi would not only improve the self-image of Sikh children but also strengthen the relationship between Sikhs and white people by providing them with a multicultural education.

Other criteria by which they distinguished themselves from the Other were predominantly gender specific. One such dimension relates to their social lives, particularly with regard to going out with boyfriends. There was a general consensus that when it came to having boyfriends, Sikh girls, in common with other Asian girls were severely disadvantaged when compared with white and West Indian girls. The vast majority also thought that Sikh males in general were far less restricted than their sisters. Thirty-seven per cent said that they would like to go out with boys but that they were restricted by their families. In contrast, twenty-six per cent risked having disputes with their parents by going out with boyfriends covertly and only three per cent said that their parents allowed them to have boyfriends. These respondents who were not permitted by their parents to go out with boys complained bitterly about the differences between themselves - as Sikh girls - and white and Afro-Caribbean females as well as about the differential treatment they received *vis-a-vis* their brothers and male cousins. Not all respondents, however, wished to emulate their white peers. Thirty-four per cent drew comparisons that emphasised the advantages of being a Sikh girl *vis-a-vis* unstable marital and sexual relationships in the wider society.

In examining other aspects of leisure time activities, it was evident that these young Sikh females drew clear distinctions between themselves and their white and West Indian peers as well as with male Sikhs. A majority (seventy per cent) spent most of their spare time at home: watching television and videos, listening to music, doing their homework (if they were still studying), helping to entertain family friends, looking after younger siblings and generally helping their mothers. Their social lives tended to be lived within the community and they were not permitted to go out in the evenings with their friends. However, most of them were sometimes allowed to go out in the daytime - shopping - with their friends, going to McDonalds, meeting friends in town and some played sport including badminton, tennis, netball and ice skating. In contrast to these girls, thirty per cent of my respondents faced far fewer restrictions, in so far as they went out in the evenings with their friends and were, in general, not restricted to social activities within the community. For instance, they went to discos, parties and pubs. Most of those who went to discos and parties did so with parental knowledge whilst going to pubs was far more problematic, since the majority of those who went there did so either covertly or in open defiance of parental wishes. These young women believed that pubs were no go areas for them because, in general, Sikh parents saw them as places where alcohol was consumed, whereas discos and private parties were seen to be less threatening to their morals as people go there to dance and socialise rather than just drink alcohol!

All respondents, even those who enjoyed relatively more freedom, made comparisons between their own recreational lives (as Sikh girls) and those of

Others. Perceived differences were therefore accorded ethnic significance i.e. 'because we are Sikhs'. Forty-two per cent believed that English and West Indian girls were extremely fortunate in being allowed out unconditionally and they wished to emulate them fully in this respect. A further thirteen per cent also wished to enjoy these freedoms but they also pointed to some of the disadvantages faced by English and West Indian girls whose parents allowed them 'too much freedom'. Here, ambivalent attitudes were expressed, since on the one hand they wished to become more like the Other but at the same time, they believed that Sikh parental discipline was of a superior kind. Only a tiny minority did not wish to emulate the Other at all and, instead, drew sharp distinctions which served to enhance the advantages of being a Sikh female.

The remaining twenty-five per cent of all respondents thought that they were similar and different to their white and West Indian peers. They were similar because they too went out in the evenings to discos, parties and pubs and they too had boyfriends. The main differences were seen to involve being allowed out less frequently and having to return home earlier than English and West Indian girls. Another difference related to their social lives within the Sikh community.

To summarise, the Sikh females in my study continually compared and contrasted their lives with those of the Other, especially white people and Afro-Caribbeans. The differences, as they saw them, were explained largely in terms of religion and socio-culture and were therefore reduced to their ethnicity. Comparisons with other Asians were also made, but the similarities tended to outweigh the differences in the topics under discussion. The vast majority believed that women of Asian origin (Punjabi Muslims, Pakistanis, Bangladeshis, Gujaratis, other Indians etc.) fared much the same as themselves when it came to marriage, boyfriends and leisure time activities. Such commonalties, especially with other Indians brings us to the question of whether my respondents considered Sikhs in general and themselves in particular to be Indian or of Indian origin.

Before Operation Blue Star the politics of Khalistan had not yet entered the world of my respondents. Only a very small minority displayed any knowledge of the meaning of the term. Moreover, when asked, the vast majority (ninety-eight per cent) said that they did consider themselves to be Indian. Indeed, it was noticeable that they often used the terms Sikh and Indian interchangeably. There was hardly any evidence to suggest that they believed in an independent Sikh state, outside India's borders. In exploring their reasons for considering themselves to be Indian, I found that their feelings of being Indian were largely related to parental and ancestral origins, to a socio-cultural heritage, which can be traced to the subcontinent and to an experience of being rejected as English by the white majority.

> Yes, I am Indian and I'm Sikh. I'm not really English, even though I was born here and I do behave like an English girl sometimes. But I'm Indian, cause by mum and dad are Indian, my grandparents are from the Punjab in India. We have relatives who visit us and my dad goes to India. We go to Sikh functions, we speak Indian languages, we eat Indian food. We are different from the English, our culture is different, it's from India. We have the arranged marriage. Gujaratis are like us in some ways, like they

have the arranged marriage. If you speak to other Indian boys and girls and if you say you are English, they will argue it out with you - they say we are Indian originally. We can't change our blood, our colour. But, you know, even if we accepted ourselves as English, I don't think that the English will accept us, as English. Some white people call us horrible names and a few are really nasty. Indians don't call their people horrible names. I think that even though we are born here and we live in England, we don't see it as our real home - India is our real home.

The last sentence in the quote (India is our real home) is especially important with regard to the politicisation of a Sikh identity, particularly in relation to the politics of separation. Statements such as this before the events in Amritsar were very common and displayed a certain sense of loyalty to and identification with the motherland; India. Throughout my study at this time, I was unable to detect any indication that the vast majority of these young Sikh females perceived that Sikhs in India were being victimised or discriminated against by the Indian state. Some references to historical antagonisms between Muslims and Sikhs were made but there was no reference to inter-communal violence between Sikhs and Hindus. A central question which therefore arose was how had the storming of the Golden Temple and subsequent events in India altered these perceptions and loyalties? A short follow-up study was conducted to examine this topic.

The vast majority expressed feelings of shock and hurt as well as deep disillusionment with India, especially with the then Prime Minister, Indira Gandhi. Even those who professed to be 'not very religious' nevertheless believed that a great injustice had been committed against the Sikhs when Indian troops stormed the temple. Whereas before this event, very few were conversant with the idea of an independent state of Khalistan, a majority (seventy-five per cent) now declared that they had 'heard about Khalistan'. Although most of these respondents did not have a sophisticated understanding of the politics of separation and of ethnic nationalism, nevertheless, it was evident that some of the vocabulary of Khalistan - freedom, independence, recognition of Sikhism as an official religion had entered their world.

For instance, when they were asked for their opinions on the causes of the conflict, forty-one per cent blamed the Indian government for discriminating against Sikhs and for invading the temple when Sikhs defended their rights. Twenty per cent thought that the Hindus were jealous of Sikh success, sixteen per cent believed that the Indian authorities did not recognise Sikhism as a separate religion from Hinduism and that the Sikhs wanted to be independent and the remaining twenty-three per cent said that they were rather confused about the conflict. When asked whether they thought some Sikhs were justified in taking up arms in India, thirty-nine per cent said that they were right to do so, in order to be 'free' and many drew comparisons with Sikh struggles during Mughal times; forty-four per cent, however, whilst supporting justice for Sikhs, in principle, did not support violence of any kind and the remaining eleven per cent did not know how to answer this question.

I'm very sad really, because it's like a civil war out there, Indian people fighting with Indian people. I'm not too sure about why this happens. Politics, that's why. I have been reading about it in the papers and some of my relatives have come from India. They say that it's now very bad for Sikhs, they are being killed out there by Hindus. I don't agree with fighting, violence. I think it's better to have peace but they should not hurt Sikh people. I hope things will get better. I don't know anything about independence. I don't really understand it very well.

Events in the Punjab, however, had gone some way in raising the political consciousness of these young Sikhs in the mid 1980s. During this time, there were protests, rallies and demonstrations organised by various Sikh organisations, including youth associations in different cities in Britain. However, the majority of the female respondents were unable to attend such meetings and it could be said that their politicisation had taken place at the attitudinal level and had not yet been translated into action. This reflected gender and generational divisions within the Sikh population in Nottingham. The Gurdwara committees were predominantly male in composition and leadership, as were the youth organisations. Additionally, the majority of these young females were still studying and living with their parents and were therefore not yet independent either economically or domestically.

How had the events in the Punjab effected their identities, particularly their Indianess? When they were asked, firstly, whether they still considered themselves to be Indian and secondly, whether they thought that Sikhs should have their own country - Khalistan. Their replies indicated that there were some distinctive changes. Whereas before Amritsar, ninety-eight per cent had declared that they considered themselves to be Indian, only twenty-five per cent said that India was still their country of origin and they hoped things would improve. Thirty-five per cent said that they no longer inclined to call India home and wished for independence and the remaining forty per cent, however, were rather confused about the situation and preferred to 'wait and see'.

The research on these young Sikh females both before and after the events in India demonstrated that there was a distinctive Sikh identity. In the early 1980s, i.e. before the storming of the Golden Temple, this identity was derived largely from a combination of three dimensions - which I identified as the ancestral, religious and socio-cultural dimensions. After the events in the Punjab, a political dimension was added, in so far as, the majority of these girls, now demonstrated an awareness of Sikh politics in India and a heightened consciousness of being Sikh. However, whilst this distinctive ethnic identity did exist, I do not wish to suggest that it was inflexible and static or that it was the only identity that they exhibited. Indeed, my study also indicated that the vast majority had multiple and situational identities.

British Asian identities

I have already shown how, in specific contexts, for example, with regard to endogamous marriage, the boundaries between Sikhs and non-Sikhs were firmly maintained and that, consequently, in this context, a Sikh identity was paramount. However, in other situations, the boundaries were negotiable and flexible and were widened by these young women to include the Other. For instance, whilst Punjabi Hindus, Gujaratis and Pakistani Muslims were considered as members of the Other with regard to marriage, in other situations, they were considered to be fellow members of a wider group - British Asians or just Asians. One such example involved the friendship patterns of my respondents. A study of peer group relationships and the composition of their best friends, revealed that they were far from encapsulated within the Sikh community. Most had Sikh friends as well as other South Asian friends, white and West Indian friends. However, when it came to their best (girl) friends, nearly half of them said that their best friends tended to be Sikhs and other Asians. In exploring the reasons for this, I found that they identified culturally and socially with other Asians. Such commonalties of culture included features of British Asian youth sub-cultures, such as bangra music and dancing, as well as items of media culture imported from India - especially, films, videos and magazines about their favourite movie stars. Additionally, most felt that they had more in common with other Asian girls than with white and West Indian females due to the social restrictions they faced and certain shared cultural traditions, especially the arranged marriage.

A pan-Asian identity also manifested itself in discussions about racism. When asked whether they believed that Sikhs received more favourable treatment than other Asians (Gujaratis, Pakistanis, Bangladeshis etc.) in Britain, all respondents replied negatively and instead said that Asians in general faced racial prejudice and discrimination. Examples were cited of attacks against individuals from different Asian communities and against Asian owned businesses in Nottingham at that time. The vast majority of these young women also had access to information through community networks and ethnic channels regarding acts of violence against Asian communities in other parts of the country. They were thus, for instance, aware of attacks on Pakistanis in Bolton, on Bangladeshis in Tower Hamlets, on Gujaratis in Leicester and on Sikhs in Southall. In this context, non-Sikh Asians were seen to be 'one of us' - members of a wider group - Asians who were all vulnerable to racial hostility and discrimination. This particular aspect of a pan-Asian identity would seem to be one that was largely reactive, to externally imposed constraints. In this respect, it is not unlike some of the other identities of these Sikh girls, particularly, their black British identities.

Being English or black British

When asked whether they ever thought of themselves as English, seventy-six per cent replied negatively, only twenty per cent said that they sometimes did so and four per cent did not know. The vast majority of those who did not wish to describe themselves as English believed that the colour of their skins made them unacceptable as English to the white majority. In addition, they thought that although they shared certain cultural traits with their white peers which made them different to their own parents, they also had distinctive ethnic traditions which distinguished them from their English peers. Furthermore, they believed that their parental origins considerably weakened any claim to being 'completely English'.

> Even if we wanted to call ourselves English, the white people would not want us to do that. Because we are not the same colour and our parents

are from India. I read a report once which was about an Indian doctor who was born here. He was scrubbing his hands before an operation. One of the white doctors said to him why wash so hard? We know you are Indian . You read things like that and you understand the real world. ... I've got some English culture - like the dress, fashion, the language, pop music, I do go out and I do have English friends. But I don't feel English, I might act English sometimes, but deep inside, I know I'm not English. My culture is different, my colour is different and my way of living is different.

In contrast to the above, twenty per cent of my respondents said that they sometimes 'felt English', especially when they interacted with their white people. In such situations, according to these girls, they spoke English, wore English clothes, ate English food and shared other cultural traits with their English friends. Moreover, most stated that they were opposed to many of their parental traditions and that this made them feel more English than Indian. However, most were also aware of rejection by some white people. For example:

> I am a mixture of both, Sikh and English. I live in England and I have mostly English ideas and attitudes. I feel more English than Indian because my attitudes conflict with the Indian ways, especially marriage, boyfriends, going out. When I am with the English, I feel very English. But then, when I'm at home with the family and Indian friends, I am less English and more Sikh. I can understand the English people better than my parents and aunts from India because I'm part English myself. Like some of my relatives say 'you are not being friendly with English people'! and I reply 'there are some quite nice ones'. My English friends say 'how can you eat that' (Indian food) and I say 'it's nice, why don't you try it?' So, I'm part of both sides ... Do English people accept me as English? Yes, my friends do, but I know that there's a lot of prejudice and that some white people don't want us here.

A black British identity?

The term black appeared to be problematic for Sikhs. When asked whether they considered to be black British, ninety-two per cent replied that they were British but that they did not think of themselves as black. Their rationale was explained largely in terms of cultural and racial differences between themselves and people of Afro-Caribbean or African descent. The following was a typical reply:

> I live here and I have my rights, sort of thing. I have a British passport. But am I black? No, I don't really think so. I'm not white, but I'm not black either. Coloureds are different, I mean, West Indians, Jamaicans, have different cultures from ours. They don't believe in our religion, they don't speak our language, they are a different race from us. We are originally from Asia, they are not. The colour is almost the same, but they do

look different, don't they. Jamaican girls have a lot more freedom than us, they are more like English girls.

Thus, the replies I received to this particularly phrased question in no way suggested that these young Sikhs had constructed a black identity based on a recognition of shared experiences of racial hostility and a common structural position with non-whites in general. However, their answers to other questions regarding their perceptions of racial prejudice and discrimination against Asians and Afro-Caribbeans in Britain, strongly indicated that in certain contexts, they did recognise commonalties with non-whites in general and that although they did not wish to apply a black label to themselves in reply to my question, there were times when they implicitly acknowledged that Asians, Afro-Caribbeans and other non-white people constituted a wider group - a group whose members were actual or potential victims of racism. Thus, this aspect of their identity was a predominantly reactive one and was highly contextual.

I asked my respondents: 'Do you think that Asians have the same chances of getting jobs as white people with the same qualifications? Do you think that West Indians have the same chances as white people with the same qualifications? Do you think that Asians have a better chance of getting jobs than West Indians with the same qualifications'?

In reply to the first two questions, eighty per cent and eighty-one per cent respectively thought that Asians and West Indians did not have an equal chance of getting a job as a white person. In reply to the third question, ninety-three per cent said that they did not think that there was any difference between Asians and West Indians in terms of their employment chances. When asked to expand on these answers, these respondents emphasised their belief that racial discrimination was an obstacle faced by all those who are not white, so that, in this respect, Asians and West Indians were seen to be members of an in-group , who faced considerable hostility from the majority society.

I think that a white person is bound to get the job because they don't think its our country. I mean, if you are not white, like if you are Indian, African, Jamaican, anyone black, will find discrimination.

Racial discrimination - it don't make no difference if you are Indian or coloured, you will find it difficult to get a good job because the English don't want black people to take good jobs from them.

This recognition of commonalties of experience between Asians and other non-white people, was also evident when discussing other forms of exclusion. For example, I asked my respondents 'Do you think that most white people accept you and other Asians who are born here as English and do you think that most white people accept West Indians who are born here as English'? A strong majority (seventy-nine per cent) thought that they were not accepted and only fifteen per cent that most English accepted them. In relation to West Indians, seventy-five per cent believed that they too were not accepted and only twelve per cent thought that they were accepted as English. In elaborating on this sense of common rejection, they clearly used labels black and coloured and, moreover, it was evident that they were not merely using such terms to refer to West Indians, but that they were also, significantly, using them to refer to themselves and other Asians.

> I think that most English people don't think that coloureds should be here, all blacks, including Indians. They don't really make a big difference between Indians and Jamaicans, they look at the colour and they see we are not white. We are different to the English because of our culture. West Indians are more like the English than us, but I don't think that they are accepted completely either, because of the colour. Because white people can't accept black people, all of us.

When their views on racism were examined, it became clear that, blackness for these young Sikh females, was far from being irrelevant to them. Indeed, the vast majority did identify with other non-white people in specific contexts, especially with regard to the effects of exclusion. However, there was very little evidence to suggest that these young Sikhs had become politicised around the notion of blackness. For example, very few held clear views about the possibility and implications of black political solidarity. Moreover, the majority, probably due to their age and gender, said that they did not wish to attend anti-racist demonstrations and rallies organised by multi-racial, multi-ethnic organisations even though they supported the aims of such demonstrations. Thus, in this respect, despite their rejection of the term black when responding to my question, there was an underlying degree of blackness, but one which was contextually specific and politically immature.

Conclusions

In this article, I have demonstrated how young Sikh women in Nottingham managed to construct Sikh and other (multiple) identities up to the mid-1980s. The study indicated that there was a strong and distinctive sense of being Sikh and that the boundaries between us (Sikhs) and them (non-Sikhs) were drawn, for purposes of identification, by reference to ancestral, religious and socio-cultural criteria. In addition to these dimensions of difference, a Sikh identity, especially *vis-a-vis* the white majority, was reinforced by feelings of rejection brought about through experiences of racial prejudice and discrimination.

In the first half of the 1980s, before the storming of the Golden Temple, young Sikhs in my study exhibited feelings of loyalty and belonging to India and there was no conflict between being Sikh and being Indian. After the events in the Punjab, however, their Indian identities were considerably weakened whilst Sikh identities became more pronounced. Only a minority were still willing to describe themselves as Indian in contrast to the majority who either declared pragmatically that they would 'wait and see' or that they wished for an independent Khalistan. It would appear that the politics of Sikhism in the Punjab had begun to exert some influence on their emergent identities and on their views on politics and Sikhism, albeit mainly at the attitudinal level.

Whilst a Sikh identity was indeed very much in evidence, however, it was neither rigid nor was it singular. Indeed, I have shown that young Sikhs had access to situational and multiple identities and that the extent to which such identities became relevant depended on the contexts in which they found themselves and the opportunities and constraints that existed both within the ethnic group and in the wider society.

Finally, the emergence and perhaps development of wider identities encompassing non-Sikhs, especially British Asian and British black identities, are ones which have implications for black politics in Britain. My respondents were young and were still financially and socially dependent on their parents when the main study was conducted. They were not yet politically active but, I think that their constructions of pan-Asian and black British identities, could be interpreted as signs of potential strength for black politics and solidarity. Only a further study on these young Sikhs in the 1990s will reveal whether and in which contexts, they have matured to become politically conscious and active as Sikhs, as black British, as British Asians etc.

Notes

1 The sample consisted of 102, sixteen to twenty year old girls of Sikh origin who were either born in the United Kingdom or had arrived in this country when five years of age or under. A combination of methodologies - interview questionnaires, group discussions and some participant observation was used.

2 Some of the main requirements as set out in the Code of Conduct can be summarised as follows (Cole and Sambhi, 1978):

i) All men are to be called 'Singh' - a lion - and all women 'Kaur' or princess, thus signifying equality between the different castes.

ii) All members of the Khalsa are instructed to observe the Five Ks - Kesh (long, uncut hair); Kara (a steel bangle to be worn on the right wrist); Kangha (a comb); Kirpan (a sword) and Kacha (decent underwear).

iii) Smoking and drinking alcohol are discouraged.

iv) The eating of halal meat is forbidden.

v) Women are instructed not to wear purdah although they are encouraged to cover their heads with a *chuni* (veil/scarf) in the gurdwara and in the presence of the Holy Book.

vi) Initiated men are required to wear turbans.

vii) Sikhs are expected to marry endogamously and to live a married life rather than become ascetics or recluses.

viii) A Sikh should be a monotheist, should meditate on the teachings of the Gurus, study the Holy Book and should not believe in idolatry, magic, omens and sacrifices.

ix) Sikhs should not observe caste distinctions.

10 Street credibility and identity: Some observations on the art of being black

Claire Alexander

I had been in the field less than a month when I was taken on my first expedition with the boys[1] into the West End for their usual Friday night outing. Outside a pub in Covent Garden, I was introduced to two new members of the group, Nathan and Arif: 'This is Claire; she's an anthropologist and she's studying black men. She wants to know why we all hang around on street corners with ghetto blasters, mugging old white women'. Nathan, who is about 6'2", and very fierce looking, fixed me with a steely glare and said, 'We don't all do that you know'. After a dramatic pause, he added, 'Any white woman will do'.

What this episode illustrates, and what became a recurrent theme during my fieldwork, was what might be described as a kind of double consciousness of identity. Amongst my informants, in London, this yielded both a knowledge of the external image of black youth, and of the gap between this image and the individual, which allowed for the manipulation of identity and expectations on a day to day basis. All were acutely aware of the stereotypes and expectations surrounding black youth; all had at some stage been constrained and restricted by these and all had at times used them to their own advantage. A major concern with my informants was that these images should not be regarded as the sole definition of black identity.

It was the articulation of this concern which forms the main aim of my research. It contends that external ascriptions of identity, by both the media and the majority of academic work to date, have created a plethora of stereotypes and images that have attempted to impose definitions of what it is to be black. The reality of such definitions was rooted in a long-standing equation of black identity with race, and a belief in the cultural vacuity of black life which precludes ethnic status and denies identity choice. To be black is therefore portrayed as something inherent and essential rather than a created category with socially ascribed meanings and features. What has been lacking in the portrayal of black youth was a recognition that the categories surrounding any discussion of race, ethnicity black identity and so on, were socially constructed, that they were not fixed in meaning and that they were not inevitably linked to the experience of the individual.

It was, perhaps, closer to the truth to say that black youth experiences external impositions as an objectified reality, which was seen as providing a series of roles and identity choices which they can inhabit or vacate according to the situation. This was not, I would stress, to deny the salience of racism in affecting the life choices and aspirations of black youth: it does, however, endow them with an element of control at the level of lived experience which has been for too long ignored. In short, I would claim that there was no one thing which was being black; it was rather a series of roles and dramatic choices which work within and upon the limits imposed by society.

This paper, then, is divided into two parts: firstly a consideration of the ways in which discourses of race and ethnicity have been conflated to essentialise black cultural expression; and secondly, some of the ways in which these constructions were manipulated - and subverted - in lived experience. Its observations were based on my recent study of a small number of black British young men aged between eighteen and twenty-five years old. It should not, therefore, be taken as a general statement about all black youth, male and female, uniformly experienced and negotiated. Indeed, that would be replacing one definition of being black merely with another.

In, his autobiography, Michael Jackson hits back at media critics. 'They say ... that I want to look more white. More white? What kind of statement is that?' (1988, p. 209). What such statements illustrate was that there was a general and clearly defined notion of what it means to be black. Moreover, it implies that there was a whole range of activities, attitudes - or physical characteristics - which were not black and were, therefore - by definition - white. While it was true that African-Americans, or indeed, black Britons, have long laid claim to a collective identity as a means of political action, I would argue that the content of this identity has been popularly ascribed by external forces and has been linked to notions of race, which precludes processes of change and of choice.

The conflation of black culture and identity with race has retrenched and gained strength with the emergence of so-called *New Racism* (Barker 1981). By focusing on cultural difference as the inevitable consequence of a biologically determined ethnicity, identity has become absolute, dehistoricised and essentialised. As Gilroy has noted, further, the essentialist approach to ethnicity has formed as much a part of anti-racist discourse as that of the New Right. Thus, he writes:

> the commonsense ideology of anti-racism has also drifted towards a belief in the absolute nature of ethnic categories and a strong sense of the insurmountable cultural and experiential divisions within (1992, p. 50).

Such an approach leads inevitably to the marginalisation of social groups in a process of cultural insiderism (ibid., p. 57) and Othering, in which minority cultures were judged in relation to, and placed apart from, the perceived dominant norm. This facilitates the attribution of deviant status and legitimates processes of social control. It has also perpetuated a problem-oriented, conflict-centred approach to black life and experience, in which blacks have been persistently portrayed as either criminals or victims, or, indeed, both - 'noble savage and violent avenger' (Hall, 1992a p. 256), constrained and defined solely by these external issues.

What the insistence on reified racial or ethnic categories ignores was the cultural context within which these definitions and restrictions occur. This includes the cultural context not only of the dominant society which creates labels and folk-devils, but also of the group which was so defined. By regarding phenotype as a sufficient natural basis for social classification, the two viewpoints were conflated - there was no room for interpretation or for difference. Of course, for many, black people in Britain have no cultural context to be aware of, because they have no real culture. Any definition of black identity was assumed to be created from, and controlled by, the dominant power structure. Or, as Rutherford and others have recently argued, 'The Centre invests the Other with its terrors' (1990, p. 11).

The equation of race, ethnicity and identity assumes the inability of the Other to construct its own definitions; to choose its own identity. The assumption of the absolute powerlessness of ethnic minorities denies any possibility of change or of choice. Black people were thus seen as the passive victims of external circumstance.

It has been argued, however, that the dualism's of modernist thought have been uprooted in recent years and dislocated its traditional certainties. Particularly in the sphere of cultural expression, the voices of the margin have decentred the dominant discourses and created a 'third space' (Bhabha 1990), in which both margin and centre were interlocked and transformed. Identity was thus constituted through the interplay of political, social, cultural and historical contingency; what Hall calls 'a matter of "becoming" as well as of "being"' (1990, p. 225). Identity becomes a product of 'the politics of articulation' (Rutherford, 1990, p. 19), which has been described as 'the politics of necessary or essential correspondence of anything with anything' (Hall, cited in Rutherford, ibid.). Identity must then be viewed as relational and interdependent; it achieves significance only through interaction with others. Thus it was a product of 'representation', constantly transforming and translating itself in an ongoing process of imagination and re-creation. Within this struggle for ideological space, culture becomes not a repository of symbols (Barth 1969), but itself symbolic - a product of interaction and the subject of representation.

Rather than interplay at the symbolic boundaries of pre-existing, latent and benign ethnicities, therefore, identity must be viewed as a dynamic and incomplete process, with culture as the main bargaining counter. Central to this 'game of cultural wars of position' (Hall, 1992b, p. 25), was the articulation and contestation of perceived power hierarchies, in which social categories were created, manipulated and negotiated, both contesting and displacing differences of gender, class, sexuality - and ethnicity.

Thus, at the level of representation and in its lived expression, black identity can be drawn from any number of sources and was signalled in a variety of ways. Styles of dress and hair, use of language, styles of music and dance - all were manipulated to create meaning. It may make use of external ascriptions of meaning or, in the style of subcultural discourse, may subvert these and create new meanings; it may draw on notions of history, the cultural resources of parents or of other black groups, either within Britain or as part of a global diaspora (Gilroy 1987). Or, indeed, notions of race and ethnic identity may be replaced by other definitions such as those based on gender or, increasingly, class.

I would argue, therefore, that although at the level of structure, racist attitudes and stereotypes persist in ascribing black identity, at the level of lived experience, these categories were open to manipulation and subversion. I am not merely asserting that black life and culture exists independently of external definition, but that in interaction, these categories themselves provide some of the raw material of black identity, reclaimed and redefined in positive terms. A simple example would be the reclamation of defamatory labels for use internally to the black community. Amongst my informants, a favourite term of both abuse and affection was nigger. This encapsulated at once both the negative stereotypes of white society and a positive redefinition by its black users. A nigger was someone who behaved in a stereotypically black way - aggressive, loud, disruptive, ignorant. It was also someone who within a particular situation was seen as very much in control; an assertion of individual and group strength, deriving from the same qualities. The term was used by the boys with both purposes in mind. It was, however, a term they would only use publicly in reference to themselves, though they did use it privately to refer to other groups. Use of the term was, moreover, granted very limited bounds of acceptability - it could only be used by blacks. As one of them told me, 'It's alright black guys going around calling each other nigger, but if a white guy calls you nigger - dead mother fucker'! (Interview 12 December 1990).

The creation of black identity becomes, therefore, the enactment of individual choice from amongst a range of cultural options and attitudes that were inhabited or vacated according to the context. This choice was posited on the individual's assessment of the situation - however competent or incompetent - and the aim he or she desires to achieve. It was an essentially dramatic gesture, formed and lived out in interaction.

It would, of course, be both naive and misleading to claim for black youth a complete freedom of creative expression. Rather than endlessly sliding signifiers, black identity was bound irrevocably with historical, economic and political circumstance. Indeed, it can be seen that the constraints of power and the overdetermination of external stereotyping were a formative impulse behind this struggle. It was necessary, however, to move away from simplistic dualistic notions concerning power, hegemony and homogeneity - that we have power and they don't - to see the ways in which these notions were continually contested and redefined. At a level lower than that of social structure, then, the articulation of power becomes increasingly dispersed and spheres of interaction become more complex and more fluid. Individual black youths can thus move between different spheres, negotiating the constraints and demands of each as part of an ongoing search for control. This was particularly common in situations with other black people, where the individual wishes to define her/himself as part of an imagined community. One example would be the use of black London English amongst a peer group, another would be a knowledge of specific music or dance forms. It can also be useful in dealing with wider white society: the favourite and most utilised black stereotype amongst the boys was the myth of black male sexuality - or as one called it 'the legend of black male sexuality'. The limitations, if not the contradictions of such an approach were obvious. Despite the inherent ambiguities of these constructions, however, such encounters allow for a degree of negotiation in interaction - they create space. Space may be either won or lost, but as Hall writes:

> it is never a zero-sum cultural game; it is always about shifting the balance of power in the relations of culture; it is always about changing the dispositions and the configurations of cultural power, not getting out of it (1992b, p. 24).

To illustrate these points, I would like to conclude with two examples from my own fieldwork. The aim here was not to provide a detailed analysis, but merely to explore the complexity of the lived attitudes and standpoints within apparently simple situations. For the purposes of illustration, I have deliberately chosen two incidents which were concerned with constructions internal to the black community; it was hoped that these will serve to challenge notions of a homogeneous and essentialised ethnic or racial group, and demonstrate the wars of position being waged within these encounters.

I

Just before completing my fieldwork in London I decided, as a farewell gesture, to hold a good-bye party for those people I had been living and working with for the past months. The plan was to bring all my main informants together to thank them and wish them well before I disappeared back into the country to write up my research. I consulted with Ricky, my flatmate, about the food and the music, and duly invited all the boys, together with Angelina, her brothers and some of their friends.

Although this was the first time the two groups had been brought together, individuals from each had met previously, so there was ostensibly little reason to expect anything other than a fairly relaxed and enjoyable evening. Instead, after initial acknowledgements, the party divided, with Angelina, her brothers and their friends in the kitchen, and the boys occupying the living area. Protagonists of both groups glared suspiciously at each other, each trying to situate the Other and measure the degree of threat posed to their own position and sense of control. After an hour or so, Shane ventured into the kitchen, and approached Darnell, 'So, where are you chaps from then?' Darnell glared at Shane disdainfully, sucked his teeth and turned away. He later said to me with some degree of scorn, 'Where did you find these guys, then? Nobody says "chaps". He ain't no black man'.

When Angelina informed Shane that they lived in Harlesden, Shane started to look extremely nervous and retreated into the living room. The boys self-image was more than a little shaken by the presence of a group from Harlesden - an area with a large black population and something of a reputation. Feeling unable to compete as typically black in the way they felt was expected, they turned the music from ragga to American club mixes, closed ranks and started busting splits. Talking loudly about jobs and cars, and posing as upwardly mobile young and sophisticated city blacks, they sought to regain control of the situation, while Darnell, Rommell and their friends talked as loudly about blues parties and sound systems, perpetuating their image as ragamuffins, as real blacks, and finally disappeared into my bedroom to build spliffs and listen to their own ragga tapes.

This episode centred around two distinct, and in some ways opposed, images of being black, which were related not to external definitions, but to stances within and in relation to the black community. Both groups were concerned to position themselves in relation to the other black group, in such a way as to maintain control of their position. This was defined entirely in terms of internally contested images of what the black community represented and their position in relation to it. Community was thus constructed as at once a source of unity and strength, and a locus of weakness and differentiation.

Thus, because the boys felt excluded from the community image occupied by Angelina and her brothers, and unable to fulfil its incumbent expectations, the response was to negate this image by bringing in a class element. This attempted to define their position against the more negative elements associated with community images and replace them with an image of wealth and sophistication aimed at undermining the other group. This in turn forced the others into the role of typical blacks, which they upheld by casting the boys as sell-outs, as somehow not really black. Each group then wielded the appropriate cultural markers of this identity in opposition to the other group. It was significant that this division made use of external social images of what race represented; in a negative way by the boys, and through positive redefinition by Darnell and the others. The distinctions were primarily perceived in territorial terms, to which other images were then attached and which served to polarise two groups otherwise largely undifferentiated in terms of background, origin and occupation. These oppositions were perpetuated even after the party with Angelina and her brothers leaving for a house party in Harlesden and the boys heading for a club in the West End.

II

For several months, one of the boys, Frank, was employed at a clothes shop in East Ham. It was common knowledge that the area was worked by a number of black youths, who entered shops and took what they liked, unhindered by the shop assistants who - rightly or wrongly - feared for their lives. However, when they raided Frank's shop during his lunch hour, Frank felt it was incumbent on him to defend his territory. He therefore rushed out, found one of the thieves and warned him - with a baseball bat - to keep out of his way. The boy, hardly surprisingly, returned the threat. Frank, for the next few days, armed himself with a kitchen knife, ready for the attack, which never happened.

At its most abstract and simplistic, this incident can be seen to reflect the often documented proclivity of black youths towards violence and criminality. Muggers, drug dealers, rioters - the black raider was just one more example of black deviance. What was of significance here, however, was not external perceptions, but the way that these stereotypes were brought into play within this event by its protagonists. These provided those involved with a range of beliefs and expectations which were constantly shifting and transforming attitudes and alliances.

The attitude of the raiders themselves was unknown, although they were clearly trading upon one of the most developed stereotypes of black youth as armed and dangerous. The attitude of the boys was, however, complex, and raised a number of questions concerning what being black actually meant within this context. As black youth themselves, they felt that the incident transgressed unspoken rules of conduct internal to the black community. Firstly, all the boys felt that the raiders should not have entered the shop because it disrespected Frank, who was also black. Secondly, and conversely, it was generally agreed that Frank should not have taken the side of the shop, which was not a black establishment, against the black raiders.

At one level, then, the boys clearly identified closely enough with the raiders as black youth, to assume the existence of shared values and norms - of a community. This identification was, however, subverted by a distinction based upon a different articulation of blackness, which was appropriated both as a self-image and as an attribute of the other as occasion demanded. This drew on a negative image of community constructed through deviance, which fragmented any unified definition and allowed for both processes of individual identification and distinction.

For Frank and the rest of the boys, then, the raiders represented an image of the typical - or stereotypical - black youth. Frank's confrontation with the raiders can be seen as an attempt to distance himself from this image. For the others, however, Frank's action was seen to be merely stupid. The raiders were, after all, violent individuals who in their role as typical blacks were - by definition - better equipped to handle themselves in any confrontation. It was significant that, in choosing to confront the raiders, Frank appropriated for himself the same images: in the days that followed, he constantly asserted to us that he, as a black man, could handle any attack, and as a symbol of this - as if to complete the image - he started carrying the knife; something he never normally did. The reality behind the image was somewhat anticlimactic, but revealing. Frank, who obviously knew nothing about weapons, put the unsheathed kitchen knife down his sock, cut his leg open running for a bus and had to have nine stitches in his calf.

Conclusion

This paper does not pretend to offer a definition or redefinition of black British youth identity. What it hopes to show is that black identity cannot be encapsulated and circumscribed by external definitions propped up by theories of natural racial or cultural characteristics. For too long, the black communities of Britain have been regarded as the passive recipients of external constraints, or the desperate searchers after an identity based on myth and illusion. For blacks, as for whites, culture and identity is continually created and recreated; it alters over time and according to different circumstances. Put simply, there is no one thing which is being black; it is rather an imagined and dramatic creation of the individual using a range of cultural, historical and social artefacts. I am not saying that as a category black becomes meaningless - especially for those it designates. What I am saying is that a more dynamic approach needs to be employed and that this requires us to reinstate the role of the individual as an active and creative part of his or her environment. This study aims to explore some of the ways in which new identities, new ethnicities are being imagined and enacted on the street.

Notes

1 Boys was a term used by the group of young men to describe themselves.

11 Back in the pavillion: Cricket and the image of African Caribbeans in Oxford[1]

Ossie Stuart

Introduction

The Caribbean male has been given an enduring image in British popular culture by the game of cricket. In stark contrast to the Rasta, the Yardie or the illegal immigrant this male image was one of superiority; on the sports field at least. The aggressive, almost animal like, fast bowler and the sophisticated and cultured batsman were each manifestations of an image of natural talent fostered by what was thought to be the ideal Caribbean environment.

Unlike the game anywhere else in both the Old or New Commonwealth, the game of cricket in the Caribbean was denied any significant social meaning. Rather than difference, in class or age for example, the homogeneity of Caribbean cricket was always emphasised. With regard to social class, the playing of cricket was a key, the badge of social status and importance throughout the rest of the cricketing world. In the Caribbean it was hardly considered relevant. It was assumed that in order to reach the top as a West Indian cricketer all that was required was the natural talent, a deep love of the game and the childhood enthusiasm to play the game in ones bare feet using local materials, preferably a roughly hewn bat and a coconut!

Of course, this image fails to capture either the reality of the game in the Caribbean or the region in which it was played. The single unified team which represents the Caribbean at all international test matches was called the West Indies. Yet the apparent unity this name implies hardly exists immediately beyond the cricket boundary. The Caribbean was not a single entity, just a geographical phenomenon. Apart from this game and one or two convenient trading agreements between nations, a unified West Indies does not exist. Furthermore, the West Indies team only represents the English speaking Caribbean, not countries of the Caribbean as a whole. Absent from the West Indies team were players from the Spanish, French and Dutch speaking Caribbean.

It was also important to remember that cricket was no longer the natural game of the Caribbean male of today (if it ever was). All the major cricket playing Caribbean nations have seen a sharp decline in the game's popularity.

So much so, it's now questionable if the game of cricket is still the most popular game in the Caribbean. This was one consequence of the tremendous economic and social change that has taken place in this region during the past thirty years.

The economic, social and cultural dominance of the United States of America in the Caribbean has grown considerably since the end of colonialism. The influence of former colonial powers has declined accordingly. In the case of the English speaking Caribbean, no longer does any of them look to their former colonial masters for economic, social and cultural leadership. Instead, the United States has usurped this role.

The influence of the United States has not left sport in the Caribbean untouched. Today a young schoolboy's dream to play cricket for their nation comes only second or third to other, more recent, sporting ambitions. The place of cricket has been taken over by American imports such as basketball, American Football and baseball. Satellite television and the success of West Indians recruited by the big American teams has ensured that these sports have become the most popular across the Caribbean. Even the minor league American clubs in New York, Seattle or Washington D.C. can offer Caribbean young men wages that the biggest cricket clubs in Georgetown, Kingston, Bridgetown or Port-of-Spain simply cannot match.

Despite this reality the image of Caribbean cricket endures in Britain. Local Caribbean cricket clubs in Britain both benefit and suffer from this image. These clubs have been shaped and influenced by the same assumptions behind the construction of the image of Caribbean cricket. In Britain these clubs have relied upon the personification of the black male as having an undifferentiated Caribbean descent. As an African Caribbean, it was easy to ascribe every black British a Jamaican identity. In cricket the national differences between Barbadians, Trinidadians and Antiguans, significant as they are, are glossed over. The British African Caribbean clubs also conspire in the creation of this image. They need it to persuade a diminishing number of young British school boys of African Caribbean descent to identify with Caribbean cricket. By doing so, these British youths will ensure the continuing survival of these clubs.

The African Caribbean Cricket Club in Oxford was no different from any other of its kind in Britain. It both labours under and mobilises the identity ascribed to it. However, the reality of this cricket club was also far from the identity ascribed to it. Its survival has depended on its ability to mobilise its ascribed identity. This has made it easier to attract local funding. Evoking a Caribbean identity was used to encourage young British born men brought up on the exploits of recent West Indian cricket stars such as Viv Richards, Curtly Ambrose and Richie Richardson to play cricket.

However, the reality was that these clubs were not Caribbean at all. Though they chose to mobilise aspects of Caribbean identity, this has only form and meaning, in the British context. As an example, it was not possible to talk of a unified Caribbean identity in the Caribbean itself. This identity can only be constructed without, in the United Kingdom. Even this unified African Caribbean identity only operates on a particular level. The clubs themselves do not conform to this image. The majority of them in Britain were begun in the nineteen sixties by former migrants from specific Caribbean countries, who still dominate these clubs. As opposed to the unified one, other identities were mobilised in different arenas to bolster the power of rival groups within these clubs.

The consequence was that these clubs were a microcosm of the contradictory identities which confront all Caribbean organisations in Britain. This chapter is a small insight into how the historic identities ascribed to the Oxford Caribbean and Casuals Cricket Club have been mobilised and re-invented and new ones constructed as it dealt with change throughout its thirty year history.

Britain and Caribbean cricket

There were a number of Caribbean organisations in Oxford. The Afro-Caribbean Association (ACA) was possibly the major vehicle of local African-Caribbean political activism today. Affiliated to it were the majority of the City's black Churches, the Roots Black Youth Club, the Caribbean Sunrise Club and, since 5 May 1992, the Oxford Caribbean and Casuals Cricket Club. The ACA was the body through which the Council relates to the Caribbean population. It was this body which qualifies for the general funds available to the African-Caribbean section of Oxfordshire's ethnic minorities. Also, co-ordinated through this body were the many other schemes for which local funding has been earmarked.

Two recent examples were the funds received from the Oxfordshire Health Authority for a project aimed at reducing the incidence of stroke and high blood pressure in the local African-Caribbean elderly population. Also a Council grant was given as the ratepayer's contribution towards the cost of the projected Afro-Caribbean Centre, responsibility of which has been given to the ACA. The remainder of the money was due to come from a Trust Fund, for which the ACA was primarily responsible for.

This, and other similar, organisations in Oxford have come to rely upon the same ideology which underpins the image of Oxford's African-Caribbean Cricket Club I have just described. Namely, the common sense ideology which has drifted towards a belief in the absolute nature of ethnic categories and a strong sense of insurmountable cultural and experiential divisions: divisions which were assumed to be the main features of ethnic difference (Barker 1981).

The authority with which to speak on behalf of the majority of people of African-Caribbean origin who live in Oxford was derived from the assumption that ethnic categories in Britain were fixed and absolute. The irony was that this unites such organisations with New Right racist ideology. Race, in this discourse, was exclusively perceived as culture and identity rather than skin colour or biology. Black and people of South Asian descent in Britain were deemed to have fundamentally different cultures to white people. Furthermore, these cultural differences were fixed, unchanging and unmediated by time.

Absent from this ideology was the idea that race needs to be viewed much more continentally, as a precarious discursive construction (Gilroy 1987). Or to put it in, perhaps, a better way, rather than thinking of identity as an already accomplished fact, instead identity should be understood as a production which was never complete, always in process, and always constituted within, not outside, representation (Hall 1991).

This singular insight by many people of African-Caribbean descent confronted with all the ambiguities of living as a citizen in Britain. As will be demonstrated by the Oxford Cricket team, a substantial well of imagination has been required to create identities appropriate to the varied and interesting experience of being a black citizen in Britain over the last forty years. Or as Hall would say: 'being placed by the European presence and the attempt to place it by those of African-Caribbean descent'.

This paper is a criticism of the assumptions behind many of the anti-racist and equal opportunity strategies adopted in Oxford. Such strategies have also relied upon the assumed existence of natural and permanent cultural identities. It was not acknowledged that such identities were arbitrary and contingent on context and history. No allowance was given for the fact that they were always shifting and changing, never fixed - always becoming.

Though an African-Caribbean Cricket Club has existed in Oxford for more than thirty years, its role, its very existence has shifted and changed as the local context and history has done. Of its permanence, the words of one of my informants were most appropriate,

> We do not exist yet, we are kept alive by the memories and stories of our players. We have some senior players who are sixty years old, they are important because they will show the younger kids what it means to play for the Oxford Caribbeans.

One trap I am closer to falling into with those whom I criticise, was the ideological platform which makes African-Caribbeans visible in only two roles; either as the victims or the problem. The centrality of racism in Oxford was one of the main reasons for the existence of the Oxford Caribbean Cricket Club. Oxford was, and still was, a racially divided city when the first migrants began to arrive in the mid to late 1950s.

It was in this environment that the club was created. The very act of positioning and re-positioning in Oxford and within local Caribbean culture has ensured the Club's survival. These players, through the Club, have situated themselves and continue to re-situate themselves against European identities, other black people, other teams and other Caribbean identities.

Oxford and black people

Oxford does not have the problems that confront inner city areas of Britain such as Handsworth, Brixton and St Pauls, Bristol. Yet like these places a discourse of race has been a significant influence upon the lives of the migrants who settled there in the late 1950s. As I will describe below, race also continues to impact upon the lives of their British-born offspring. Oxford's population was 109,000 in 1991, of that ten per cent were of New Commonwealth origin. Out of this figure four per cent were of Caribbean descent. Oxford's economy at the time of mass migration in the 1950s was made up of the retail trade, transport, the Car Factory and the University.

Migrants were encouraged to come to Oxford from, in the main, Barbados and Jamaica. They found racial barriers in housing, employment and later, education. Migrants were barred from state subsidised housing due to the residency qualification and were exposed to extortionate Rackman-style rents. The majority had to put up with overcrowded and rotten poor quality housing. The lucky few who could afford purchasing a house were prevented from living where they chose through a conspiracy between estate agents and those white people who wished to sell.

The barriers to equal employment were similarly controlled. Men, mainly from Barbados, were able to find work on the buses - indeed that was why they were brought to Oxford in the first place. Likewise, women, mainly from Jamaica, were brought to the city to work in the health service as nurses, auxiliaries and cleaners. However there was a colour bar in the employment market. Both the unions and employers at the car factory conspired to prevent migrants from joining the factory work force which was the best paid in the city. The retail trade operated an informal colour bar and the City Council did not encourage black people among its personnel.

Though things did begin to change towards the end of the 1960s - widespread discrimination and an informal colour bar persists in many parts of Oxford's economy to this day. The main forms of employment today are the Universities, printing and publishing, the Car Factory, electrical engineering, the health service and the local Council. Only the last two provide job opportunities for Oxford's local African Caribbean population.

The blatant racial discrimination in housing and employment during those earlier years was discrimination based upon the colour of a person's skin. Today this form of crude measure has been replaced by a new form of discrimination. This was an emphasis on difference through cultural identity rather than skin colour.

The poor performance of African Caribbean children in Oxford's schools has resulted in an industry to support these victims. Redress and support through Section 11 tutors or specially funded multi-cultural support institutions were the preferred remedy rather than eradicating poor teaching practices. In a racialised education system, teachers were no longer allies, they were, instead, perceived as adversaries.

Even issues of local concern to sections of the ethnic minority population have become racialised, as a result, isolated. The City Council regularly hive off such matters into special committees, or refer them to individual community experts who advise the all white Council body. Finally, a single Sunday programme meets BBC local radio's obligation to the ethnic minority populations. Independent Commercial Radio has yet to notice that there was a sophisticated black population in Oxford!

Finally, as traditional employers of black workers decline, such as the Rover Car Factory, the building trade, they are not being replaced by new employment opportunities. Youth unemployment looks set to remain higher than average among young African Caribbean males in Oxford, especially.

Oxford Caribbean cricket

This study was gender specific. I am looking at men of African Caribbean descent playing cricket. However, this was a study of how one cultural symbol - cricket - was mobilised as part of the construction of an African-Caribbean identity in an urban British town. There were other symbols which play a similar role in the making urban ethnic identity, some of which either involve or were mobilised by women. This study was, therefore, a metaphor for construction of urban identity in Oxford. The absence of the female image was in no way a suggestion that they play no part in this process.

From the pages *Beyond the Boundary* (James 1963) comes the clear message that cricket empowered the poorest and most disadvantaged in Caribbean society, those of African descent. Ironically, just like soccer in Africa during the first five decades of this century, cricket coincided with, and expressed, the dramatic changes that were taking place right across the Caribbean. The movement of former African slaves into the cities coincided with their importance to the local economies and to the political world as the plebiscite was opened up. The role of players of African descent in the stunning victories in the 1930s and 1950s against the then colonial master, England, served to underwrite this sense of new confidence. At a time when the glorious exploits of Weeks, Warrel, Walcott, Ramadin and Valantine were on the lips of every West Indian, every young boy played street cricket and dreamed of emulating their heroes.

For men, cricket represented social status, social mobility, it meant modernisation and it meant male West Indian success. Though our image of Caribbean cricket was the unified West Indies team. This was not a Caribbean reality. Ironically, at a time when the glorious exploits of Weeks, Warrel, Walcott, Ramadin and Valantine were on the lips of every West Indian, the attempt to create a region as one political and economic unit was crumbling on the vast political and economic differences between the island nations which make up geographicaly the Caribbean.

This image has merely been reinforced when we come to the United Kingdom As with local African-Caribbean cricket, the image of a unified and homogeneous African-Caribbean community was but an illusion. Furthermore, far from representing the whole African-Caribbean population in Oxford, the cricket club only represented a few individuals.

The first club to be established in the City was begun in 1962. The Club was named the Caribbean Casuals. The term Caribbean in this name was misleading. Far from being an amalgamation of players who had migrated to Oxford, this team revolved around two Barbadian families, who allowed their friends to play. Initially they only played other African-Caribbean teams in other cities and towns in South-East England that were being formed at about the same time.

In an earlier paper I laid great emphasis upon the racism these players experienced. They encountered severe difficulty in obtaining pitches to play on. Other long established clubs refused to give former migrants games in their first team despite the obvious talent of these new arrivals. Finally, when the Casuals Cricket Club did enter the local Oxford league, they found that they were not only competing against the opposite team. They also had to compete against the bias of the umpires too. In fact, it was dissatisfaction with the standard of umpiring which contributed to the decision to leave the league in 1973 and only play friendly matches from then on.

Despite this obviously discriminatory atmosphere, to suggest that this was the primary explanation for the Clubs' existence was far too simplistic. Though the racial climate was an important factor, it was not the determining one. It should not be forgotten that many other people of African-Caribbean descent chose to play for other local teams at the same time and prospered. Rupert Evans and Michael Laudett, two of Oxfordshire's top county players are of African-Caribbean descent. Yet they have rarely played for either the Casuals or its rival in Oxford, the Cowley West Indians (of which I will say more in a moment). Furthermore, many of the players from both these clubs also played for other local clubs too.

Their reason to return to the two African-Caribbean Clubs was usually based more up on convenience than on racism. For many players, identification with one or other of the Clubs revolves around family and friendship as well as questions of discrimination.

The other club in Oxford - arch rivals to the Casuals - was initially called the Cowley West Indians. It was founded in about 1970. It was the team for those who were not the friends of the two dynasties who ruled the Casuals. People who had a cricketing talent on entering Oxford usually went to either the Casuals or the Cowley West Indians depending on their relationship to each. If you were not attached to either you played for a long established club.

Like the Casuals, the Cowley West Indians Club was run by one or two individuals. Also, like the Casuals, during the first decade of its existence the club was content to play friendly matches against other West Indian teams across the South-East of England. Unfortunately, ended in 1980, when the main actor behind the Club decided to retire, taking their entire kit with him; as far as he was concerned it all belonged to him.

This obliged the Cowley West Indians to begin all over again. This time, with the help of a small businessman, they persuaded the Council to lease them a pitch in Cowley. The early 1980s was the time of municipal equal opportunities, when Council largesse towards the ethnic minorities was at its height. This businessman, aware of the political realities of the day, forced the Club to change its name to the Oxford Caribbeans Cricket Club to ensure the best possible opportunity to meet the requirements to receive Council funding.

The funding of projects for the benefit of the ethnic minorities was all the rage in Oxford at this time. The Council provided funding for the Roots Youth Club, the Caribbean Sunrise Club and, by 1985 had agreed to part fund the Asian Community Centre. The change in name helped the Oxford Caribbeans Cricket Club to attract funding for new kit and to obtain planning permission to turn their Cowley base into a clubhouse and pitch. However, there were serious shortcomings with this strategy. Competing with other interest groups, they were unable to win the required funding to commence building their club house. This was vital because in 1981 the Oxford Caribbean Cricket Club had entered the league Oxford Cricket Association League.

Though they had won Division Two for three years running since promotion in 1982, the Oxford Caribbeans Cricket Club were prevented from playing Division One cricket because their pitch and facilities were too poor. In 1985 the Oxford Cricket Association League Management made it clear that they would not allow the Oxford Caribbean Cricket Club to play premier division cricket until and unless it had improved its facilities dramatically.

With no future Council funding available, the Oxford Caribbean Cricket Club was in trouble, playing Second Division Cricket would eventually force their best players to leave. Already their younger players were beginning to drift out of cricket altogether. The Club was about to fold when out of the blue the Casuals, their arch rivals, offered to merge with them.

This was unexpected because of the long standing rivalry between the two Clubs. On the rare occasions they played each other over the years, the Casuals had won easily. Some members of the Casuals disliked the black youth approach to cricket they associated with the Oxford Caribbean Cricket Club. In turn, some members of the Oxford Caribbean Cricket Club resented the perceived arrogance of the Barbadian mafia. Yet, neither Club could ignore the advantages that would be gained from a merger. This would provide the Oxford Caribbean Cricket Club with Premier Division standard facilities; in return it would give the Casuals access to younger, fitter players and a renewed period of Premier Division Cricket. So at the beginning of 1986 season the Oxford Caribbean and Casuals Cricket Club entered the Premier League.

Despite the advantages the merger brought, it was far from smooth, the white players in the Casuals, especially, had feared that they would be sidelined. Some players in the Oxford Caribbeans feared the power of the Barbadian mafia. In fact, the fears of both groups were realised. The white players in the Casuals were indeed sidelined, but they were too old anyway. Other younger white players play for the united Oxford Caribbean and Casuals Cricket Club today. The Barbadian mafia, who wished for the merger, does indeed dominate the Oxford Caribbean Cricket Club.

Explanation

So what does all this mean? There has been a tendency to ascribe a fixed, homogeneous and absolute identity onto black organisations like the Oxford Caribbeans Cricket Club. To do so, fits the political realities of race and discrimination in Britain as we have known it for the past decade. Oxford has only understood this section of the ethnic minority population as a simplistic group, with the same needs, interests and, finally with the same problems. As victims or the problem, this population was misunderstood. Worse, although the new racist discourse can be found at the heart of Oxford's political and social life the ethnic minority population was pushed to margins of community life.

This ascribed image was patently false when one looks closely at the Oxford Caribbeans Cricket Club. To even suggest that these three clubs represent African-Caribbean identity was also far from the truth. At best these clubs have been vehicles for the status of elders of two Barbadian families. They have mobilised a version of Barbadian identity, one which lays great emphasis on a notion of Barbadian excellence at the game of cricket, to maintain their authority and influence within the clubs they played for.

Those who sought to challenge this particular construction, including other Barbadians who sought other interpretations of Barbadian identity, were the ones who left to play for other clubs. Despite the names of these clubs, they have never embraced a universal black identity, except when in need of Council funds. Even when they did it was strictly circumspect. The businessman's desire to change the name of the Club was hotly contested by many of the players who felt that it would dilute their links with the West Indies. They did not want to be seen as merely a British ethnic minority team.

Nevertheless, this businessman used his key relationship with the club as evidence of his claim that he was a significant community leader of Oxford's African-Caribbeans. Though his relationship with the club was ended with the merger, he still perceives himself as one of Oxford's leading African-Caribbean citizens.

It was clear that these clubs have both rejected images ascribed to them and spurned the opportunity to identify themselves as the local African-Caribbean clubs. Yet they have succumbed to the images ascribed to them by the opposing teams in the Oxford Association League. These clubs, village teams with longer traditions, have always seen these clubs as a kind of local West Indies team with the big image which goes with it. They want the club to excel in fast bowling, flamboyant big scorers, yet, also be impatient with spin. They want the same challenge faced by the England team. Both the Oxford Caribbeans Cricket Club and the Casuals have obliged, pandering to this image. Players of the teams have frequently described their cricket as being in keeping with the West Indian tradition.

Please remember that one of the central attributes which they recognised as being in keeping with West Indian cricketing tradition, fast bowling, has not always been thus. Furthermore, there has been a reluctance to allow African-Caribbeans of South Asian descent to play for the Club's First XI. The image remains of the African-Caribbeans being solely of African descent. So, like everybody else, the clubs construct and select specific images from the Caribbean to produce a new identity in keeping with their experience in Britain.

As Stuart Hall reminds us, communities in Britain were positioned and repositioned in relation to the dominant presence. Yet, that does not mean that there was no room for these populations to actively create and re-create identities These identities were always in production, shaping and being shaped by their environment. In the case of local cricket in England, this game has been shaped and transformed by such clubs to such an extent that if the term traditional English cricket meant anything in the past, it has no meaning now.

Notes

1 I wish to thank the Wingate Foundation for supporting this research.

12 Politics of identity

Stuart Hall

I want to say a little bit about the distinction between political mobilisation and African Caribbean identity, and some of the problems that writing such a history would present because of the way in which we need to reconceptualise what it is we mean by identity. Which is to say that this is hanging around, as it were, as a quite unclarified concept. There has, I think, been a series of transitions between two very different conceptions of identity - a shift to a post-identity period, if you understand what I mean. The word is under erasure; we all use it, we don't quite mean what we used to mean by it - that is to say, something relatively fixed by position, fixed by a long historical association, fixed by ancestral and inherited position. We don't quite mean something like that.

We know that in contemporary societies identities are more flexible, more open, more labile, more fluid, less predictable, more dramaturgical, more dependent on performance, less dependent on - as it were - inherited tradition. We know that the shift has been made, but then out there beyond yawns a kind of endlessly sliding world where identities are just kind of pinpoints in the firmament. We occasionally inhabit them, show up having been summoned to them and then get lost, or we lose ourselves, etc. We know that is not a way of talking about the question of identity.

And so, somewhere, there is a third way, it seems to me, which people are trying to grapple towards in this area. And it is this, why it is that we need a third way and what that might be, that I just want to say one or two words about.

But first of all - I can't even begin to try to produce a sketch, but if you thought of writing the history of African Caribbean political mobilisation in Britain since large-scale migration began, in terms of identity and identification, rather than in terms of other things, you could identify a number of important clusters. I can't put it in any more unified way than that. In the very early stages, when people were hailed as immigrants, hailed as coloured, and came to think of themselves as West Indians. This is one moment, but notice that in all this talk about identity here, I have to use two perspectives - how they are addressed and how they inserted themselves into the position of address. And that is because, it seems to me, identity, although it has to be spoken by the subject - collective or individual - who is being positioned, it is not a question of what the inside wants to locate only. And it's not a question of how the outside, or the external dominating system, places you symbolically: but it is precisely in the process - never complete, never whole - of identification.

And, therefore, one of the shifts that I would make myself is to stop talking exclusively about identity and begin to talk about identification. Which is the process by which groups, movements, institutions, try to locate us for the purpose of regulating us; try to construct us within symbolic boundaries in order to locate us, to give us resources, or take resources away from us. And in order to exist within that kind of symbolic framework, we try to manipulate or respond to it by saying 'Well, I'm sort of like that', or 'Sometimes I will show up like that, if there's enough money' or 'I refuse to be like that, as you call it' and 'instead I want to call it that'.

Now all those four things have to do with how any identity is produced for oneself, as part of a conversation around social positioning at any time. I think that one needs these two sides always. So just think about what I said about that first moment. Actually, West Indian is to me the most interesting identity of all, particularly in relation to what Ossie Stuart said, because, of course, it is the last least ancestral identification there was. Nobody from the Caribbean came here in the 1950s thinking of themselves as West Indian. You know, I'd never seen another West Indian. I'd occasionally glimpsed the odd Barbadian - he was the strangest thing I ever saw. But when Karl Jackman came, incidentally to teach me Latin in the sixth form, and opened his mouth, I thought I'd never heard a sound like that. I discovered I was West Indian in London - that's where you discovered you were West Indian. And never completely, because one also always remained partly Jamaican, Barbadian, etc. So the island jealousies were also maintained alongside the discovery of a kind of pan-Caribbeanism, the location of which was principally Notting Hill or Brixton, or somewhere like that. So even in that very simple moment, when African Caribbean migrants are not yet placed anywhere within any stable internal domestic symbolic system, already there are different ways in which they are placed and placing themselves in relation to the system. If you think of the next phase, which is a very important one, it is the phase in when that system begins to settle down and when racism becomes a much more clear political and social cultural formation, and when people are beginning to experience themselves as excluded. That is, of course, the moment, especially in the wake of the Civil Rights Movement, of the first notion of this group, that had never called themselves black ever before in history, discovering at a particular historical moment that they could answer up to the name black.

It is also the moment of the production of an Afrocentric identity amongst, especially, black youth. Now people said earlier today that, of course, Afrocentric identity around Rastafarianism, around reggae, etc., was a metaphor in Britain for something that was happening elsewhere, in Kingston. Let me remind you, it's a metaphor in Kingston too. So it's a metaphor of a metaphor of a place - Africa - which when actually the Rastafarians arrived, the Africans said: And who are you? Where do you think you're going to? Of course you come from here 400 years ago, but do you think Africa's been sitting down, waiting for you to row back? No, we've moved on, Africa is somewhere else'.

The Africa that was being spoken of was, of course, in a political sense, of absolutely central effectivity. But whether it was literally one place from which some little descent could have been traced, so that when people said 'I am African, they really meant something ... What they principally meant was I am anything but British'. It was a counter-identification. It was what enabled people to tell how the hell they've got here with a counter-narrative. They were the symbolic characters that sustained them as Rastafarians and expressed as a counter-narrative of the oppressed, of the excluded. It was one of the few ways in which people borrowed the symbolic language - a certain kind of symbolic language, of Christianity - and upturned it in order to reach for a way of talking their own history, of narrativising their own history. So another way of thinking of identity and the production of identity, is in terms of the story that people are able, in certain situations, and have to produce in order to give a popular historical account of who they are, where they came from, how they got into this fix. And usually, since history doesn't have to do with the past, but with the future - where these people are going to end up and why.

Identities are as important about where you're going as where you're coming from. Where you're coming from are the resources that you put together in order to make that story give some semblance of sense and in order to locate the individual coherently in relation to it, but it is about mobilising those symbolic resources in relation to the future. It tells you where these people want to get to and why they don't want to go that way. It enables them to mobilise, it's part of mobilisation. Now that period is dominated by the formation of identity in relation to racism, of course, so one sees the function of symbolic exclusion on the part of the host society - to set a group out, by not using only race, but also colour. So when we say race, we put it in quotation marks because, of course, we don't mean literally biological race, we mean all those racial and colour characteristics that can be used as symbolic marks of exclusion. That's why we need quotation marks around it. It doesn't mean that it doesn't mean anything - it doesn't mean what you probably think it means, if we use it in the literal sense. But, of course, it's powerfully symbolically important, and those who are excluded can use it, try to borrow it, try to upturn it, in order to give themselves an alternative or counter-position in relation to gaining access, gaining space - winning space - and creating some constituency or collectivity.

Now, if you take that view, that is partly because that collectivity - whatever you call it, the people, the nation, the community - as a singular homogeneous thing, does not exist. The reason why one needs the narrative is to make a unity out of that which is not yet a unity. The whole argument about class has been turned upside down because people imagine that the class was already unified and, for some mysterious reason, it just never turned up in one place. Actually, it was all over the place and people hoped by inserting this signifier, which could collect enough of people's common interests, common experiences, to make them a more unified social and political force. That's what I mean by saying that the language which refers to the past - 'We have always been here' - is a way of saying 'We haven't always been together, but if we just find out what we have in common, we could produce ourselves as something which is common and create a more coherent political force'.

So always, the terms of identity is Janus-faced: it's pointed in the two directions. It looks backward, mythically it constructs and invents its past sometimes. The question is not whether they're literally true, or not, but whether in the situation (this is why identities are situational) they provide resources out of which to produce yourself. To produce yourself, collectively or individually, in a space which gives you more leverage - which is exactly what Claire Alexander was talking about. Claire was not talking about a kind of open-ended field where anybody could make up to be what they want: she wasn't talking about that kind of wild American post-modern version of identity, you know, like a smorgasbord, a supermarket identity, where you go and choose up five, ten tins of whatever you feel like today. We're not talking about that, we're talking about operating a very constrained system, but nevertheless, even within those constraints, it is possible to use the identity question as a way of levering spaces open; even when that very leverage doesn't put you in some new, wholly positive, wholly integrated situation - it simply wins you a bit of space. A lot of the contradictions remain open. The point that she made about using the language - it's funny in the way black men use the stereotype of them by white society actually to perform in order to win themselves a bit of space. Though it's not actually a joke at all in the way in which black men internalise the language of sexism, which is used about women in their own community. So they also talk about black women as bitches. So you don't get rid of the contradictory material out of which new identities have to be produced. You don't produce another whole positive space in which everyone is going to fit and we're all going to be black like that for the next fifty years; but, positionally, it is possible to be black like that in relation to the forces and symbolic material which is arrayed around, which is trying to position us. They try to position us and we are trying to find some space within the positioning. That's what the identity and the struggle - the identity dialectic - seems to me to be about. So understand it positionally in that way.

If you move to that last moment then, that last moment is a very contradictory one. It now has very much more to do with blackness trying to find its space; not so much in relation to a kind of reconstruction of the invented past - that Afrocentric moment - but very much in relation to the experience within the diaspora itself. That is when the question of can you propose questions arises: can you be black and British? Are they mutually exclusive identities? What would it be like to try to be black and British? And what would it be like for the British for some blacks to try to be British? Because that question is not a question which is posed for the black community only. It is posed for everybody.

That is why, if you go back to the questions you were asking at the beginning of this morning, the question about white ethnicity, my answer to the question - should we worry about white ethnicity? - well, if you're trying to construct white ethnicity as some whole space of enunciation and action from which we can move: don't bother, it's been there for a very long time. Just inhabit it and press on. But if you want to know whether one ought to be concerned about how white ethnicity is constructed and how it acquires the power of the norm, my answer is yes, yes, we ought to be concerned about that. Because in part, its symbolic power arises from the fact that it is not an ethnicity. Precisely, it is the norm by which everything else becomes an ethnicity. So the activity of making the British, not hate themselves - there's no question of moralism and guilt-tripping - but of their recognising that they too are a quite interesting island people, with a rather interesting history; who have been marching all over the world a long time and have just come home and need to settle down in a corner here, and are in a long decline; and have had some interesting historical experiences, of course. And our history has been part of you - you drank our tea and rotted your teeth with our sugar, and you took us half way round the world - we share a mutual story. Your ethnicity and mine. I mean, to think about Englishness from the ground; not of the norm and the minorities, but just of a lot of different ethnicities - some interesting, some not - would make a very important shift.

And it would make that shift because, at the same time, black identities are moving into that space more self-consciously - that is to say, occupying the double consciousness of being black and British, and in Europe, and listening to American music - and are willing to play, situationally, one of those identities off against another. That is to say, consciously beginning to edge into a more hybrid, more pluralistic notion of what black experiences are about. Not that blackness doesn't count, not that it doesn't have a history, not that it doesn't have a specificity, but that it is a variety of different things. To be black in this society is many different things, and it cannot be defined exclusively in relation to racism. Now racism is the most constraining, confining, oppressive structure, through which we have related for a long time, and in a very face-to-face sense, since migration, with the host society. But the experience of being black in the world, and of the range of expressive and creative forces which are accessible to it; of the variety of cultural languages that it can now speak, cannot be funnelled through the tiny eye of the negative experience of racism. Because that is simply to accept that I am nothing but the inverse of how I am seen. You know, they see me as black, and so I am black and I can only speak with one voice, through one experience from that. It is not possible to occupy black identity the end of the 20th century in the heart of Europe in that monological way.

So what you are seeing now, at the end of a twenty/thirty year history, is blacks increasingly understanding the multiplicity of identities that they are going to need to get from one side of the street to another. But at the same moment, alongside that, there is exactly the reverse temptation. That the processes of exclusion, marginalisation, of being dropped out of the quest for modernity at the end of the 20th century, could be so awful and could be so inaccessible to the marginalised and those on the periphery, that they can only survive the next phase by climbing into the bunker.

Now these are the real choices in the current situation, which is a diaspora experience. Now the identities here, of course, are drawing on a lot of traditions from the past. African Caribbean people draw from what they imagine they inherited expressively from the African tradition, what they imagine they've brought here from the cultures of the Caribbean, which was already a creolised culture. They are drawing on the music that they listen to and they share with other people in the black diaspora in the New World. They belong to five different worlds - that is what they are. That is what C.L..R. James said: they are interesting because although they are absolutely minute - you can hardly find them on the map - they are actually the product of drawing together, synthesising, of syncretizing a variety of different cultures. And what is interesting about their culture is precisely not that it is pure and can be traced back without being transformed at all, back to the year dot, but precisely that, inspite of the ruptures that have marked their history, they have produced something quite new, out of the hybridisation of different cultural forces.

Now to live with hybridity, I believe, is the politics of the 21st century. Everybody, everybody - Bosnia, Herzogovinians, everybody is going increasingly, in an interdependent world of migrated peoples, to live with - I don't mean symbolically, I mean materially too - to live with hybridity, to live with impurity, to live with the fact that there are no pure origins left. And the temptation not to accept the translation of identities, but to defend ourselves with tradition; that is to say, not to use tradition as a resource to produce yourself anew, to lay your claim on the modern anew, but to use the past as an area of retreat. That is what I call fundamentalism, and there's much of it around in the past - Thatcherite Britain, and in Germany, and in France - the retreat to a one track, monological, essentialising homogeneous notion of white European identity. That kind of fundamentalism is not exclusive to Islam; it is not to be found in most of the Islamic societies anyway; it has had much more to do with what is happening to the play of identities at this historical moment - a moment of globalisation, of uneven modernity, where societies that are left out of the modern race reach for tradition, in order to defend themselves against what it might feel like to have nothing between themselves and starvation but the World Bank. That's what creates fundamentalism - no space between you and starvation except the World Bank, and then get behind the barricade - whatever it is. And since 1979, lots of small Little England English people have been getting behind the barricades. And the moment when Europe begins to look like that hybrid, impure space of migrated peoples; the space of peoples that listen to world music; the space of peoples that move their bodies in different ways; the space of peoples who will lay claim to universalism where citizenship rights are concerned, but who will not pay the price of universal citizenship by all becoming one - who insist that they have to be treated with respect to the right of the state in terms of a universal set of rights, but who insist that they can look like Muslims and North Africans and Chinese, so long as they are prepared to pay the price of being part of a political collectivity.

The political question is what the trade-off is. There is a trade-off, there's no question about it; we oughtn't to fool ourselves that there's no trade-off. Groups cannot be absolutely culturally different and want to claim the rights of every society. You can't say, 'It's my right to shoot Salman Rushdie, but tomorrow I'm going to show up at the DHSS and expect my handout just the same'. There is a kind of trade-off there - but a trade-off of the old universalistic Enlightenment is too high: it did not respect difference enough and in the world of the 21st century, people are just going to be culturally different. They don't want to look the same and we have to recognise that the discourse of Enlightenment universalism usually meant 'Let us all be human beings - very French at the same time'. A very French type of human beings: a very French type of reasoning. It was a wonderful dream for everybody, but the Enlightenment from the 18th century onwards has had deep and profound silences - groups who were never quite as equal as everybody else and, therefore, never quite as human as everybody else.

And the respect for difference is the insistence that if you're going to be universal, let us be universal. Let us negotiate what the political price of that is, but after that, culturally, one has to take culture away from that, because people want the resources to be able to be productive, creative, to explore their own histories, to tell their own stories and to develop their own identities in the future.

Now that is where the politics of identity - if you take this less essentialist view, but don't drift it off into no-mans land, no-womans land, no-persons land - if you try to find a point where identity is positional but not essentialist; is located, is always located in more than one set of discourses. No one discourse will give you identity. So that if you ask, what are people in religious terms, you have to ask what are the sexual and gender consequences of the way in which that religious identity is being lived. It always has knock-on consequences, because no one dimension can structure identity. But if one is prepared to take that more diversified and yes, more pluralised notion of what identity is - and a more positional notion of it - there is a politics there, but it is a very difficult one. But I suspect it's the only game left on the table.

Bibliography

Akhtar, S. (1989), *Be Careful With Muhammad!*, Bellen, London.

Al-Azmeh, A. (1993), *Islams and Modernities*, Verso, London, 1993.

Al-Azmeh, A. (1994), Ethnic Relations Seminar, 10 March, St Antony's, Oxford.

Alexander, C. (1992), 'The Art of "Being Black": The Creation of Black British Youth Identities', D.Phil. thesis, Oxford.

Ali, Y. (1992), 'Muslim Women and the Politics of Ethnicity', in Saghal, G. and Yuval Davis, N. (eds.), *Refusing Holy Orders,* Virago, London.

Anderson, B. (1983), *Imagined Communities: Reflections on the Origin and Spread of Nationalism*, Verso, London.

Anthias, F. and Yuval-Davis, N. (1992), *Racialised Boundaries,* Routledge, London.

Archer, A. (1986), *The Two Catholic Churches: A Study in Oppression,* SCM Press, London.

Badham, P. (ed.), (1989), *Religion, State, and Society in Modern Britain,* Edwin Mellen Press, Lampeter.

Balibar, E. (1984), 'La société metisée', *Le Monde,* 1 Decembre, Paris.

Balibar, E (1989), 'Le racisme: encore un universalisme', *Mots,* 18, Mars, Paris.

Ballard, R. and Driver, G. (1977), 'The Ethnic Approach', in *New Society,* 16 June.

Ballard, R. and Ballard, C. (1977),'The Sikhs: The Development of South Asian Settlements in Britain' in Watson, J. (ed.), *Between Two Cultures: Migrants and Minorities in Britain*, Basil Blackwell, Oxford.

Ballard, R. (1986), 'Changing life styles among British Asians', *New Community*, 13, 2.

Ballard, R. (1990), 'Migration and kinship: the differential effect of marriage rules on the processes of Punjabi migration to Britain', in *South Asians Overseas: Migration and Ethnicity*, Clarke, C., Peach, C. and Vertovec, S. (eds.), Cambridge University Press, Cambridge.

Ballard, R. (1992), 'New Clothes for the Emperor?: The Conceptual Nakedness of the Race Relations Industry in Britain', *New Community,* 18, 3.
Banton, M. (1955), *The Coloured Quarter,* Cape, London.
Barker, M. (1981), *The New Racism*, Junction Books, London.
Barot, R. (1972-3), 'A Swaminarayan Sect as a Community', *New Community*, 2, 1.
Barot, R. (1981), The Social Organisation of a Swaminarayan Sect in Britain. Unpublished Ph.D. Thesis, School of Oriental and African Studies, University of London.
Barot, R. (1987), 'Religion and community among Bristol Hindus: The case of Sanatan Deevya Mandal', paper presented at the Colston Research Symposium on Religious Pluralism.
Barth, F. (1969), *Ethnic Groups and Boundaries*, George Allen and Unwin, London.
Belchem, J. (1985), 'English Working-class Radicalism and the Irish, 1815-50' in Swift, R. and Gilley, S. (eds.), *The Irish in the Victorian City,* Croom Helm, London.
Ben-Tovin, G., Gabriel, J., Law, I. and Stredder, K. (1986), *The Local Politics of Race,* Macmillan, London.
Bhabha, H. (1990), 'The Third Space', in Rutherford, J. (ed.), *Identity: Community, Culture, Difference,* Lawrence and Wishart, London.
Bhachu, P. (1985), *Twice Migrants: East African Sikh Settlers in Britain*, Tavistock, London.
Bourdieu, P. (1977), *Outline of a Theory of Practice*, Cambridge University Press, Cambridge.
Bourne, J. and Sivanandan, A. (1980), 'Cheerleaders and Ombudsmen: The Sociology of Race Relations in Britain', in *Race and Class,* 21, 4.
Bowen, D, (1981), 'The Hindu Community in Bradford,' in *Hinduism in England,* Bowen, D. (ed.), Bradford College, Bradford.
Bowen, D. (1987), 'The evolution of Gujarati Hindu organizations in Bradford', in *Hinduism in Great Britain*, Burghart, R. (ed.), Tavistock, London.
Bradford Heritage Recording Unit, (1987), *Destination Bradford: A Century of Immigration*, Bradford.
Bradley, J, (1993), 'Religious Identity in Modern Scotland: Culture, Politics and Football', unpublished Ph.D thesis, University of Strathclyde.
Brah, A. (1993), 'Reframing Europe - Engendered Racisms, Ethnicities and Nationalisms in Contemporary Western Europe', *Feminist Review,* 45, Autumn.
Brathwaite, E. (1974),'Carifesta: Doing It Our Way', in *New Community,* 3, 3.
Brear, D. (1986), 'A Unique Hindu Festival in England and India, 1985: A Phenomenological Analysis', *Temenos*, 2.
Burghart, R. (1987a), 'Introduction: The Diffusion of Hinduism to Great Britain', in *Hinduism in Great Britain,* Burghart, R. (ed.), Tavistock, London.
Burghart, R. (1987b), 'The Perpetuation of Hinduism in an Alien Cultural Milieu', in *Hinduism in Great Britain*, Burghart, R. (ed.), Tavistock, London.

Buzon, B. (1991), 'New Patterns of Global Security in the Twenty-First Century', *International Affairs,* 67, 2.
Carey, S. (1983), 'The Hare Krishna movement and Hindus in Britain', *New Community*, 10, 3.
Carey, S. and Shukur, A. (1985), 'A Profile of the Bangladeshi Community in East London', *New Community,* 12, 3.
Castles, S. and Kosack, G. (1973), *Immigrant Workers and Class Structure in Western Europe*, Oxford University Press, London.
Centre for Bangladeshi Studies (1994), *Routes and Beyond*, Roehampton Institute.
Chapman, M. (1978), *The Gaelic Vision in Scottish Culture,* Croom Helm, London.
Chapman, M., McDonald, M. and Tonkin, E. (1989), 'Introduction - History and Social Anthropology', in Chapman, McDonald and Tonkin (eds.), *History and Ethnicity*, ASA Monographs 27, Routledge, London.
Citron, S. (1991), *Le Mythe National* , Editions Ouvrières, Paris.
Cockcroft, W.R. (1974), 'The Liverpool Police Force, 1836-1902' in S.P. Bell, *Victorian Lancashire,* David and Charles, Newton Abbot.
Cohen, Abner (1969), *Custom and Politics in Urban Africa*, Routledge, London.
Cohen, Abner (ed.), (1974), *Urban Ethnicity*, ASA Monographs 12, Tavistock, London.
Cohen, Abner (1980), 'Drama and Politics in the Development of a London Carnival', in *Man* N.S. 15.
Cohen, Abner (1993), *Masquerade Politics: Explorations in the Structure of Urban Cultural Movements*, Berg Publishers, Oxford.
Cohen, Anthony (1982), (ed.), *Belonging: Identity and Social Organisation in British Rural Cultures*, Manchester University Press, Manchester.
Cohen, Anthony (1983), 'Anthropological Studies of Rural Britain, 1968-1983: a position paper', ESRC, London.
Cohen, Anthony (ed.), (1986), *Symbolising Boundaries: Identity and Diversity in British Cultures,* Manchester University Press, Manchester.
Cohen, Anthony (1990), 'The British Anthropological Tradition, Otherness and Rural Studies', in Lowe, P. and Bodiguel, M. (eds.), *Rural Studies in Britain and France,* Belhaven Press, London.
Cohen, P. (1988),'The Perversions of Inheritance: Studies in the Making of Multi-Racist Britain' in Cohen, P. and Bains, H.S. (eds.), *Multi-Racist Britain*, Macmillan, London.
Cohen, W.B. (1981), *The French Encounter with Africans. White response to Blacks 1530-1800,* Indiana University Press, Indiana.
Cohn, B. (1987), *An Anthropologist Among the Historians and Other Essays*, Oxford University Press, Delhi.
Cole, W.O. and Singh. S.P. (1978), T*he Sikhs, Their Religious Beliefs and Practices*, Routledge and Kegan Paul, London.
Colley, L. (1992), *Britons: Forging the Nation, 1707-1837*, Pimlico, London.
Collins, S. (1952), 'Social Processes Integrating Coloured People in Britain', in *British Journal of Sociology,* 3, 1.
Collins, S (1957), *Coloured Minorities in Britain*, Lutterworth, London.
Commission for Racial Equality, (1992), Legal Division, London.

Crissman, L. W. (1967), 'The segmentary structure of urban overseas Chinese communities', *Man* , 2.
Cross, M. (1991), 'Editorial', *New Community,* 17, 3.
Dahya, B. (1974), 'The nature of Pakistani ethnicity in industrial cities in Britain', in *Urban Ethnicity,* Cohen, A. (ed.), Tavistock, London.
Deljarrie, B. and Wallon, B. (1988), *La Ligue des droits de l'Homme. Un combat dans le Siecle,* Etudes et Documentation Internationales, Paris.
Desir, H. (1989), 'SOS Racisme, Hier et Demain', *Hommes et Migrations,* 1118, Janvier, Paris.
Donald, J. and Rattansi, A. (eds.), (1992),*"Race", Culture and Difference,* Sage, London.
Drury, B.M. (1988), 'Ethnicity Amongst Second Generation Sikh Girls: A Case Study in Nottingham', unpublished PhD thesis, University of Nottingham.
Drury, B.M. (1990), 'Blackness: A Situational Identity'. Paper presented at a Conference on 'New Issues in Black Politics', CRER, University of Warwick.
Drury, B.M. (1991), 'Sikh Girls and the Maintenance of an Ethnic Culture', *New Community,* 17, 3.
Dubow, S. (1989), *Racial Segregation and the Origins of Apartheid in South Africa, 1919-1936*, St Antony's/Macmillan, London.
Duffield, M. (1984), 'New Racism, New Realism: Two Sides of the Same Coin', *Radical Philosophy,* 37.
Eade, J. (1989), *The Politics of Community: the Bangladeshi community in East London,* Avebury, Aldershot.
Eade, J. (1990), 'Nationalism and the Quest for Authenticity: the Bangladeshis in Tower Hamlets', *New Community,* 16, 4.
Eade, J. (1991), 'The Political Construction of Class and Community: Bangladeshi political leadership in East London' in Werbner, P. and Anwar, M. (eds.), *Black and Ethnic Leaderships: The Cultural Dimensions of Political Action*, London and New York, Routledge.
Eade, J. (1992), 'Quests for Belonging' in Cambridge, A.X. and Feuchtwang, S. (eds.), *Where You Belong: Government and Black Culture*, Aldershot, Avebury
Eade, J. (1993), 'The Political Articulation of Community and the Islamisation of Space in London' in Barot, R. (ed.), *Religion and Ethnicity: Minorities and Social Change in the Metropolis,* Kuk Paros, Kamppere.
Eisenstadt, S.N. (1968), 'Introduction', in *On Charisma and Institution Building*, Weber, M. [Selected Papers, Eisenstadt, S.N. (ed.),] University of Chicago Press, Chicago.
Ekeh, P. (1990), 'Social Anthropology and Two Contrasting Uses of Tribalism in Africa', *Comparative Studies in Society and History,* 32, 4.
Ennew, J. (1980), *The Western Isles Today*, Cambridge University Press, Cambridge.
Erikson, R. (1984), '"Indians" and "Africans" in a Hindu Gujarati community', unpublished mss, Dept. of Social Anthropology, Cambridge University
Feuchtwang, S. (1980), 'Socialist, feminist and antiracist struggles', *MIF,* 4.

Feuchtwang, S. (1990), 'Racism: territoriality and ethnocentricity', in Cambridge, A.X. and Feuchtwang, S. (eds.), *Antiracist Strategies*, Avebury, Aldershot.

Feuchtwang, S. and Cambridge, A.X. (1992), 'Conclusion' in Feuchtwang, S. and Cambridge, A.X. with Eade. J, and Clarke. J. *Where You Belong: Government and Black Culture*, Avebury, Aldershot.

Finnegan, F. (1982), *Poverty and Prejudice: Irish Immigrants in York 1840-1875*, Cork University Press, Cork.

Ford, G. (1992), *Fascist Europe. The Rise of Racism and Xenophobia*, Pluto Press, London.

Fortes, M. and Evans-Pritchard, E.E. (1940), *African Political System.*, Oxford University Press, Oxford.

Foster, J. (1974), *Class Struggle and the Industrial Revolution*, Methuen, London.

Frykenberg, R. (1989), 'The emergence of modern "Hinduism" as a concept and as an institution', in *Hinduism Reconsidered*, Sontheimer, G.D. and Kulke, H. (eds.), Manohar, New Delhi.

Galissot, R. (1985), *Misere de l'antiracisme*, Arcantere, Paris.

Gallagher, T, (1987), *The Uneasy Peace*, Manchester University Press, Manchester.

Garigue, P. (1953), 'The West African Students' Union', *Africa*, 20, 3.

Geertz, C. (1973), *Interpretation of Cultures*, Basic Books, New York.

Ghua, R. (ed.), *Subaltern Studies I*, Oxford University Press, Delhi.

Gilroy, P. (1987), *There Ain't No Black in the Union Jack: The Cultural Politics of Race and Nation*, Hutchinson, London.

Gilroy, P. (1992), 'The End of Antiracism', in Donald, J. and Rattansi, A. (eds.), *"Race", Culture and Difference*, Sage, London.

Gilroy, P. (1993a), *Small Acts. Thoughts on the Politics of Black Culture*, Serpent's Tail, London.

Gilroy, P. (1993b), *The Black Atlantic: Modernity and Double Consciousness*, Verso, London.

Goering, J. (1993), 'Reclothing the Emperor while Avoiding Ideological Polarisation: A comment on Roger Ballard's essay', *New Community*, 19, 2.

Gordon, R. and Spiegel, A. (1993), 'Southern Africa Revisited', *Annual Review of Anthropology*, 22.

Goulbourne, H. (1991), *Ethnicity and Nationalism in Post-imperial Britain*, Cambridge University Press, Cambridge.

Guidice, F. (1992), *Arabicides*, La Decouverte, Paris.

Gupta, D. (1983), 'Racism Without Colour: the Catholic Ethnic and Ethnicity in Quebec' in *Race and Class*, 25, 1.

Hall, C. (1994), 'Nation, Empire, Gender: the White Brotherhood of Britain in the 1860s', Ethnic Relations Seminar, 24 February, St Antony's, Oxford.

Hall, S. (1990), 'Cultural Identity and Diaspora', in Rutherford, J. (ed.), *Identity: Community, Culture, Difference*, Lawrence and Wishart, London.

Hall, S. (1991), 'Old and New Identities, Old and New Ethnicities' in King, A.D. (ed.), *Culture, Globalisation and World System*, Macmillan, London.

Hall, S. (1992a), 'New ethnicities' in Donald, J. and Rattansi, A. (eds.), *'Race', Culture and Difference*, Sage, London.

Hall, S. (1992b), 'What is this "Black" in Black Popular Culture?' in Dent, G. (ed.), *Black Popular Culture,* Bay Press, Seattle.

Halstead, M. (1988), *Education, Justice and Cultural Diversity: An Examination of the Honeyford Affair 1984-5*, Falmer, London.

Handley, J, (1947), *The Irish in Modern Scotland*, Cork University Press, Cork.

Hankins, T.L. (1970), *Jean D'Alembert: Science and the Enlightenment,* Cambridge University Press, Cambridge.

Hardy, F. (1990), 'Hinduism', in *Turning points in Religious Studies*, King, U. (ed.), T. and T. Clark, Edinburgh.

Hargreaves, A. (1988), 'The French Nationality Code Hearing', *Modern and Contemporary France* , 34, July.

Hewitt, R. (1986), *White Talk, Black Talk,* Cambridge University Press, Cambridge.

Hickman, M.J. (1980), 'The Problematic Irish: An Analysis of the Presentation of Britain's Relationship to Ireland in School Texts', MSc. dissertation, University of the Southbank.

Hickman, M.J. (1990), 'A Study of the Incorporation of the Irish in Britain with Special Reference to Catholic State Education: Involving a Comparison of the Attitudes of Pupils and Teachers in Selected Catholic Schools in London and Liverpool', PhD. University of London.

Hillyard, P. (1993), *Suspect Community*, Pluto Press, London.

Jackson, M. (1988), *Moonwalker,* Heinemann, London.

Jackson, P. and Smith, S.J. (eds.), (1981), *Social Interaction and Ethnic Segregation,* Academic Press, London.

Jackson, R. (1984), 'The concerns of religious education and the characterization of Hinduism', *British Journal of Religious Education*, 6.

Jackson, R. (1985), 'Hinduism in Britain: Religious nurture and religious education', *British Journal of Religious Education,* 7.

Jackson, R. (1987), 'Changing conceptions of Hinduism in "time-tabled religion"', in *Hinduism in Great Britain*, R. Burghart (ed.), Tavistock, London.

Jackson, R. and Nesbitt, E. (1986), 'Sketches of formal Hindu nurture: Hindu supplementary classes in England' *World Religions in Education,* (Shap Mailing) CRE, London.

Jacob, M.C. (1981), *The Radical Enlightenment. Pantheists, Freemasons and Republicans,* Allen and Unwin, London.

James, C.L.R. (1963), *Beyond the Boundary*, Hutchinson, London.

Jayawardena, C. (1968), 'Migration and social change: A survey of Indian communities overseas', *Geographical Review*, 58.

Jayawardena, C. (1980), 'Culture and ethnicity in Guyana and Fiji', *Man,* N.S. 15.

Jazouli, A. (1992), *Les Années Banlieues,* Seuil, Paris.

Jeffery, P. (1976), *Migrants and Refugees: Muslim and Christian Pakistani Families in Bristol,* Cambridge University Press, Cambridge.

Jenkins, R. (1986), 'Social anthropological models of inter-ethnic relations' in John R.and Mason D. (eds.), *Theories of Race and Ethnic Relations,* Cambridge University Press, Cambridge.

Joly, D. (1987), 'Pakistani Associations' in *Immigrant Associations in Europe,* by Rex, J., Joly, D., and Wilpert, C., Gower, Aldershot.

Jones, C. (1977), *Immigration and Social Policy in Britain,* Tavistock Books, London.
Junod, V. (1952), 'The Coloured Elite in London'. Unpublished mss, Department of Social Anthropology, Edinburgh.
Kaarsholm, P. and Hultin, J., (eds.), (1994), *Inventions and Boundaries: Historical and Anthropological Approaches to the Study of Ethnicity and Nationalism,* International Development Studies, Roskilde.
Kalka, I. (1991), 'The Politics of the "Community" among Gujarati Hindus in London', *New Community,* 17, 3.
Kanitkar, H. (1979), 'A School for Hindus'?, *New Community*, 7, 2.
Keith, M. (1994), 'Making the Street Visible: Criminalisation, Racialisation and the Bengali Community of East London', Ethnic Studies Seminar, 10 February, St Antony's, Oxford.
Killingley, D., Killingley, S.Y., Nowicki, V., Shukla, H. and Simmonds D. (1984), *A Handbook of Hinduism for Teachers,* Grevatt and Grevatt (2nd rev. edn.), Newcastle-upon-Tyne.
Kirk, N. (1980), 'Ethnicity, Class and Popular Toryism, 1850-1870' in Lunn, K. (ed.), *Hosts, Immigrants and Minorities*, Dawson, Folkestone.
Knott, K. (1986), *Hinduism in Leeds: A Study of Religious Practice in the Indian Hindu Community and in Hindu-Related Groups,* Leeds Community Religions Project Monograph Series, Dept. of Theology and Religious Studies, University of Leeds.
Knott, K. (1987), 'Hindu temple rituals in Britain: The reinterpretation of tradition,' in *Hinduism in Great Britain*, R. Burghart (ed.), Tavistock, London.
Knott, K. (1991), 'Bound to Change? The Religions of South Asians in Britain', in *Aspects of the South Asian Diaspora*, S. Vertovec (ed.), Oxford University Press, New Delhi.
Knott, K. (1994), 'From Leather Stockings to Surgical Boots and Beyond: The Gujarati Mochis of Leeds', in *Desh Pardesh: The South Asian Presence in Britain,* Ballard, R. (ed.), Hurst, London.
Knott, K. and Toon R. (1982), 'Muslims, Sikhs and Hindus in the UK: Problems in the estimation of religious statistics', Religious Research Papers No. 6, Department of Sociology, University of Leeds.
Knowles, C. and Mercer, K. (1990), 'Feminism and antiracism: An exploration of the possibilities' in Cambridge, A.X. and Feuchtwang, S. (eds.), *Antiracist Strategies,* Avebury, Aldershot.
Lawrence, E. (1982), 'In the Abundance of Water the Fool is Thirsty: Sociology and Black 'Pathology', in *The Empire Strikes Back*, Hutchinson, London.
Lebow, R.N. (1976), *White Britain and Black Ireland: The Influence of Stereotypes on Colonial Policy,* Institute for the Study of Human Issues, Philadelphia.
Lees, H.S. (1979), *Exiles in Erin: Irish Immigrants in Victorian London,* Manchester University Press, Manchester.
LeLohe, M. (1990), 'The Asian Vote in a Northern City', in *Black Politics in Britain,* by Goulbourne, H., (ed.), Avebury, Aldershot.
Leveau. R, and Wihtol de Wenden, C. (1988), 'La deuxième génération', *Pouvoirs,* 48.

Levinas, E. (1987), *Collected Philosophical Papers,* trans. Alphonso Lingis, Martinus Nijhoff Publishers, Derdrecht.
Levi-Strauss, C. (1976), *Tristes Tropiques*, trans. Doreen, J. and Weightman, D., Penguin, Harmondsworth.
LICRA/MRAP, (1987), *Droit et Discrimination 15 ans d'application de la loi contre le Racisme,* LICRA/MRAP.
LICRA/MRAP, (1989), *Le Racisme en Justice 1972-1989,* LICRA/MRAP.
Little, K. (1947), *Negroes in Britain*, Kegan Paul, London.
Lloyd, C. (1993), 'Racist Violence and Anti-Racist Reactions: a view of France' in Bjorgo, T. Witte, R. (eds.), *Racist Violence in Europe,* Macmillan, London.
Lloyd, C. (1994), 'Universalism and Difference: The Crisis of Anti-Racism in Britain and France' in Rattansi, A. and Westwood, S. (eds.), *On the Western Front: Studies in Racism, Modernity and Identity,* Polity, Cambridge.
Logan, P. (1988), 'Practising Hinduism: The Experience of Gujarati Adults and Children in Britain'. unpublished Report, Thomas Coram Research Unit, University of London Institute of Education.
Long, M. (1988), *Etre Francaise Aujourd'hui et demain*, Tome I, Documentation Francaise, Paris.
Lonsdale, J. (1990), 'Mau Maus of the Mind: Making Mau Mau and Remaking Kenya', in *Journal of African History,* 31, 3.
Lonsdale, J. (1992), 'The Moral Economy of Mau Mau', in Berman, B. and Lonsdale, J., *Unhappy Valley. Book Two: Violence and Ethnicity*, James Currey, London.
Lyon, M. (1972), 'Race and Ethnicity in Pluralistic Societies', *New Community*, 1, 4.
Lyon, M. (1973), 'Ethnic Minority Problems: An Overview of Some Recent Research', *New Community*, 2, 4.
Mare, M. (1993), *Ethnicity and Politics In South Africa*, Zed, London.
Marks, S. (1992), 'The Origins of Ethnic Violence in South Africa', in Kaarsholm, P. (ed.), *Institutions, Culture and Change,* International Development Studies, Roskilde.
Marks, S. (1994), 'The Tradition of Non-Racism in South Africa', 8 March, Somerville College, Oxford.
Mason, P. (1974), 'Race, Resistance and the IRR', *New Community*, 3, 3.
McDonald, M. (1987), 'Rituals of motherhood among Gujarati women in East London,' in *Hinduism in Great Britain,* R. Burghart (ed.), Tavistock, London.
Mestiri, E. (1987), 'Une Génération Charnière. Entre marginalité et intégration', *Hommes et Migrations,* 1104 Juin.
Michaelson, M. (1979), 'The Relevance of Caste among East African Gujaratis in Britain', *New Community,* 7, 3.
Michaelson, M. (1983), Caste, Kinship and Marriage: A Study of Two Gujarati Trading Castes in England. unpublished Ph.D. Thesis, School of Oriental and African Studies, University of London.
Michaelson, M. (1984), 'Gujarati communities in Britain,' paper presented at the Symposium on Gujarati Ethnicity, Centre of South Asian Study, School of Oriental and African Studies, University of London.
Minister of the Interior Circular, Circular 26 May 1981, Paris.

Modood, T. (1988), "'Black', Racial Equality and Asian Identity", *New Community*, 14, 3.
Modood, T. (1990a), 'Catching up with Jesse Jackson: Being Oppressed and Being Somebody', *New Community,* 17, 1.
Modood, T. (1990b), 'British Asian Muslims and the Rushdie affair', *Political Quarterly,* 61, 2.
Modood, T. (1992a), 'The End of a Hegemony: The Concept of 'Black' and British Asians'. Conference paper given to the CRER annual conference on 'The Mobilisation of Ethnic Minorities and Ethnic Social Movements in Europe.'
Modood, T. (1992b), 'If Races do not Exist, Then What Does? Racial Categorisation and Ethnic Realities'. Paper Presented to the conference to mark Michael Banton's retirement, 'Social Order in Post-Classical Sociology', University of Bristol.
Morris, H.S. (1968), *The Indians of Uganda,* Weidenfeld and Nicolson, London.
MRAP, (1984), *Chronique du flagrant racisme,* La Decourverte, Paris.
Murphy, D. (1987), Tales of Two Cities: Travel of Another Sort, John Murphy, London.
Murshid, T. (1993), 'Bangladesh: the Challenge of Democracy - Language, Culture and Political Identity', *Contemporary South Asia*, 2, 1.
Murshid, T. (1995), *The Sacred and the Secular: Bengal Muslim Discourses, 1871- 1977*, Oxford University Press, Oxford.
Murshid, T. (forthcoming), 'Education, Ethnicity and Identity with particular reference to Asian pupils in London', Trentham Books, Stoke-on-Trent.
National Council of Hindu Temples (UK), (nd), *Hinduism: An Introduction to the World Oldest Living Relgion,* National Council of Hindu Temples (UK).
Ndem, E.B. (1953), 'Negro Immigrants in Manchester'. Unpublished mss., Department of Social Anthropology, Edinburgh.
Nesbitt, E.(1987), 'British Punjabi Hindu Children and Their Religious Tradition, Punjab Research Group Discussion Paper Series No. 11.
Nesbitt, E.(1989), 'Valmiki and Ravidasi Children: A Spectrum Of Identity', paper presented at the 15th Symposium on Indian Religion, Oxford
Nye, M. (1991), 'A Hindu community in Edinburgh: Regionalism and religion', paper presented at the 5th annual conference, British Association for South Asian Studies, London.
Odhiambo, E.S.A. (1990), 'From the Kenya State to the Civil Society of the Luo Nation', Conference on 'State and Society in Africa and Eastern Europe', February, Bellagio.
Odhiambo, E.S.A.and Cohen, D. (1989), *Siaya. The Historical Anthropology of an African Landscape,* James Currey, London.
Patterson, S. (1963), *Dark Strangers,* Tavistock, London.
Patterson, T. (1992), 'Irish Lessons: Access to Social Security Benefits for Irish and Other Minority Ethnic Communities in Britain', M.A. (Econ.), University of Manchester.
Peach, C., Robinson, V., Maxted J. and Chance, J. (1988), 'Immigration and ethnicity', in *British Social Trends since 1900,* Halsey, A.H. (ed.), Macmillan, London.

Peel, J.D.Y. (1989), 'The Cultural Work of Yoruba Ethnogenesis', in Chapman, McDonald and Tonkin (eds.), *History and Ethnicity*, ASA Monographs 17, Routledge, London.
Peroti, A. (1986-7), 'La Mobilisation des Étudiants de France et le Code de Nationalité', *Presse et Immigrés en France,* Paris.
Philips, D. (1974), 'Riots and Public Order in the Black Country, 1835-1860' in Stevenson, J. and Quinault, R. (eds.), *Popular Protest and Public Order,* George Allen and Unwin, London.
Pocock, D. F. (1976), 'Preserving The Religious Life: Hindu Immigrants In England', *Contributions to Indian Sociology,* 10.
Politzer, G. (1947), *Revolution et Contre-Revolution au XXe siecle, Reponse a Or et Sang,* Editions Sociales, Paris.
Radcliffe-Brown, A.R. and Forde, D. (1950), *African Systems of Kinships and Marriage,* Oxford University Press, London.
Ranger, T.O. (1969), *The Recovery of African Initiative in Tanzanian History,* University College, Dar es Salaam.
Ranger, T.O. (1970), *The African Voice in Southern Rhodesia, 1898-1930*, Heinemann, London.
Ranger, T.O. (1983), 'The Invention of Tradition in Colonial Africa', in Hobsbawn, Eric and Ranger, Terence (eds.), *The Invention of Tradition,* Cambridge University Press, Cambridge.
Ranger, T.O. (1993), 'The Invention of Tradition Revisited', in Ranger, T.O. and Vaughan, O. (eds.), *Legitimacy and the State in Twentieth Century Africa*, St Antony's/Macmillan, London.
Ranger, T.O. (1994), 'The Tribalization of Africa and the Retribalization of Europe', 19 January, St Antony's College Seminar, 'Tribe, State and Nation', Oxford.
Raychaudhuri, T. (1988), *Europe Reconsidered. Perceptions of the West in Nineteenth Century Bengal*, Oxford University Press, Delhi.
Rex, J. (1979), 'The Future of Black Culture in Britain', *New Community*, 7, 2.
Rex, J. and Mason, D. (eds.), (1986), *Theories of Race and Ethnic Relations,* Cambridge University Press, Cambridge.
Rex, J. (1992), *Ethnic Identity and Ethnic Mobilisation in Britain.* Monographs in Ethnic Relations, 5, CRER, Warwick University.
Rich, P. (1984), *White Power and the Liberal Conscience. Racial Segregation and South African Liberalism, 1921-60,* Manchester University Press, Manchester.
Ridd, R. (1994), 'Muslims in a Changing South Africa: their Position and Prospects', Report for the Nuffield Foundation.
Robinson, C. (1983), *Black Marxism,* Zed Press, London.
Robinson, V. (1986), *Transients, Settlers and Refugees: Asians in Britain*, Clarendon, Oxford.
Robinson, V. (1990), 'Boom and gloom: The success and failure of South Asians in Britain', in *South Asians Overseas: Migration and Ethnicity*, C. Clarke, C. Peach and S. Vertovec (eds.), Cambridge University Press, Cambridge.
Rude, G. (1959), *The Crowd in the French Revolution*, Clarendon, London.
Rutherford, J. (1990), *Identity: Commmunity, Culture, Differrence,* Lawerence Wishart, London.

Ruthven, M. (1990), *A Satanic Affair: Salman Rushdie and The Rage of Islam,* London.
Said, E. (1978), *Orientalism,* Routledge and Kegan Paul, London.
Said, E. (1993), *Culture and Imperialism,* Chatto and Windus, London.
Saifullah Khan, V. (1976), 'Pakistanis in Britain: Perceptions of a Population', *New Community,* 5, 3.
Saifullah Khan, V. (1979a), 'Work and network: South Asian women in South London' in Wallman, S. (ed.), *Ethnicity at Work,* Macmillan, London.
Saifullah Khan, V. (ed.), (1979b), *Minority Families in Britain: Support and Stress,* Macmillan, London.
Samad, Y. (1992), 'Book Burning and Race Relations: Political Mobilization of Bradford Muslims', *New Community,* 18, 4.
Samad. Y (1993), 'Imagining a British Muslim Identification', Conference on 'Islam in Europe: Generation to Generation', St Catherine's, Oxford.
Samad, Y. (1995a), 'Kashmir and the Imagining of Pakistan', *Contemporary South Asia,* 4, 1.
Samad, Y. (1995b), *A Nation in Turmoil: Nationalism and Ethnicity in Pakistan, 1937-1958,* Sage, Delhi.
Sankange Familly Scrapbook, (nd), Harare.
Saville, J. (1987), *1848 The British State and the Chartist Movement,* Cambridge University Press, Cambridge.
Schnapper. D, (1990), 'Les juifs et la nation' in Birnbaum P (dir), *Histoire politique des juifs de France: Entre Universalisme et Particularisme,* PFNSP, Paris.
Schwartz, B.M. (ed.), (1967), *Caste in Overseas Indian Communities,* Chandler, San Francisco.
Sharma, U.M. (1969), 'Hinduism in a Kangra Village'. unpublished Ph.D. Thesis, School of Oriental and African Studies, University of London.
Shaw, A. (1988), *A Pakistani Community in Oxford,* Basil Blackwell, Oxford.
Silverman, M. (1988),'Questions of Nationality and Citizenship in the 1980s', *Modern and Contemporary France,* 34, July.
Silverman, M. (1992), *Deconstructing the Nation: Immigration, Racism and Citizenship in Modern France,* Routledge, London.
Spear, T. and Waller, R., (eds.), (1993), *Being Maasai,* James Currey, London.
Strathern, M. (1991), *Partial Connections,* Rowman and Littlefield Publishers, Maryland.
Strathern, M. (in press), 'Nostalgia and the New Genetics' in *The Rhetoric of Self-Making* (ed.), Battaglia. D. University of California Press, Berkeley.
Stuart, O.W. (1989), 'Good Boys, Footballers and Strikers: African Social Change in Bulawayo, 1933 - 1953', Ph.D. thesis, School of Oriental Studies, University of London, 1989.
Stuart, O.W. (1992), 'Race and Disability: Just A Double Oppression?', *Disability, Handicap and Society,* 7, 2.
Stuart, O.W. (1994), 'Response', 19 January, St Antony's College Seminar, 'Tribe State and Nation', Oxford.

Swift, R. (1985), 'Another Stafford Street Row: Law, Order and the Irish Presence in Mid-Victorian Wolverhampton' in Swift, R. and Gilley, S. (eds.), *The Irish in the Victorian City,* Croom Helm, London.

Taguieff, P.A. (ed.), (1991), *Face au Racisme,* La Decouverte, Paris.

Taylor, S. (1992), *The Irish in Britain - A Profile of Discrimination and Prejudice,* Report of The Race Equalities Unit, Haringey Council, London.

Temu, A. and Swai, B. (1981), *Historians and Africanist History: A Critique,* Zed, London.

Thapar, R. (1989), 'Imagined religious communities? Ancient history and the modern search for a Hindu identity', *Modern Asian Studies,* 23, 1.

Thompson, E.P. (1963), *The Making of the English Working Class,* Penguin, Harmondsworth.

Touraine, A. (1988), 'La Revolution n'est plus ce qu'elle était', *Projet* 213 No Special: L'heritage de la Révolution Francais aujourd'hui', Paris.

Trarieux, M.L. (1902), 'Le Programme de la Ligue des Droits de l'Homme', in *Bulletin Officiel de la Ligue des Droits de l'Homme,* Tome 1, Paris.

Ullah, P. (1985), ' Second Generation Irish Youth: identity and ethnicity', *New Community,* 12, 2.

Vail, L. (ed.), (1989), *The Creation of Tribalism in Southern Africa,* James Currey, London.

van der Veer, P. (1991), 'Hindu "Nationalism" and the Discourse With "Modernity": The Vishva Hindu Parishad', in *Fundamentalism Observed,* Morty M. and Appleby S. (eds.), University of Chicago Press, Chicago.

van der Veer, P. and Vertovec, P. (1991), 'Brahamanism abroad: On Caribbean Hinduism as an Ethnic Religion', *Ethnology,* 30.

Vertovec, S. (1990), 'Religion and ethnic ideology: the Hindu youth movement in Trinidad', *Ethnic and Racial Studies,* 13, 2.

Vertovec, S. (1992a), *Hindu Trinidad: Religion, Ethnicity and Socio-Economic Change,* Macmillan, London.

Vertovec, S. (1992b), 'Community and Congregation in London Hindu Temples: Divergent Trends', *New Community,* 18, 2.

Vertovec, S. (in press), 'South Asian Religions in Britain: Impacts and Developments', in *Religious History of Great Britain 1789-1992,* Mews S. and McLeod H. (eds.), Bayard Preese, Paris.

Wallman, S. (ed.), (1979), *Ethnicity at Work,* Macmillan, London.

Watson, J. (ed.), (1977), *Between Two Cultures,* Basil Blackwell, Oxford.

Werbner, P. (1985), 'The organisation of giving and ethnic elites', *Ethnic and Racial Studies,* 8, 3.

Werbner, P. (1990), *The Migration Process: Capital, Gifts and Offerings among British Pakistanis,* Berg, Oxford.

Werbner P. and Anwar, (eds.), (1991), *Black and Ethnic Leaderships in Britain: the Cultural Dimensions of Political Action,* Routledge, London.

Werbner, P. (1991a), 'Introduction' in Werbner P. and Anwar, (eds.), (1991), *Black and Ethnic Leaderships in Britain: the Cultural Dimensions of Political Action,* Routledge, London.

Werbner, P. (1991a), 'Introduction 2' in Werbner P. and Anwar, (eds.), (1991), *Black and Ethnic Leaderships in Britain: the Cultural Dimensions of Political Action,* Routledge, London.

Werbner, P. (1991b), 'The Fiction of Unity in Ethnic Politics: Aspects of Representation and the State among Manchester Pakistanis' in Werbner P.

and Anwar, (eds.), (1991), *Black and Ethnic Leaderships in Britain: the Cultural Dimensions of Political Action.* Routledge, London.
Werbner, P. (1992), 'On Mosques and Cricket Teams: Religion and Nationalism among British Pakistanis', conference paper, May, Torino.
Werbner, R. (1993), 'Arguments of Accountability: Historical Narrative, Crisis and Social Biography in Zimbabwe'. Paper presented to the Institute of Commonwealth Studies.
Wihtol de Wenden, C, (1988), *Les Immigrés et la Politique,* PFNSP, Paris.
Williams, R. B. (1988), *Religions of Immigrants from India and Pakistan: New Threads in the American Tapestry*, Cambridge University Press, Cambridge.
Williard, G. (1989), 'Fascisme contre Revolution' *Differences,* 87 Mars, Paris.
Willis, J. (1993), *Mombasa, the Swahili and the Making of the Mijikenda*, Oxford University Press, Oxford.
Wuthnow, R. (1989), *Communities of Discourse: Ideology and Social Structure in the Reformation, the Enlightenment and European Socialism,* Harvard University Press, Harvard.
Yuval-Davis, N. (1992), 'Fundamentalism, Multiculturalism and Women in Britain' in Donald, J. and Rattansi, A. (eds.), *'Race', Culture and Difference,* Sage, London.
Zola, E. (1988), *J'accuse ...!*, Editions Complexe, Brussels.

Index